D1251072

English-Canadian Furniture of the Georgian Period

Frontispiece
Small Sideboard
Montreal, c. 1800-15

This small sideboard or serving table combines many of the elements common to finer Canadian furniture — austere but English-derived design, mixed woods, simple string inlays, adaptations toward economy, and wholly secondary pine. The sideboard is of mahogany, with solid top, sides, and legs, and mahogany veneer over secondary pine in the skirt. The front is slightly bowed. The pine drawer fronts are veneered with bird's-eye maple panels and mahogany edge banding, as well as mahogany beading strips. Panels of bird's-eye maple veneer are also in the tops of the legs. The parallel stringing of the legs, skirt, drawer fronts, and top edge is of maple and dark stained maple in triple lines. (See also figs. 91, 92.) The original plain drawer knobs, of mahogany, are common on Georgian-period furniture. The lozenge keyhole inlays are of bone. (See also figs. 100, 140, 224, 228, 285.) The spade feet on square-tapered legs are very unusual on Canadian pieces (see also figs. 194, 275), and only the front legs are footed. This sideboard is one of an identical pair, the other in a private collection. The pieces were acquired in Montreal, around 1868 or 1869, by Donald Alexander Smith, later Lord Strathcona.

Height: 91 cm (35⅝ in.);
Length: 125 cm (49¼ in.)
Montreal Museum of Fine Arts

ENGLISH-CANADIAN FURNITURE OF THE GEORGIAN PERIOD

Donald Blake Webster

Foreword by
Charles F. Hummel

McGraw-Hill Ryerson Limited
TORONTO MONTREAL NEW YORK ST. LOUIS SAN FRANCISCO
AUCKLAND BOGOTA GUATEMALA HAMBURG JOHANNESBURG
LISBON LONDON MADRID MEXICO NEW DELHI
PANAMA PARIS SAN JUAN SÃO PAULO
SINGAPORE SYDNEY TOKYO

to John Laurel Russell,
for his wisdom and support

1 2 3 4 5 6 7 8 9 10 BP 8 7 6 5 4 3 2 1 0 9

ISBN 0-07-082980-2

Design/Maher & Murtagh Inc.
Printed and bound in Canada

Canadian Cataloguing in Publication Data

Webster, Donald Blake, date
English-Canadian furniture of the Georgian period

Bibliography: p.
Includes index.
ISBN 0-07-082980-2

1. Furniture, Georgian — Canada. 2. Furniture — Canada. I. Title.

NK2441.W43 749.2'11 C79-094495-2

Contents

Acknowledgements

Always the last part of any book to be written, it seems, is that brief section acknowledging and thanking those who in one manner or another have contributed to the effort. In this instance the pleasure was doubled, for my wife and I have made many friends during the course of this venture and its innumerable travels over the years.

The late George MacLaren, and John Russell, to whom the book is dedicated, were particular sources of encouragement even before the project was outlined and started. Charles Foss, C.M., has been equally encouraging, and availing of the considerable resources at the Kings Landing Historical Settlement. All these people, whatever the request, have been gracious hosts, and free with their own knowledge, insights, and sources.

Museum and antiquarian colleagues have all been supportive in offering access to their collections and photographs, often in most inconvenient or difficult circumstances, and I only regret that I cannot name each one. Elizabeth Collard of Montreal, Gregg Finley at the New Brunswick Museum, John Harbinson and Charles Humber of Toronto, Barbara Riley and Fred Thorpe at the History Division, National Museum of Man, Marie Elwood and Scott Robson at the Nova Scotia Museum, Donald MacKay of Halifax, Huia Ryder of Saint John, and Philip Shackleton of Ottawa have all been particularly helpful. No less so have been those many people who welcomed us into their homes, but prefer to be cited as "private collection."

Among museum staff, William Robertson has photographed all of the pieces in the Canadiana department collections, including the colour shots, and has accompanied me to record numerous privately owned pieces in and around Toronto. Our department secretary, Karen Haslan, typed all the text, sometimes working on several drafts and versions, generally in the early moring, before the typical harried day of museum department secretaries begins.

Charles Hummel at the Henry Francis du Pont Winterthur Museum readily agreed to read and criticize the text and to write the foreword, even though he felt I would attract fire because of a few of my more opinionated statements. Charles Foss, Charles Humber, and John Russell have also surveyed parts of the text and captions. The ultimate responsibility for errors, of course, must remain mine alone.

Finally, and most important, my wife Lonnie catalogued, recorded, and measured while I photographed, advised on fine points from beginning to end, helped to make the hard choices of the final photograph selection, criticized text and proofread parts of galleys, and fed me and kept children away while I was writing. No one could expect more.

I have encountered, without exception, great curiosity about this project. As word of it has spread around, offerings of new material have arrived (and continue to), some of which fit into this volume, and some of which will be incorporated later. In thanking all those people who have contacted me on their own initiative, and I hope will continue to, I can only say that the point where I could consider the subject of stylized and formal English-Canadian furniture as exhausted has certainly not been reached However, I have arrived at a stage where a reasonable sampling from the earlier period has been compiled, and some conclusions have been reached.

D. B. Webster
June 1979

Foreword

In 1953, a square work table by Thomas Nisbet, illustrated as Fig. 283 in this book, was one of the "documented" examples of American furniture in the collections of the Henry Francis du Pont Winterthur Museum. In that year, this writer reported to Winterthur as a Fellow to begin graduate study at the Museum and the University of Delaware. In the fall of the same year, Thomas Nisbet was correctly identified as a cabinet-maker of Saint John, New Brunswick, in the *Art Bulletin of The New Brunswick Museum Art Department*. For some time, neither of the last two events had much significance in the art world.

It is true, of course, that the label identifying Thomas Nisbet as the maker of this work table had deteriorated, and only "New Brunswick," as the geographic location of Nisbet's shop, was clearly legible. The point of this foreword, however, is that everyone working in the field of American decorative arts in 1953, including this writer, assumed that the *only* New Brunswick that had any meaning for Thomas Nisbet's label and the work table was a town in New Jersey.

In fact, it was not until shortly before Charles Montgomery published the correct origin of the work table as No. 407 in his book *American Furniture: The Federal Period* (New York, 1966) that students of American decorative art began to realize that maple and birch in combination with solid and/or veneer woods were not confined to the production of furniture in the United States.

To be fair, the attitude represented by this example cannot be attributed entirely to rampant chauvinism south of the Canadian border. In 1953, American furniture had been the subject of intensive study for over fifty years, whereas before 1960 or 1961 no major book on Canadian furniture had yet appeared in print. In fact, through 1977, less than a dozen books devoted solely or in large part to examination of Canadian furniture had been made available to students, collectors, dealers, and scholars in the United States. The extensive collection of published material in the Winterthur libraries that relates to furniture throughout the world includes only thirty-four titles — twenty-four articles, eight books, and two booklets — on the subject of Canadian furniture. Moreover, the publication in 1963 of *The Antique Furniture of French Canada* by Jean Palardy was such an exciting event that it may have contributed toward lulling students in the United States into believing that it was easy to differentiate between furniture produced in Canada and in the United States.

With publication of *English-Canadian Furniture of the Georgian Period*, the first of two projected volumes, Donald Webster has succeeded in making chauvinism the last refuge of careless students of furniture in the United States. In this book, which uses the English Regency style as its terminus, he begins his illustrations with a late eighteenth-century mahogany and white pine easy chair from Sheffield, New Brunswick, that could just as easily pass for a New England example if its history were unknown. A drinking stand shown as Fig. 107 is still in the Winterthur collection and was illustrated as No. 388 in Charles Montgomery's catalogue of the Museum's Federal period furniture. It is made almost entirely of mahogany with only a small piece of secondary wood, the axle, made of birch. A quite similar stand appears in *Sheraton Furniture* by Ralph Fastnedge. What could be more symbolic of the often close, sometimes too close for comfort, relationship of Anglo-American and Anglo-Canadian furniture?

This book would be invaluable if the author had done nothing more than vividly remind us of the results of settlement in Canada of Loyalist families from the United States, of long-standing relationships between Canadian and United States citizens with common ancestors and descendants, and of similarities between the origins — England, France, Germany, Ireland, and Scotland — of cabinetmakers who immigrated to Canada or the United States.

But he has done a great deal more. He has built on the essentially regional studies of Charles Foss, George MacLaren, Jean Minhinnick, Jean Palardy, Huia Ryder, and Philip Shackleton, to present an encyclopedic overview of styles and types of Canadian furniture in the Georgian period. Further, he has succeeded in providing a well-arranged catalogue of the stylized and formal furniture of early English Canada. Not only does Donald Webster succeed in grouping related forms, but he also groups related elements of design and decoration of those forms, which permits easy comparison and is a great service to students of furniture.

He has succeeded so well in achieving this goal that it may be tempting to pass by, or gloss over, the introductory chapters of his book in order to peruse the body of illustrations and related reference material. That would result in a great loss to the reader. In his chapters, the author presents strong, well-argued opinions that should stir debate in Canada and provide fuel for argument among historians who regularly examine aspects of culture, intellect, and society in the United States. His view that fashion dictated ugliness in the third quarter of the nineteenth century will surely send brickbats and salvos in the direction of the Canadiana Department of the Royal Ontario Museum from colleagues in both countries. No reader of this book will be able to state that Donald Webster conceals his viewpoints.

Of great interest is the success with which he delineates the strong relationship between furniture, economic history, and climate. He notes that concentrations of population and bases of prosperity, all necessary to create sufficient markets, simply did not exist in Canada to the extent that they did in colonial America and the new Republic. The settlement of English-speaking Canada in the nineteenth century corresponds to what had already transpired in the English-speaking colonies of the seventeenth century that later became part of the United States. Moreover, because of the extreme climate, much of early Canadian life centred on the kitchen and fireplace. This had a decided influence on the types of furniture demanded for everyday life. This material makes for stimulating, thought-provoking chapters that must be read in order to fully understand and appreciate the illustrated catalogue that follows.

The theme that Canadian antiquarians have neglected the collection and study of stylized and formal furniture of early English Canada, while concentrating on Anglo-Canadian primitive furniture and French-Canadian products, forms the strong impetus for Donald Webster's book. It was shocking to learn that the surviving corpus of known Anglo-Canadian furniture made before 1830 is much less than the number of examples of American furniture in the Winterthur collection alone. Equally shocking is the author's revelation that there is only one Anglo-Canadian cabinet-maker represented by a large body of known furniture and considerable documentation in the form of family letters. That craftsman is John Warren Moore of St. Stephen, New Brunswick, who was active much later than the Georgian period. Thomas Nisbet, mentioned at the beginning of this foreword, is represented by a number of labelled pieces that survive, but none of his records have been discovered.

It seems clear that with publication of this book, the number of surviving examples of Anglo-Canadian furniture is bound to grow. Donald Webster correctly states that a truly definitive work on Anglo-Canadian furniture remains "a long way off." The state of recognition and awareness in Canada today of what Anglo-Canadian cabinet-makers achieved prior to 1830 is strikingly similar to the attitude that prevailed in the United States between 1900 and 1940. During that period, any example of very elaborate or sophisticated antique furniture that could not be precisely documented was automatically assigned an English provenance. While the author also notes that English-Canadian furniture is difficult to isolate and identify with any degree of certainty, it is quite likely that a number of pieces of furniture that have disappeared into the antiques market in the United States since the 1920s will once again assume their rightful identities. Indeed, a portion of this book that appeared as an article in *Antiques* (January, 1979) has already brought to Mr. Webster's attention a dining table and two sets of chairs purchased in New Brunswick in 1927 but now reposing in Philadelphia. The sorting and reattribution of antique furniture that will take place in the United States as a result of the publication of this book can only have a salutary effect.

Similarities and differences between Anglo-Canadian and Anglo-American furniture before 1830 are highlighted by Donald Webster's excellent study. Just as the environment of the United States transformed the experience of cabinet-makers here, the Canadian environment changed cabinet-making in English-speaking Canada. In 1968, Professor George Kubler of Yale University, speaking about Spanish, French, and English traditions in the colonial silver of North America, observed that silversmiths of those nationalities knew more about each other in Europe than in America. Thanks to Donald Webster, we now have an opportunity to examine common denominators and uncommon facets of cabinet-making in Canada and the United States before 1830.

Charles F. Hummel
Winterthur, Delaware
May 1979

Introduction

It has always struck me as very odd that one of the most distinguished areas of the European-derived decorative arts, the stylized and formal furniture of early English Canada, has for so long been neglected by Canadian antiquarians. I have even heard expressions of disbelief that finer furniture was ever made at all in Georgian-period Canada. For all I know, doubts may yet exist. This is most unfortunate, for it is obviously the finest examples in any aspect of the decorative arts that are the most important, and that must govern the standards of comparative judgement applied to the whole range.

To be sure, the majority of sophisticated Georgian furniture in Canada is English, either early settlers' goods or imports, or recent antiques trade imports. There also remains, particularly from later on in the 19th century, a considerable quantity of American manufactured furniture. Thus, years ago, existing and much scarcer Canadian furniture of the same period was habitually considered to be probably English or American, and was automatically discounted by all but a very few Canadian-interest antiquarians just on that basis. No one then made much attempt to sort it out.

It was not until I began this project some ten or eleven years ago and started recording examples that the real reasons for the elusiveness of the finer early English-Canadian furniture came into sharp focus. It is, very simply, sometimes quite difficult to isolate and identify with any degree of certainty, and must be approached on a piece-by-piece basis. Being derivative in style and form of British designs and fashions on the one hand, and very similar to northeastern American furniture on the other, it has none of the well-defined and neatly assessable characteristics that allow for ready identification. Unlike French-Canadian or Ontario-German furniture, for instance, the stylized English-Canadian furniture does not typically permit instant recognition across a room. It must be scrutinized closely; it is easy to confuse with English or American furniture, and clues to regional differences lie in detail rather than substance. With some examples, even close and detailed examination will not eliminate all uncertainty.

This peripatetic project of picking out the Georgian-period English-Canadian furniture has thus turned out, to say the least, to be a good deal more than I originally bargained for, but it has been great fun as well. It cannot end here, of course. Fresh examples periodically appear, a great deal needs to be done in the area of tying cabinet-makers to their production, and the differentiation of regional characteristics (if they are valid at all beyond wood usage patterns) is still indistinct. With all this not completed, the project must continue, and this volume should be taken for what it is, a survey in the nature of a first report.

One should perhaps not admit to such conclusions, but I have found no examples or evidence of truly "Great" Georgian-Canadian furniture, or any which could credibly be described with superlative adjectives. The conditions, structure, and environment of English-Canadian society at the time, with foremost attention devoted to the occupation and development of a vast raw land, just could not foster or support that sort of lavishness and opulence. Instead, I think it must be said that the furniture of this period, in whatever fashions or styles it followed, was generally most likely to be closer to the minimum rather than maximum expression of those styles.

The best of Georgian-Canadian furniture is by any standard well-designed and skilfully constructed, but it is understated, simplified, and generally unadorned. While it must obviously be judged by accepted qualitative standards, it must also be judged by the circumstances of its own time. If one applies, as we must, the broader standards of material history superimposed on those of narrower antiquarian assessments, we cannot validly view this furniture in the same light as that of Britain or the seaboard United States, where the conditions of time and place were so vastly different.

The Canadian furniture is in any event relatively spare; it represents the art of the possible rather than of the ideal; it is considerably more limited in its range of forms and styles, and it must be assessed for what it historically represents as well as for what it currently is.

As is detailed further on, the concept of the cultural cloak, the idea that a society's visibly enduring past, both in architecture and the decorative arts, provides a quiescent influence for cultural stability is more important, I believe, than is generally allowed in North America. Without preservation and protection of the cultural cloak, the parameters of contemporary culture would extend perhaps only twenty years past and forward, with a potential total turnover of living environments once a generation. Some cities in their renewal and redevelopment zeal have approached this, leaving a mood of rootlessness, without sense of belonging or of community among their citizens. Societies need stronger material bases than that. Politicians and urban planners now, however, seem to have a more refined sense of the meaning and benefit of the cultural cloak idea than have some antiquarians, yet it is the latter who are in many ways the actual keepers of the past.

The main problems in dealing with the more sophisticated levels of English-Canadian furniture are always going to be, first, basic identification, and then maker-attribution. The simpler examples of this furniture, while they are Canadian, are also North American. The shadings of regional differences, as mentioned earlier, are sometimes so deceptive and subtle as to all but defy isolation.

Since recognition of the cultural cloak, and the popularity of antique collecting, came much earlier and more strongly to the United States than to English Canada, an inestimable quantity of good Georgian-period Canadian furniture has been exported over many years via the antiques trade. This export traffic has gone on at least since the early 1920s, and perhaps earlier, and has been slowed in very recent years only by the price levels of good Canadian furniture in Canada rising above U.S. levels for similar American furniture.

As happens in the antiques business, a great deal of this furniture was given American nationality. After two or three or more changes of hands, except for pieces showing strongly Canadian characteristics, the origin of most of this furniture would now be next to impossible to establish with any degree of reliability. I often note in *Antiques* magazine, for example, and in American auction catalogues, pieces which in spite of their American attributions appear to be possibly of Canadian origin. There are, as well, many known Canadian pieces in American private collections (just as there are many American pieces in Canada), and some of these have been included with the illustrations.

The quantity of known pieces does not, of course, alleviate the problem of ongoing identification. Very little Georgian-Canadian furniture is self-identified by maker markings, and only two makers are known to have used paper labels. The majority of pieces must still be sorted out from inherent evidence and by comparison, at best rather inexact. Confusions and mysteries in this field, I am afraid, will always remain.

American correspondents have more than once mentioned to me how fortunate are people working on the decorative arts in Canada, as compared to the United States. We are still at a very early stage of decorative arts studies, and can experience the thrill and plain sport of the original chase, much like a fisherman being turned loose on a remote lake that has never been fished before. While we have fresh territory to explore and can initiate wholly original work, similar first ground-turning in the American decorative arts was done over fifty years ago. Our American colleagues of this age are thus instead in a position of screening for nitty-grit in often already well-turned subject matter. This is perhaps a logical progression over the decades in any field, but hardly as pleasurable as fresh discovery and assessment.

I occasionally provoke argument in lectures by blandly stating that no book yet written in this generation on Canadian decorative arts, present offering included, is definitive or the last and final word on the subject, nor is any likely to be. In this first stage of decorative arts studies, any scholar who delayed writing until every scrap of his subject was in place, with nothing left to add, would likely not survive long enough to publish at all.

The existing bibliography on Canadian decorative arts represents almost wholly initial work, and it is in the nature of initial work in any field to be incomplete and perhaps erroneous. All of this work, however, forms a base from which other scholars will sooner or later refine, digest, clarify, add material, and expand detail, all to the end of filling out rough pictures with more precise and in-depth second- and third-generation studies.

Putting together any complete and, particularly, valid picture thus requires decades. There are never sufficient resources to exhaust a subject in any single study, nor has any single individual wisdom sufficient to determine all truth. Time is required for assessments and reconsiderations of past work; and time is required for successive studies by fresh minds employing different approaches. In the end, complete pictures of any nation's early decorative arts and material history are the result not so much of creation as of gradual evolution. Truly definitive work in the Canadian decorative arts remains a long way off.

Sideboard, from Hepplewhite. See fig. 194.

Some General Considerations

All furniture, though it may be handsome, elegant, or even opulent, is still basically utilitarian. Unlike painting, sculpture, or the fine arts generally, furniture in any situation, from manor house to log cabin, by its very nature must serve some practical purpose. Otherwise there would be little reason for it to exist and occupy space.

Furniture, too, reflects directly the economic and social situations and status of the people for whom and by whom it is made. Thus it must be viewed in context of the conditions of its own time, as well as of what it is considered today. Though everyone uses furniture, one would not at any period have expected to find luxurious furnishings in dirt-floored huts, any more than the European landed nobility would have accepted pine-plank tables or plain ladder-back chairs as salon furniture. Individual conditions of lifestyle mandated the differences we find today in the qualitative levels, and their relative distributions, of early furniture.

Obviously excellence is excellence, and poor quality is poor quality, whatever its time frame. Age alone cannot magically create qualitative superiority, only rarity. Since many people collect with historical rather than qualitative motivations, it is certainly short-sighted to make contemporary antiquarian judgements solely on grounds of our present view of the aesthetic qualities of the utilitarian remains of other generations. Within a broad consideration of antiquities as evidence of their own time, however, rather than just as isolated and aged objects, qualitative assessments and comparisons must still be made.

Many North American and British antiquarians feel that the furniture and architecture of the English late-Georgian age, coinciding with the American-Federal period, represented a high water-mark in human-inspired design. (European antiquarians, conversely, sometimes confuse opulence with elegance.) At the taste-making level of society the excesses of the baroque age had passed, though they were to re-emerge in the ugliness dictated by fashion in the third quarter of the 19th century. The late Georgian and American Federal period was an age both of rationality and understatement in design, and of neo-classical taste based on ancient Mediterranean forms. The furniture of this period was, in a phrase, comfortable, rich, and human — pleasing and radiating an enveloping warmth to the eye and the soul. Supreme good taste, for a time, was also fashionable, a most fortuitous benefit which can hardly be considered true of all ages.

Canada as a modern nation-state suffers from the unfortunate mischance of timing that this late Georgian age, flourishing in the homelands from which most of English-language Canada was seeded, coincided here exactly with the period of first-generation occupation and settlement of a huge land-mass with an inhospitable environment. Few conceivable conditions could have been more inhibiting to the pursuit of excellence over necessity, or to the creation and development for Canada of a large-scale material cultural base — permanent and visually gratifying.

English Canada had little opportunity for this. In the late Georgian period — a time of initial settlement in this country — the average first- and second-generation Canadian was for the most part preoccupied by such mundane concerns as a roof overhead, staying warm during much of the year, and having enough to eat through the next winter. Grand buildings were few and far between, and fewer still have been allowed to survive. Except among senior British colonial government, military, and mercantile people, elegant domestic furnishings and *accoutrements* were just not a major concern.

This country was undergoing first settlement, all within one generation, of the Maritimes, southern Quebec, and southern Ontario, a vastly greater land area and distance span than had ever been settled that rapidly before. Whatever was not immediately useful was unnecessary. In a raw land with Canada's climate, the simple accumulation of possessions was superfluous. Except by sea, on lakes, or by fully navigable rivers, domestic goods, to say nothing of heavy cargoes, were transportable only with the greatest effort and difficulty. What roads existed were deep mud, frozen ruts, or dust, according to season, and so rough as to cause high losses not only of cargoes but of vehicles. Shipments inland from ports of landing were best limited to light, durable essentials.

Reflecting all of these conditions, stylized and reasonably sophisticated English-Canadian furniture in Georgian styles is rare by any standard. What we might call simply "good" furniture was probably never very widespread, even in its own time. It was produced in small quantities by a few specialized makers. Much has also since disappeared, either forever, fire being the universal leveller of early cold-climate, wood-fuelled houses and buildings, or at least from sight through more recent antiques market dispersal and exportation.

A rough but realistic estimate would indicate that not over 2–3000 refined pieces — well designed and proportioned, of good woods and construction, and of certain Canadian origin — survive today. That may be, if anything, a high estimate. Remaining outstanding Canadian pieces — handsome, gracious, and perhaps truly elegant — number at most in the several dozens.

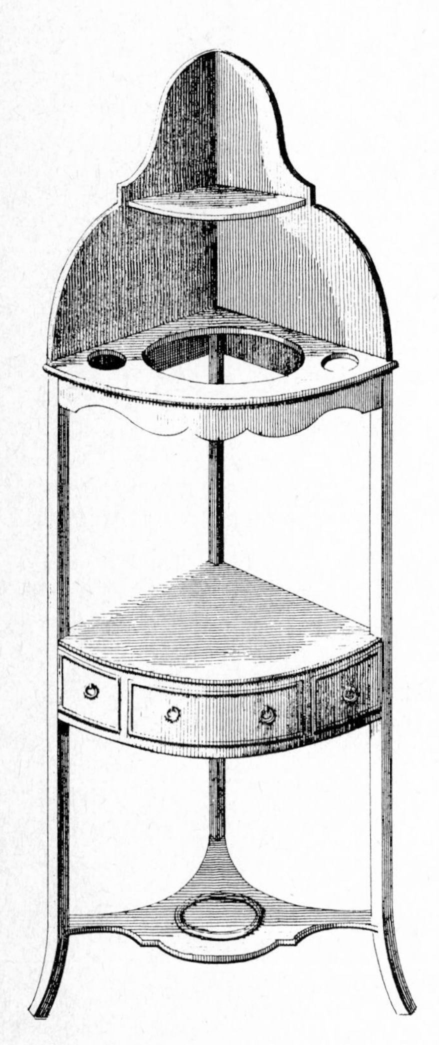

Corner Wash-Stand, from Sheraton. See fig. 258.

Stylized Canadian-Georgian furniture was only a small proportion of all furniture produced in Canada through the 19th century. There is also no apparent correlation between population sizes, *vis-a-vis* Britain and the United States, and quantities of formal furniture produced. The constraints of economic and environmental conditions restricted English Canada to far less fine furniture, and other decorative arts, relative to population than either the U.S. or, particularly, Britain.

Many western societies owe the essence of their national stability to their geographical and historical roots, far more than to their governmental systems or politicians of the moment. People are reminded of this, sometimes beyond what they wish to admit, by visible physical remains of their own cultural longevity and continuity. One's own visually obvious and omnipresent history is a cloak of security which offers a sense of belonging and of community, and is an unmatchable cultural stabilizer.

This is one of the underlying strengths of Britain, France, Spain, Italy, and Greece, certainly of the Far East, to a considerable extent of the United States, and of French Canada. All have this material cultural cloak. Whatever temporary political aberrations may happen, with tangible, visible antiquity, people at least have an awareness of who they are and what they come from. This cultural cloak, to contemporary populations overwhelmingly attentive to present-day concerns, is best expressed by its quiet preservation and continuing presence.

The misfortune of timing for Canada, in being able to enjoy at most only the periphery of the elegance of the late-Georgian period, was reinforced by the accelerating pace of the 19th century. The late-Georgian age also saw the coming of the end of a thousand years of craft-determined technology and production, based on individual human training, initiative, skills, and experience. The close of the Georgian period thus proved as well to be the end of the last chance to achieve a broad, unique material foundation, determined by man rather than the machine, the makings of a cultural cloak. The age of dependable artificial power and of industrial homogenization, embodied in universal application of the steam engine, was upon Canada almost immediately.

Within a few decades there was very little difference between virtually every physical object made here and the same object made anywhere else. By 1850 to 1860 the majority of furniture came from factories, not cabinet-makers. By 1880 the popular standard of excellence was no longer the best that man could make, but had shifted to the most expensive item in the store or the mail order catalogue. English Canada in effect had progressed too quickly from the trauma of first settlement to the beginnings of mechanization, to have really been able to achieve or retain a large base of physical and visible material history. The country suffers for it to this day.

Because of a material antiquity too sparse to command automatic attention, Canada has also been quite late in discovering the benefits of architectural and antiquities preservation for cultural identification and stability. Thus in many cases we are now forced to a position of saving not necessarily the best of what was created — it is too late for that — but merely what is left, with happenstance of survival rather than original excellence as the determining factor.

Quebec and the eastern United States are in rather better shape, not solely because of an earlier realization of the concepts and benefits of preservation, but more because of longer periods of settlement and history. In these regions there has been simply a much longer time span of building and craft production, from the early 17th century, and there is thus more physical evidence of the heritage remaining. The cultural cloak in Quebec and the American northeast, however, is also considerably more deeply ingrained and appreciated than in English Canada, and this has certainly aided preservation awareness.

In furniture the same is true. That stylized and formal English-Canadian furniture was ever created at all is still barely recognized, and the idea even now comes with considerable amazement to many. In the popular mind, early Canadian furniture is still synonymous with the pioneer syndrome and utilitarian country pine, scraped clean and glossily refinished. Thus as the contemporary fashion for the pioneer past has grown, the market has followed.
Of the several companies now "reproducing," for instance, "early" Canadian furniture, all focus on simple, production-adapted, 19th-century country designs in pine. This is perhaps not disturbing in itself, for country or provincial furniture is popular everywhere. What is disturbing, how-

ever, is that country and even rude furniture is all too readily accepted in Canada as the ultimate in antiquarian taste. No one has yet tried reproducing the best of Canadian furniture, in mahogany, cherry, or maple, and few people other than assiduous collectors know what it is.

On the other hand, collecting based on qualitative judgements, long established with Quebec antiquities, as with collectors in the fine arts and exotic realms, has finally penetrated to English-Canadian antiques. Far more excellent pieces of Georgian-period furniture are now identified, known, and appreciated in private homes, for instance, than was certainly the case a few years ago, when most good furniture was blindly considered as "probably English" or "probably American." As well as collectors and museums, a few discerning dealers have also aided this trend.

Since extant stylized Georgian furniture is so uncommon, the best of these pieces can almost be considered as national treasures. This raises the question, now that this furniture is gradually becoming better recognized and more widely sought, of continued preservation and of continuity of information.

Preservation, it would seem, is becoming less of a problem, and for this we can probably look to the economic and investment aspects of collecting. Private collectors are increasingly accepting the credo that they cannot really own their possessions. They are merely the caretakers of them until the time inevitably comes for their collections, in one way or another, to pass on to succeeding possessors and caretakers. This concept alone, however, still does not mandate what care the collector may give his pieces while in his possession. Extreme damage or even partial destruction is always possible, through accident, individual negligence, or plain stupidity. In North America, Quebec alone has inserted the power of the State into private antiquities and art collecting, a draconian and unnecessary intrusion that becomes, like prohibition, counter-productive as it creates underground activities.

In fact, the collector with a substantial outlay in his holdings, whatever they be, is in the position of the investor who keeps his stock certificates or bonds in a drawer at home, rather than in a vault. Whether or not he often or ever considers the concept of temporary custodianship, he must in any event take all precautions just to protect his investment. Thus collectors are increasingly likely to see that restoration or repair is accomplished very carefully, to maintain wintertime humidifiers, to keep household fire risk at the lowest possible level, and to maintain considerable security. With an increasing appreciation of the qualitative levels of Canadian furniture and all antiquities has come a rapidly escalating price-value structure. Since no collector-investor is likely to jeopardize his investment, this more than anything else has resolved many past excesses.

The severe problem of continuity of information is also being slowly resolved. In the past many good Canadian pieces have been removed, particularly into the American market, without information as to place or context of origin. Most will then always be considered, in the absence of contrary identification, as American pieces. Until a few years ago, few dealers or auctioneers passed on much information, if they had indeed ever sought or recorded any, to collector-buyers. So, many excellent pieces of furniture, even within Canada, have been transported without record from their historical and geographical origins, and now to whatever extent is possible must be sorted out solely on a basis of inherent and comparable characteristics.

This information problem, particularly with better pieces of furniture, is also finding an economic solution. With the increasing application of qualitative judgements to Canadian antiques, and with escalating values, has come the idea that information is part of the investment. Collectors paying four- and five-figure prices want to be as certain as possible about what they are buying. Thus the better dealers, who are the most likely to handle the best pieces, now record and pass on whatever background information they have, not so much out of historical commitment but out of the valid assumption that information and documentation add to value. Collectors more and more are further researching their pieces, as well they should. Thus financial reality, as well as generally assuring preservation, is likely also to assure information gathering and continuity by private collectors.

The pace of negligent destruction, discard, loss, or severe alteration of everything from early buildings, to archaeological sites, to antique furniture has at least slowed, due to both government (legislative) and individual initiatives. With every person who decides to leave the original paint on an early chair, or every organization or entrepreneur who finds it is feasible to restore and utilize rather than demolish an early building, something has been gained. One attribute of the material cultural cloak is that it lies quietly, providing broad awareness by its very presence, but not necessarily requiring personal understanding. Its impact is no less. The cultural cloak, as the dollar-spent in economics, has as well a multiplier effect created by its ever-expanding influence.

Canadian decorative arts and material history studies are still in a stage of initial sod-busting rather than of harrowing and refining. In spite of this, however, Canadian material history studies are in an increasingly healthy state. Albeit slowly, the cultural cloak is taking shape, and there is no longer real cause for fear that the physical past will simply be allowed to disappear or be sacrificed under the weight of contemporary concerns.

Pembroke Tables, from Hepplewhite. See figs. 177-180.

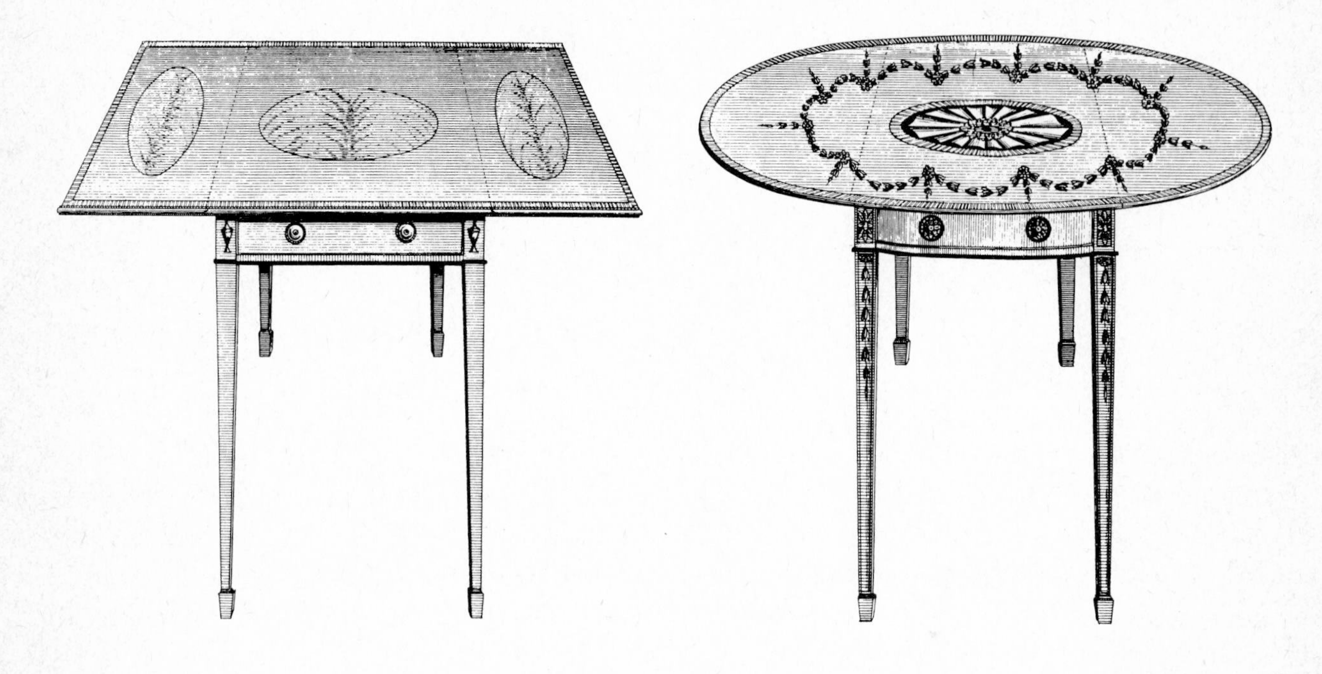

Styles, Forms, and Fashions

Earliest Settlement

The period of the finest English-derived cabinet-making in Canada spans a time frame of only some seventy years, from roughly 1780 to 1850. Numerous English, Scottish, and American settlements, however, had been established somewhat earlier than this. Halifax, for example, was founded and incorporated in 1749 by Governor Edward Cornwallis, who arrived that year with 2500 English settlers. Among them was the first recorded cabinet-maker to work in English Canada, Edward Draper, along with fourteen joiners and turners all capable of making basic furniture.

Yorkshire farmers settled the Bay of Fundy and Minas Basin areas in the 1760s and '70s. German-speaking settlers founded Lunenburg in 1753. Following the expulsion of the Acadians in 1755, and the final defeat of France, pre-Loyalist colonial New Englanders moved north in small but steady numbers, settling both on the southwest coast of Nova Scotia and in the Annapolis Valley. The first contingent of Scottish settlers arrived at Pictou in 1773. Thus Nova Scotia, particularly, already had a diverse English-speaking population even before the beginning of the American Revolution.

Most if not all of these earlier communities, however, were scattered and small in population, with near subsistence-level economies and living standards. Clustered along the southwestern Nova Scotia and Bay of Fundy coasts, they were also societies oriented toward the sea, not inland. Britain, or the American colonies to the south, were both home to these first-generation inhabitants, and the source of virtually all domestic amenities from pottery to shoes to window glass — except those that were self-made.

The early years were undeniably hard. The Reverend George Patterson described the paucity of furnishings, and virtually every other domestic amenity, among the Nova Scotia Scots in the 1780s, in his *The Memoir of Rev. James MacGregor, D.D.*

> Their furniture was of the rudest description. Frequently a block of wood or a rude bench, made out of a slab, in which four sticks had been inserted as legs, served for chair or table. Their food was com-

monly served up in wooden dishes or in wooden plates, and eaten with wooden spoons. Money was scarcely seen, and almost all trade was done by barter.

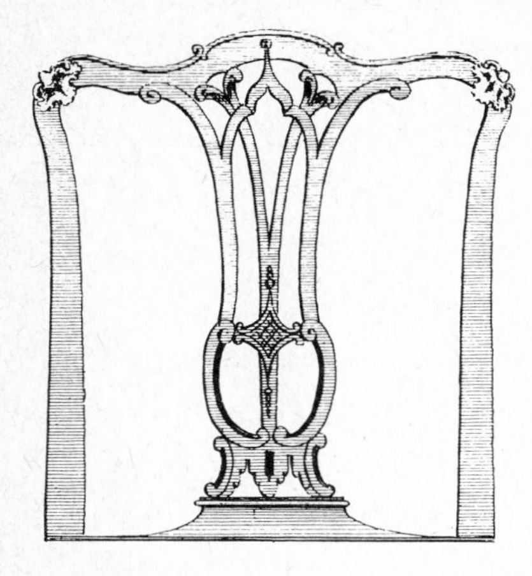

The specialized skilled crafts or occupations which developed because of demand, in the coastal settlements of English Canada before the American Revolution, were largely those on which the population depended for its immediate existence. Ship and boat builders, lumber millers, blacksmiths, coopers, wheelwrights, carpenters, and joiners were all essential.

With area population bases rarely numbering beyond dozens or at most hundreds of people, specialists such as silver-makers and pewterers, glass blowers, potters, sheet-metal (tinned iron and copper) workers, and also cabinet-makers were largely superfluous; their time had yet to come. Their particular products were readily imported from the huge British, craft-industrial establishment, as colonial mercantilism mandated, and these craftsmen probably could not have made a living anyway in economically undeveloped communities. The situation, in fact, is different today only in degree. One would not expect to see an individual skilled in, say, jewellery enamelling or advertising graphics locate in a remote 200-person northern village with much expectation of practising his specialty locally.

The skills and long experience that produced the finest of the early silver, ceramics, glass, and furniture that we so much admire and treasure now as antiques were, exactly as such skills are today, rather on the outer fringes of the economic mainstream. These craftsmen, in any event, could be patronized by only a minuscule proportion of the immediate population, for their output, after all, represented luxury and pretensions to elegance, and not the necessities of life. People in small colonial communities who could hardly afford inlaid mahogany sideboards could perfectly well make do with plain plank tables and rough benches, and did. Any carpenter could make those most constant necessities — coffins.

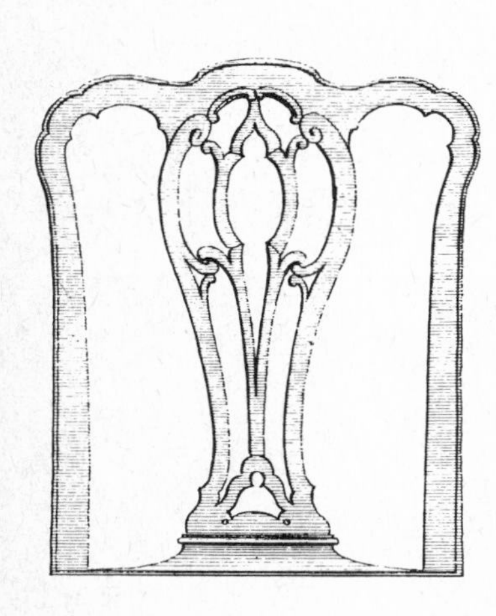

Economic Prerequisites

The viability of such specialized, esoteric commercial crafts and skills in any time period has required one of two conditions. In essentially feudal or autocratic states, special classes, such as the Church in New France, and the landed, moneyed nobility in England and Europe, provided outlets for luxurious objects and patronage for their makers. In more modern and less socially structured times, such skills, to be viable, have required large and preferably growing population bases, infrastructures with a high degree of economic interdependence, rather than subsistence-level independence. This also implies, of course, some reasonable level of economic prosperity and sufficient stability for the development of actual wealth — in a word, large towns or cities.

This is essentially why, in British-inhabited Canada before the Loyalist influx of the 1780s, we simply do not find the immigration or native development of the skills and experience necessary to build stylized and formal furniture. The population concentrations and bases of prosperity, i.e., sufficient markets, simply did not exist as necessary preconditions.

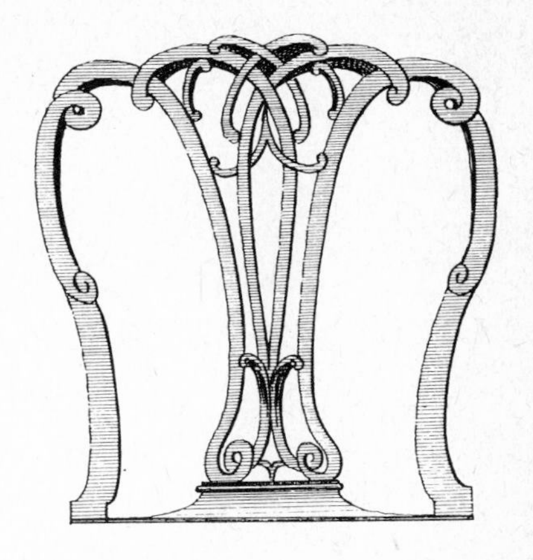

Loyalist and Scottish Migrations

The American Loyalists, arriving between 1782 and 1784, many dispossessed and poor but a few wealthy, constituted a sizeable population. Nova Scotia had been, at best, thinly settled. The Loyalists became the foundation of New Brunswick. To the west, Loyalists migrated into the Eastern Townships of Quebec, the north shore of Lake Ontario, and into the Niagara Peninsula, all previously unsettled areas.

Almost simultaneously, the beginnings of the Highland Clearances motivated a large dispossessed Scottish population toward British North America. In a constant stream beginning with the Pictou settlement of 1773, the Scots arrived in large numbers well into the 19th century, perhaps most heavily immediately following the end of the Napoleonic Wars. Though preferring to settle in eastern Nova Scotia and Cape Breton Island, replacing the French who had been removed after 1760, by the close of the War of 1812 the Scots had reached the new lands of southern Ontario.

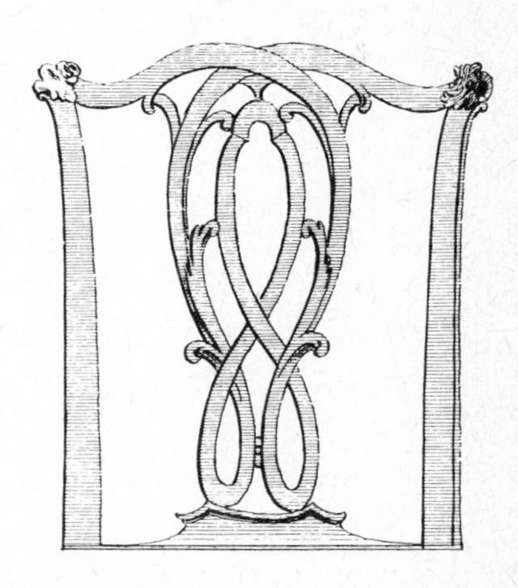

"Backs of Chairs," from Thomas Chippendale, *The Gentleman and Cabinet-Maker's Director*, 1762. See figs. 8-18.

Before the coming of the Loyalists, and the Scottish migrations of the late 18th and early 19th centuries, we can safely presume that those people who could afford finer furniture brought it from Britain or the New England colonies. Less affluent households somehow fended for themselves.

New Brunswick and Nova Scotia to this day still contain a considerable quantity of both English and New England 18th-century furniture, most of a basically good but rarely opulent quality. Family histories (sometimes questionable) maintain the furniture was brought or shipped later by immigrant British or Loyalist forbears. Unlike domestic necessities such as utility pottery, simple glass, or hardware and nails, there is no evidence of any early commercial importation of furniture; only of its transport as personal effects. Importation of furniture came only at the beginning of the 19th century. Though dealers have also imported considerable English furniture in recent years, virtually all of the good 18th-century American furniture that is now known in the Maritimes appears originally to have come as settlers effects.

Survival Rates

It is difficult to judge from hindsight just what sorts of furniture and furnishings were generally favoured in Georgian-period Canada. There are few descriptive contemporary references, particularly those dating before the 1820s, but these indicate that rusticity was much more the norm than elegance. For a view of styles and quality in the best of indigenous furniture, we must instead look very largely to what still exists today.

There seem to be no extant examples of English-Canadian furniture, from any area, that one could reasonably consider to have been produced before about 1785. Even in Quebec and Montreal, the centres of English military and mercantile life after the fall of New France in 1760, there is no record of migration or activity by skilled English or Scottish craftsmen for at least another twenty years.

It was the end of the American Revolution, rather than just of the Seven Years War, which finally brought reasonable political stability to Canada, and ended not only more than a century of recurring English-French warfare on the North American continent, but a long period of English colonial tensions as well. After this, the spread of highly specialized crafts and trades followed very closely in time the pattern of land settlement and of population growth.

In the 18th and early 19th centuries, though possession of one or two better pieces of furniture, likely passed on within a family, was perhaps not uncommon, the small quantity of early formal furniture surviving today does not suggest this was in any way typical. Even as late as the 1830s, contemporary descriptions refer constantly to the sparseness of furnishing and the simplicity of furniture. The great majority of Georgian-period households, certainly, were equipped with the minimum essentials of plain and even rude home-made or carpenter-built softwood furniture, without style and of the simplest sort.

This early home-made furniture simply has not survived. Made for hard and often temporary usage (though "temporary" could be a long time), and meant to be replaced, it was generally broken up or burned when it became unstable or was no longer needed. Like earlier Canadian earthenware utility pottery, every known example of which has been excavated from some archaeological context, the survival rate to our day of early rough furniture has been essentially nil.

Stylized furniture of special quality, incorporating good woods, proportions, and craftsmanship, is something else. Pieces of this calibre, brought from the "old country," or purchased or commissioned from local specialist cabinetmakers, were treasured by most families and passed on from one generation to another. The original owners cared for such furniture, since it was pleasing to the eye and an indicator of economic and social status, and it had, after all, been expensive to acquire. Home-made furniture offered no such motivations for preservation. Ultimately, then, good furniture took on familial contexts as well, as "grandmother's dining table" or "uncle's favourite chair." The result, in the long run, has been a somewhat higher survival rate for good furniture than for rough necessities. Losses over the years, probably still substantial, have been due far more to accidental fires than deliberate discard.

"Desk & Bookcase," from Chippendale. See fig. 78.

Origins of Cabinet-Making

The earliest specialized production of furniture in the 18th century seems to have been of simple ladder-back and Windsor chairs. There was constant demand for such pieces, as chairs were more difficult for settlers to make themselves than were assembled-plank tables, benches, cupboards, or open shelving. George MacLaren, in *Antique Furniture by Nova Scotian Craftsmen*, mentions that the fourteen joiners and turners who came to Halifax in 1749 with the Cornwallis expedition made "chairs with rush seats," certainly ladder-back types. None of these particular chairs is known to have survived but many other professionally made 18th-century chairs do exist.

All Canadian Windsor chairs are patterned on American rather than English forms, with rods forming the full backs. (See figs. 54–58.) The English Windsor chair type, with its central and often pierced back-splat flanked by rods, strangely enough does not seem to have been made at all in English Canada. Earlier Windsor chairs, too, are restricted to a few bow-backed, continuous-back-and-arm, square-backed, and comb-backed forms, often with "bamboo" turnings. The far greater variety of "kitchen" Windsor chairs, from pillow-backs to arrow-backed, rabbit-eared, and gunstock types, appear only in the 19th century, from myriad small factories particularly in Nova Scotia and Ontario.

The earliest recorded furniture factory in Canada was the Windsor chair shop of Joseph DeGant, believed to have been established about 1780 in Halifax. Numerous DeGant chairs survive (see fig. 54), identifiable by the marking, *DEGANT/WAR* [*ranted*]. *HAL*[*ifax*] stamped or branded on the bottom of the shaped plank seat. Later Windsor chair-makers often marked many of their products in the same manner, as did American chair-makers.

Cabinet-making and chair-making finally began to flourish in the 1780s and '90s, with newly immigrated makers setting up shops and small factories wherever sufficient markets existed. A letter of April 16, 1787, from Robert Woolsey in Quebec to James Morrison at Montreal, is more specific than most.

> . . . You told me when at Montreal that Windsor Chairs cou'd be had always. Major Cox wou'd wish to have a dozen painted green. The backs of them are to rise with around, not square tops, and arms. Don't lose any time in telling me whether you have found a Cooper to answer the description I gave you.

Stylized Furniture

Though home- and carpenter-made furniture, and simple production furniture on the order of Windsor and ladder-back chairs, were the norm, and in frontier areas remained so for decades, indigenous and highly elegant furniture in various degrees of style began to appear in urban areas between 1785 and 1790. Many of the very finest pieces of English-Canadian furniture were, in fact, made before about 1810.

MacLaren notes thirty cabinet-makers, including the first, Edward Draper, as working in Nova Scotia by or before 1810. Huia Ryder lists twenty-four operating during the same period in New Brunswick. Jean Palardy, in a very incomplete listing, notes seventeen English and Scottish cabinet-makers in Quebec before 1810, and Elizabeth Collard has found nine others in Montreal alone.

Styles — Late Chippendale

The prevailing style for formal furniture during this period we can only call generic late Chippendale, as was then the current mainstream in England and the United States. This focussed on such forms us tall pendulum clocks with domed or serpentine broken-arch cornices. Tables and chairs generally had straight and square cross-sectioned legs, occasionally moulded, the so-called "Marlborough" leg that by the 1770s was rapidly supplanting cabriole legs on English furniture. Full cabriole legs, as an earlier 18th-century form, are rare and generally an archaic characteristic on Canadian furniture. Chairs had simple vase-splatted backs, usually pierced but occasionally solid, and often with eared back frames. Chest of drawers typically were flat-faced and rectangular, with straight-edged tops and plain extended square bracket bases and feet.

Sheraton-Hepplewhite

Somewhat later in date in Canada than the generic Chippendale style, but overlapping it, were the basic Hepplewhite and Sheraton-derived types. The makers of even the better pieces focussed on the main characteristics of these forms, for example, thin, square-tapered or round, reeded legs, but then adapted, often heavily, for simplicity in detail and embellishment. Unlike the Chippendale, Canadian Sheraton or Hepplewhite furniture even approaching an adherence to real purity of style is virtually unknown; adaptation is all but universal.

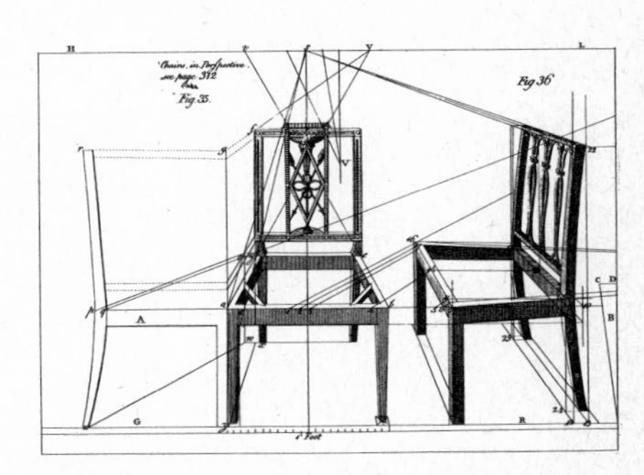

"Chairs in Perspective," from Thomas Sheraton, *The Cabinetmaker and Upholsterer's Drawing-Book*, 1792.

While the Chippendale-based forms, at least before 1800 or so, for the most part are stylistically straightforward, in the 19th century stylistic mixtures and hybrids became quite common. Particular details, such as chair or chest of drawer legs, or chair back formations, or reeding, fluting, or the addition of columns, were often used in strange contexts and mixtures. It is not unusual to see isolated characteristics of two or even three basic English design forms incorporated into the same piece of furniture. This occurred particularly with archaic 17th- or early 18th-century details included in later design forms, with the Sheraton and Hepplewhite styles which were often intermixed, and as Chippendale-Hepplewhite, Sheraton-Regency, and Sheraton-American Empire combinations. English-Canadian furniture of this early 19th-century period may be generally quite simple, but it is never uninteresting.

American Federal

Considering the extremely strong influence of New England, New York State, and Pennsylvania, both as places of origin of immigrants, and because of easier north-south rather than east-west trade and travel contacts, the derivations of English forms called American "Federal" dominated large segments of English-Canadian cabinet-making. This should perhaps even be used in Canada as a term for basic design influences, rather than looking back to original English design forms which, geographically and culturally, were often a stage removed.

Classical Revival—French Empire

The prime exception in earlier Georgian Canada to the *mélange* of styles which make up the American Federal designation is the French Empire, and the rationale seems historical rather than cultural. The Classical Revival, and particularly the classical Egyptian-derived forms emanating from France during the Napoleonic period, had a profound influence in the United States, and became very popular there shortly after 1800. This Classical Revival–French Empire style became the guide for some of the greatest of early 19th-century American cabinet-makers, perhaps most notably French-trained Charles-Honore Lannuier of New York.

Classical Revival—English Regency

In Britain, the same basic French Empire influences in furniture, sometimes called "Egyptian" combined with the heavily ancient-Greek-influenced English Classical Revival derived largely from architecture, resulted in an early 19th-century stylistic cousin, the so-called English Regency. It is the Regency derivation, rather than the French Empire directly, that became fashionable in Canada, and for good reason.

France and the United States had become allies during the American Revolution; in some ways the American Revolution was but another chapter in a century of English-French warfare. The French Revolution and its aftermath then made Britain, to say the least, extremely nervous, and Napoleon and the Empire after 1800 became a direct military threat perhaps equalling that of Germany in 1940. The possible influence of revolutionary France and the Empire on Quebec was a secondary colonial worry, but worrisome nonetheless. It is in any event an understatement to say that, following the conquest of New France in 1760, Britain was determined to prevent any direct contact between France, the traditional rival and enemy, and British North America with its considerable French-speaking population.

Furniture design influences were, of course, merely a negligible offshoot of the drama in which Britain was involved between 1775 and 1815, but they are indicative of the position of British North America during that period. The English Regency furniture thus appeared in Canada in quantity, was copied, and became extremely popular after about 1810. The directly French Empire or "Egyptian" style, ultimately quite Americanized, became a strong fashion in Canada only after about 1825, by which time it was degenerating in form and already slowly declining as a fashion in the United States.

To be sure, there were all manner of exceptions, particularly in the Sheraton-Classical Revival forms of Duncan Phyfe and other makers, which were introduced into Canada at an early stage. (See figs. 71, 72, 164, 182.) There are also many early 19th-century Canadian pieces which must simply be considered as generically Classical Revival, and which defy sorting into specific Regency or Empire pigeonholes.

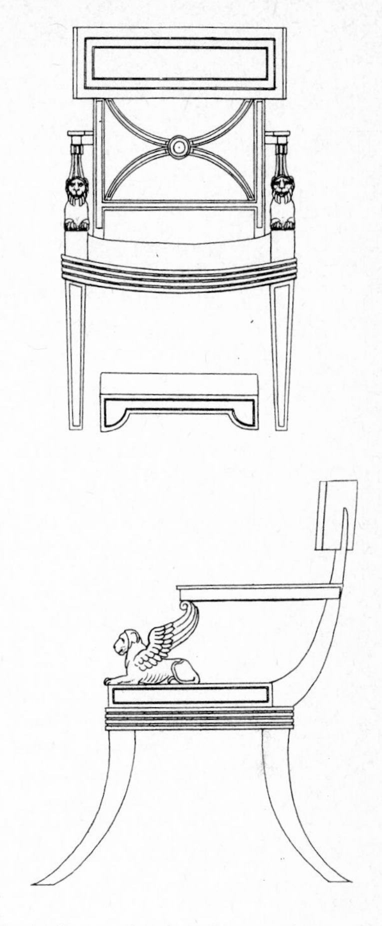

Chair form, from Thomas Hope, *Household Furniture and Interior Decoration*, 1807. See fig. 51.

American Empire

Though they came from essentially the same origins, just as family trees diverge there were decided differences between the English Regency furniture of the early 1800s as it was produced in Canada, and the Americanized Empire style as it was later introduced. The Regency forms, popular from about 1810 to about 1825, were lightly structured, never ponderous, oppressive or overwhelming, and often were delicate and flowing in lines and curves.

The later American Empire, conversely, emphasized thick and often multi-segmented pillars and columns, sarcophagus conformations, solid lion's paw feet, massive overhangs and set-backs, and often tomb-like rather than graceful proportioning. Compared with the earlier Regency, the Canadian Empire style is often heavy and architecturally neo-Stalinist. Since the English Regency is clearly a Georgian style, and the American Empire, in its late Canadian time frame, a neo-Victorian style, a separation of the two has been used as the dividing line between the two volumes of this survey.

Any prolonged observation of the products of, say, the first forty years of specialized and professional cabinet-making in English Canada leads invariably to three basic conclusions.

Simplicity of Furniture — Market Conservatism

First, even the best of the Georgian-period Canadian furniture is elementally simple compared with that of Britain or the United States. The cabinet-makers who emigrated, and in turn trained apprentices, were builders and suppliers to a population of slowly increasing prosperity, but not of English-style wealth, and particularly not of great hereditary wealth. This market also wanted primarily what was elsewhere already in fashion, of proven acceptability, and already established as symbolic of modern elegance.

We should remember here also that, unlike many later 19th- and 20th-century European immigrants who came to Canada for positive reasons, seeking expanded opportunity and an improved living standard, the same was not true of many earlier English-speaking immigrants. The Loyalists did not come to Canada of free choice, nor did many of the Scots. These people were often dispossessed and sometimes even driven from their native homes; they had lost the practical option of staying where they were. Canada was not to them at the time a country of great opportunity or even of real expectation, but merely of hope. British North America was a refuge, a haven, and the immigrants refugees. There is nothing like having lived through a period of displaced person or refugee status to engender personal conservatism.

The cabinet-makers to this population were thus followers of established and prevailing tastes, not designers, innovators, or trend-setters. New designs and styles, in architecture as well as furniture, usually did not appear widely in Canada until they enjoyed general acceptance abroad, or were sometimes even in decline there, already supplanted by newer fashions. For this reason, at least before 1830 or so, it is generally prudent to assign date frames to English-Canadian furniture somewhat conservatively, dating later rather than earlier in the time range indicated by particular style characteristics.

Equally important perhaps, unlike England with court or Royal Appointment cabinet-makers who were almost automatically taste-makers *ex-officio,* or the United States with its fashion-setting cabinet-makers of the eastern seaboard cities, there is no apparent evidence that any Canadian cabinet-makers enjoyed particular prestige, or any special influence or power over the trends of fashion. These craftsmen were providing furnishing for houses, and occasionally large houses, but not urban mansions or great country estates. More particularly, there were no special classes of patronage, by either birth or acquired wealth, sufficient to convey such taste-making power. Always, of course, in "establishment" taste the "English-is-better" syndrome prevailed as well.

Tastes in furniture dictated good design and proportion according to prevailing styles, but reduced to ultimate simplicity. Pieces of good but standard woods with an obvious emphasis on minimum expense enjoyed a ready and growing market. Opulence had little place in this environment.

Thus in Georgian-period Canadian furniture, extensive or complete veneering is rare, and marquetry unknown. Carving is uncommon and, where it exists, is of minimal extent or complexity. Inlay work, except for imported motif inlays (shells, fans, etc.), was usually simple ovals or rectangles, basic single-wood stringing, bordering, or at most, multi-wood geometric banding. Convoluted furniture in the sense of *bombe* forms, extensive block carving, elegant hand-shaped and carved-kneed cabriole legs, or complex serpentine or reverse serpentine steam-bowed chest fronts simply does not exist. Few people could afford to buy or to house adequately such pieces (and these few tended anyway to English furniture). Thus cabinet-makers, in the absence of commissions or an obvious market, could hardly afford to attempt such time-consuming works on speculation, much less innovative designs, even where they may have been capable of them.

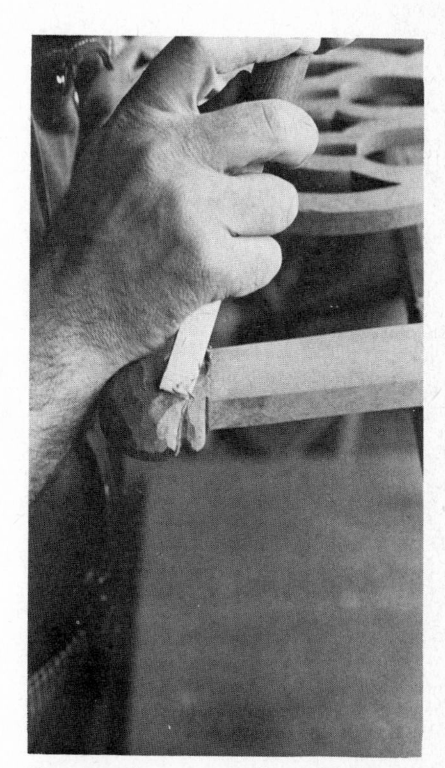

Carving the crest-rail scroll of a reproduction Chippendale chair, at the Kittinger Co., Buffalo, N.Y.

The best known cabinet-makers, people such as Tulles, Pallister & McDonald, Thomas Nisbet, and Alexander Lawrence, whose work we can be sure of, in fact were probably capable of building much more elaborate and opulent furniture than what they normally had the economic opportunity to produce. Time was money, then as now. The need to direct themselves to the realities of their actual markets, the constant necessity for economies and, always, the general preference for imports, were obvious and probably critical impediments to striving toward the limits of ability.

Climatic Constraints

The realities of economic conditions, the markets cabinet-makers faced, and the Canadian climate, in the first and second generations of settlement also seem to have governed the forms of furniture which came to be produced in quantity. Judging from the relative incidence of survival, which is at best an imperfect measure, but certainly contains some clues, some furniture types were quite obviously generally useful and necessary, and some very clearly were special circumstance frills.

Considering, for a total view, the realm of country furniture as well, chairs, cupboards, and varied multi-purpose tables were by all odds the most ubiquitous types, followed closely by chests of drawers. Stylized pieces were, of course, in the minority among these forms. If we add to this myriad box chests and plain benches, only occasionally made in sophisticated versions, we quickly conclude that general-purpose and storage furniture forms predominated, and that the average household was a quite basically furnished establishment. This, of course, only confirms past written descriptions.

Among chairs, for example, certainly Windsor and ladder-back types were common and widespread. Even the most basic of the stylized chairs, such as the simple late 18th-century Chippendale-Hepplewhite types, are scarce by comparison. Other more specialized chair forms, such as comfortable upholstered wing chairs (see figs. 1-7) or corner chairs (see figs. 32, 33), are simply rare.

This pattern carries through to other furniture types, and indicates that the Georgian period in Canada was hardly an age of comfort. As well as wing chairs, sofas were also a very rarified form. In fact, upholstered furniture of any type dating from before 1820 to 1825 is most uncommon, and there are no indications of its widespread use.

Some specialized furniture types in the earlier settlement period one would expect to have found only in affluent homes, but the paucity of other forms is somewhat surprising. Card tables, sofa tables, side or pier tables, long dining tables with extra leaves or banquet ends, desks, bookcases, and even clocks are in the minority of extant furniture. The fact, however, that of these forms sophisticated examples are nearly as common as country pieces is a sure sign that their original distribution was very limited. Some of the specialized table forms, in fact, do not even exist in country versions in Canada; they were unnecessary in single-heat-source houses.

The Canadian climate clearly was a deciding factor in the choice and use of furniture. Where both cooking and heating depended on a single central or end-wall fireplace, as in most earlier houses, eating, card-playing, womens' sewing, and virtually every other activity requiring a table surface, took place at a large and likely pine-plank central table in the kitchen near the fireplace. Specialized formal dining tables, fold-over card tables, or parlour chairs were really worth having only in large houses with enough heat sources, i.e., multiple fireplaces, to make their use viable. Who could otherwise comfortably eat, play cards, read, or socialize half frozen?

The relative scarcity and high quality of many Canadian clocks existing from before about 1825, even presuming that at least ten times as many English clocks were probably in use, suggests that a large proportion of the population was still scheduled by the sun, emptiness of stomach, and state of tiredness. Other apparent scarcities however are puzzling. The number of extant beds for example, both canopy and low post, datable earlier than 1830 is far smaller than the existing quantity of chests of drawers. Obviously many households used built-in bunks, especially for children, as bunks were much easier to curtain against icy drafts when partially surrounded by walls. The paucity of beds, in fact, suggests that unheated early bedrooms, into which one rushed only to get quickly under the covers, were a low-priority furnishing concern, and that most beds may well have been simply home-made frames, long since disposed of and replaced.

The number of clearly Canadian-made formal or even simple mirrors surviving from the Georgian period is hardly greater than that of clocks or card tables. Again presuming at least a tenfold quantity of imported mirrors, the vast majority of the population still would seem to have done without. Living without clocks is one thing; it even has virtue, but what person and, particularly, what woman, even at the turn of the 19th century would carry on without being able to have a clear view of one's own image? A general absence of mirrors is hardly believable. More likely most mirrors were acquired as pieces of imported mirrored glass, then simply home-framed, and eventually broken and discarded. Only stylized and more treasured parlour mirrors have survived.

There is no question that climate has in Canada had a considerable impact on furniture use, in patterns quite different from much of the United States, or particularly Britain. Iron heating stoves were virtually unknown before about

1815, and really came into universal use only in the 1830s. This is probably why, for example, we find so few bedroom wash-stands datable before about 1825; they were useless in unheated bedrooms. The broader influences of climate on lifestyles, however, are subjects which go far beyond furniture alone, and are for a different discourse.

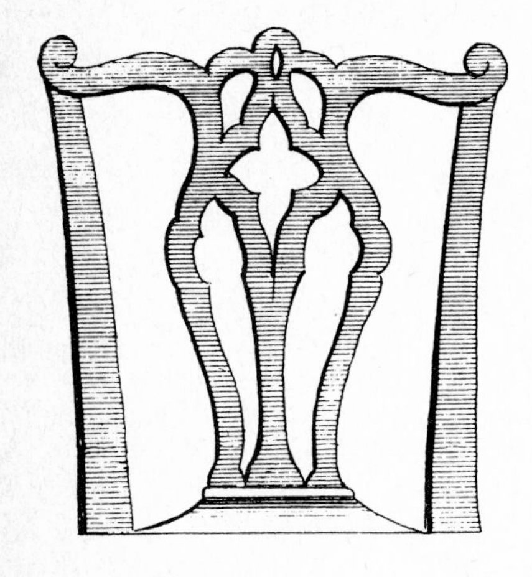

Training and Instinct

A final, obvious conclusion from prolonged observation is that most if not all Georgian-period Canadian furniture was built either from learned habit, i.e., apprenticeship training, or from examination of and adaptation from other pieces, even to plain outright copying. Cabinet-makers would occasionally sketch rough configurations of pieces they were making in their day-books, a few of which still exist, but there is little evidence of furniture having been planned or laid out from published design or pattern books of the period. Like houses built without architectural design, most furniture was made on an *ad hoc* basis, with the maker's instinct, training, experience, and visual judgement far more important than anything plotted on paper.

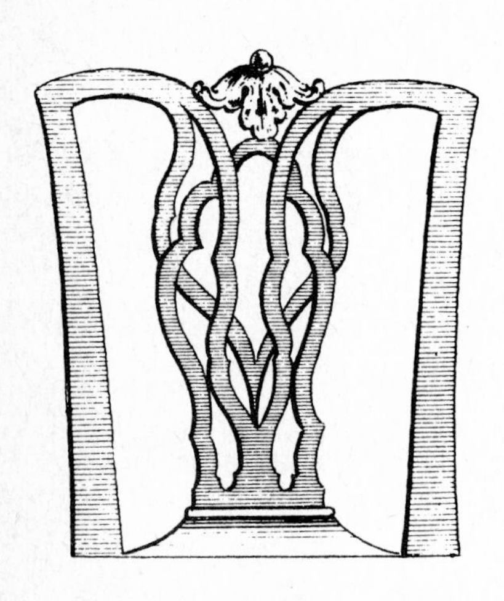

Archaic Details

Though the generic late Chippendale was the earliest prevailing formal furniture style in Canada, one cannot imply from this that earlier forms and characteristics were automatically discounted and abandoned by cabinet-makers, as might well have been the case had adherence to fashion been the only basis for Canadian furniture design. In fact, all manner of archaic or "throw-back" details, and even whole pieces, appeared in Canadian furniture long after they had, stylistically, become totally obsolete. This is one indication of furniture design having gone into a traditional realm, subject no longer to whims and changes of fashion, but only to new generations of cabinet-makers and markets.

Consider that New England "Carver" and bannister-back chairs were being made in Upper Canada even well into the 19th century. (cf. Shackleton, nos. 25-27; Dobson, no. 86.) From isolated known and datable pieces we can establish also that country Chippendale chairs were being made probably as late as 1825. (See figs. 9, 10.) Derivative but identifiable English Queen Anne period and even 17th-century characteristics appear equally late. (See figs. 15, 34, 85, 90, 91, 172, 244, 256, 307, 309.)

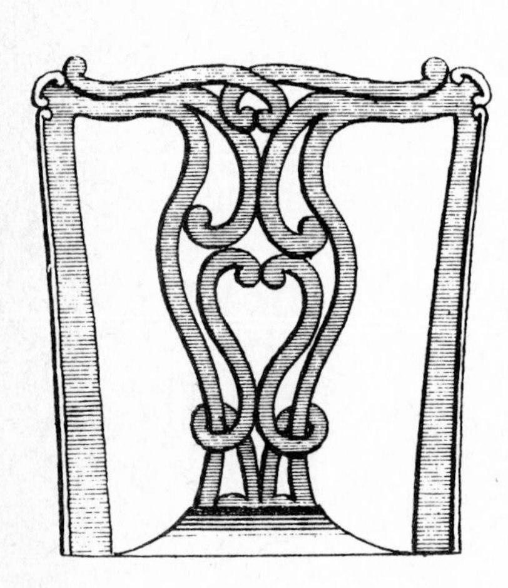

Chair Backs, from Robert Manwaring, *The Cabinet and Chair-Maker's Real Friend and Companion . . .*, 1765. See figs. 8-18.

Impact of Fashion

The short ogee-bracket foot, a stylistic characteristic of the early and mid-18th century, in Canada inexplicably appears only on Ontario-German furniture (see figs, 80, 160-1, 236-8, 256), and at a later date — the 1830s — than either square-bracket feet characteristic of the later 18th century, or the flared "Hepplewhite" on "French" feet of the early 19th century. Round, reeded "Sheraton" legs, though never a principal form, seem in Canada both to have become popular later, and to have continued to be made far longer, than "Hepplewhite" square-tapered legs. Both types, particularly on tables and chairs, by the 1830s had degenerated to plain, round turnings.

While shifts in fashion and the introduction of design changes today occur largely through commercial pressures and the deliberate creation of consumer desire through impersonal media, in the late 18th and early 19th century they came about much more through direct personal contact and social influences. The common occurrence of archaic design characteristics particularly in Canadian country furniture, and the continuing fabrication of obsolete design forms, can only be explained from a rationale of isolation and a relative lack of personal mobility. The further physically removed one is from the origins of influence and from direct contact with fashion, the less is its impact or importance.

Georgian-period Canadian furniture, though usually based on identifiably English-derived design origins, took so many divergent paths and so often included intrusive anomalies that it is very difficult to apply strictly English period or design-name designations. With earlier Canadian furniture, these designations often fail to adequately describe individual pieces, particularly with design forms that have gone from fashion into tradition, or that have had the secondary influence of an American stop-over following their English origins. In using design-descriptive labels such as "Hepplewhite" or "Sheraton," it is best to think of them in quotation marks, in a generic rather than specific sense. Likewise, such terms are often all but useless as dating expressions. Except as specific referrals to isolated details and characteristics, we could perhaps even give them up.

Cabinet-makers, especially in rural or frontier areas, had been trained in the design forms, whether fashionable or traditional, during their apprenticeships or other training. They then went on to produce what their own customers and markets would accept, and particularly, what they could afford. Except perhaps in the interests of economy, these makers were hardly about to shift their styles of production without some good reason; why should they? Since fashionable influences beyond urban centres were at most residual and gradual, there were no good reasons.

This situation, of course, was to change drastically from the early second quarter of the 19th century onward. Change became influenced by everything from the mobility of people and freight afforded by ever faster and more reliable steamships and railroads, to the development of modern advertising, and later to mail order merchandising. New fashions were introduced and becoming widespread at an accelerating rate, as the pace of human existence itself was speeding up, a process that has not yet ceased. Thus rapid change, not only in furniture design but in all other categories of physical objects, and even the desirability of change for the sake of change itself, was soon to become acceptable and normal.

Sofa, from Chippendale's *The Gentleman and Cabinet-Maker's Director*, 1762. See fig. 60.

The Question of Identification

A most immediate problem of finer Canadian furniture, considering the "it-must-be-English" syndrome, is the often very difficult matter of identifying pieces of high quality as being Canadian in origin. Georgian-period, English-Canadian furniture stylistically lies mixed in a large cultural salad, since it is derivative of the styles and forms first of both England and Scotland, and then often of the United States, which adopted these styles. Fashions in furnishings during the Georgian period were much the same throughout the English-language world. Differences in furniture between Britain and the New World thus appeared far less in basic designs and styles than in relative degrees of elaboration and opulence.

In Canada, as elsewhere, the favoured late 18th- and early 19th-century design forms were those of the basic Chippendale, Hepplewhite, Sheraton, and varied Classical Revival schools, and of individual fashion-setting designers and makers, from Robert Adam to Duncan Phyfe, and countless others. In pure form, adapted with more traditional designs, or simplified into "country" furniture, the core design characteristics of the various English schools or "periods" still usually remain apparent even in severe stylistic mixtures.

Determining even Canadian nationality, much less regionality, of furniture within the whole sphere of predominantly English styles, sometimes themselves European derivatives, can be much more difficult. Most earlier English-Canadian cabinet-makers were native English, Scottish, or Anglo- or German-American first-generation immigrants, often producing furniture in adaptations of the styles and forms originally taught them as apprentices or trainees. The apprentice-training system itself appears to have been a substantial contributor to stability and longevity of style and design.

Use of Mahogany

The most favoured wood of the best of Canadian Georgian furniture was West Indies mahogany, imported as logs into port cities such as Halifax, Saint John, Quebec, and Montreal, as in England and all American coastal cities.

These were the very cities which developed and grew as centres of commerce, wealth, and rising expectation, and which could generate the sort of excellence and elegance in craftsmanship which reached its zenith in cabinet-making. Mahogany logs were a ballast cargo, the shipping of which was pure profit, like crated window glass or brick, for ship-owners and masters. Sailing vessels had to ballast with stone in the absence of such heavy and stable consignments.

Mahogany as a cargo, however, was also far better suited to water than to overland transport. On the roads of the period heavy cargo haulage was all but impossible. Thus even within short distances from seaport cities, we find that the use of mahogany declined very abruptly, in favour of indigenous direct substitutes such as cherry and stained birch or butternut, or contrasts such as figured maple or walnut. However, even if mahogany was not used, the basic stylistic influences in furniture were as far-reaching as the range of travel and settlement of people themselves.

In Canada during the Georgian period, from roughly 1780 on, cabinet-making in mahogany was thus limited to the immediate areas of ports of landing for logs or lumber. Further shipment by river happened in a very few instances. As a result, we do not find any Canadian Georgian-period mahogany furniture attributable to non-coastal Nova Scotia, to central New Brunswick except Fredericton, on the Saint John River, to the Eastern Townships or anywhere in Quebec other than Quebec City, Trois Rivières, and Montreal, or at all, with isolated exceptions, to Upper Canada. Cabinet-makers in all of these inaccessable areas depended on native woods.

Importance of Wood Determination

The problem of identifying sophisticated Georgian-period furniture is much more pronounced in sorting out differences between Canadian and northeastern American furniture than is identifying those between Canadian and British furniture. This is so in spite of the fact that the considerable majority of early cabinet-makers were English or Scots immigrants, with somewhat fewer Americans. Very simply, the native woods of eastern Canada and New England and New York are largely identical species. Those of Canada and the British Isles are wholly different (though many British, European, and Asian species were introduced into North America in the later 19th and the 20th centuries).

We do fairly often encounter English furniture incorporating North American woods, although it is never wholly composed of such woods. A substantial lumbering trade to Britain, from both Canada and the United States, grew after the American Revolution. Most of this was building lumber, primarily white pine and spruce, shipped by the millions of board feet of sawed lumber. However, hardwoods such as maple and walnut were included as well, destined largely for room interior finishing, but also for cabinet-work.

In the early 19th century, English cabinet-makers also developed a special liking for North American curly and bird's-eye maple. Good pieces of English furniture in maple thus appear periodically, often recently imported, to confound the identification process, but these will invariably include native British secondary woods. As a case in point, we once examined (with a thought to acquiring) a handsome, bird's-eye maple flared-footed chest of drawers, dating probably from about 1810. With well-selected tightly figured wood, lonzenge-shaped keyhole inlays, and English lion's head ring drawer pulls, the chest in its configuration was perfect as a fine early Nova Scotia or possibly Upper Canada piece.

The drawer sides, however, were of a soft wood which looked like almost impossibly straight-grained pine or, more likely, larch (tamarack). The latter is quite unknown as an underlying secondary wood in Canadian furniture. A small sliver of that wood, the cell structure of which was examined microscopically, proved to be European Larch (*Larix decidua*), which is native to the British Isles, but not, in 1810, to North America. The bird's-eye maple chest of drawers was thus clearly of English origin.

Card Table, from Sheraton. See fig. 116.

Wood Identification

Positive wood identification is perhaps the single most important prerequisite to furniture identification. Generally speaking, imported woods and veneers aside, the natural growing ranges, or overlap of ranges, of species of native northeastern North American woods used in a piece of furniture will be a prime clue to where that piece was made. Unfortunately, the natural ranges of many common North American cabinet woods are geographically very large, so wood identification alone in many cases can provide only a broad idea of the regional origin of a piece of furniture.

Though some antiquarians may choose to believe otherwise, species of woods cannot always be reliably identified from naked-eyed examination alone. Standing trees, bark, branches, twigs and buds, leaves and seeds all have readily visible and identifiable characteristics. By the time wood becomes lumber or veneer, however, all of these characteristics are gone. Only the grain and cell structure remain.

Wood grain, though certainly varied between species, is at best an uncertain criterion for positive wood identification. Given a standard set of native wood samples for making comparisons, and a five-, ten-, or fifteen-power jewellers' pocket magnifier, both of which any antiquarian dealing with woods should have, with experience one can certainly examine wood grain and develop conclusions. This will usually provide genus identifications such as birch or cherry, but not species, i.e., white, grey, or yellow birch, or black, red, or pin cherry.

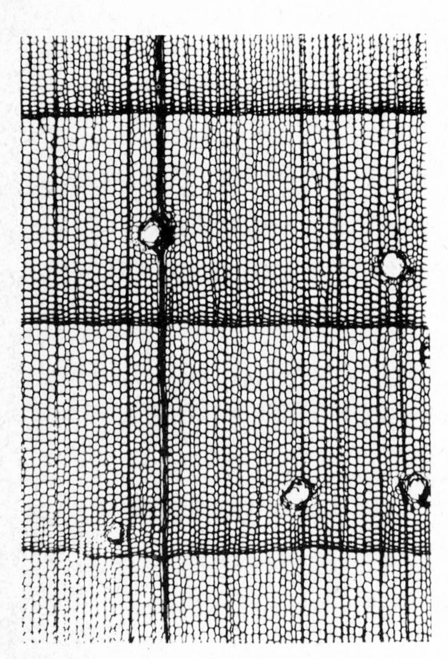

Cross-section, x 30, of white pine cell structure, from Hale, *The Structure of Wood.*

Many similar species produce similarly grained woods. Particularly, many similar species not only of European trees, but of trees world-wide, produce wood grain structures very close to those of North American species. Likewise, the conditions under which an individual tree grows — soil, moisture, sunlight, and climate — can have a profound effect on the grain and colour of its wood. Thus one cannot trust absolutely wood identifications based solely on wood grain appearance through a pocket magnifier unless all other considerations, including furniture style, hardware, construction details, and other woods, are completely supportive.

Only cell structure is an absolute characteristic, for it is as individual to specific species as are all the other components of a whole tree. Even cell structure, however, can still vary with growth conditions and sometimes be difficult to identify. Small wood slivers, preferably including both cross and lengthwise structure, can be shaved from non-visible areas of furniture. Magnified fifty to one hundred times under a binocular microscope, wood cell structure becomes immediately apparent. As in any precise identification of natural material, of course, the examiner must have background knowledge of what he is looking for, and the experience to be able to recognize what he observes, which is why wood cell identification is usually a specialized skill.

Identification by Elimination

Once the woods of a particular piece of furniture have been established, we can move on to examining possible conclusions that can be derived from them. The process now becomes one of gradual elimination, as the sorting out of various suppositions inevitably leads to an ever-narrowing range of truly supportable choices.

Secondary Woods

There is no evidence that earlier (pre-1830) Canadian furniture makers ever used imported exotic woods other than mahogany, and very occasionally rosewood, as either primary or internal secondary woods. Veneers, of course, often imported as cut and bundled sheets, are another matter. Thus if a good piece of Georgian-period mahogany furniture incorporates internal secondary woods not naturally indigenous to Canada, the possibility of Canadian origin is excluded. We just do not find deal or Baltic pine, or European larch, in the structure of Canadian furniture.

Should our hypothetical piece of furniture, for example, include any, but not necessarily all, secondary woods native only to the United States, but whose natural growth ranges do not extend as far north as Canada, then the piece is almost certainly American. There is no known evidence of any importation of middle-Atlantic or southern American woods into Canada. Earlier Canadian furniture, even the most sophisticated, uses white pine as the main and usually the only secondary wood. Only occasionally is there any other, such as poplar, spruce, or oak, except for native hardwoods used as glue blocks or specific support pieces.

Northeastern American furniture, of course, very often also includes white pine as the main secondary wood. This confuses identification, and from the Canadian view precludes any definite conclusions as to Canadian origin solely from identification of white pine. Considerable American furniture, however, has varied and mixed secondary woods, of perhaps several different species in the same piece. Such secondary mixtures are very uncommon in Canadian furniture. Poplar, particularly, is very often a combination secondary wood in northeastern American pieces, but it was used only occasionally in early Canadian furniture.

Conversely, should the hypothetical piece of furniture include any secondary woods native only to the British Isles or Europe, as in the bird's-eye maple chest of drawers mentioned earlier, then the possibility of Canadian origin is again excluded. Makers of English furniture favoured oak as their secondary wood. This is all but unknown in Canadian furniture. (See, however, fig. 91.) Other British and

European woods, however, including various species of pine which cannot visually be positively distinguished from North American white pine, will often be found as well in English furniture. Those species of European woods now also found in North America, including Scotch and Baltic pine, European larch, English walnut, and others, were introduced only in the later 19th century, and well after the Georgian period of Canadian furniture.

There is always, of course, the occurrence of pieces which are plain confounding. Montgomery (p. 29) mentions occasional English furniture which has imported secondary white pine. The possibility of furniture produced from the woods of abandoned or broken-up sailing vessels, from older imported furniture or other cabinet-work, or even from exotic long-floating logs or lumber cannot be discounted. Still, we must assume that any presence of non-native woods except for mahogany and other exotic veneers, and particularly of non-native secondary woods, is presumptive evidence of non-Canadian origin.

Native Hardwoods

The most common of the native hardwoods in sophisticated and "better country" Canadian furniture are maple (often curly or bird's-eye), birch (sometimes highly figured), black cherry, butternut, and black walnut. Ash, hickory, and beech appear only in Windsor chairs, but not in stylized Georgian-period furniture. Poplar and oak were rarely used, and only as secondary woods. Other native possibilities such as elm, chestnut, and sycamore, and cultivated fruitwoods such as apple, pear, and peach do not appear to have been used as cabinet woods at all in this time period.

Maple

Maple, either straight-grained or figured, is not alone evidence of any particular regional origin. Maple was a favourite wood for furniture in Ontario, the Quebec Eastern Townships, and the Maritimes, as well as in New England, New York, Pennsylvania, and Great Britain. Maple, however, was often mixed with other primary or external woods, and these combinations vary considerably from one area to another, depending on wood availability.

A very typical primary wood combination in Ontario was curly or bird's-eye maple and cherry, often striking and eye-catching. The maple was sometimes used as a veneer over pine, or occasionally inlaid, while the cherry generally served for main structural sections — legs, stretchers, tops and sides, and table-tops or leaves. Maple and walnut combinations appear as well, but less commonly, and their origin in Canada is limited to the Niagara Peninsula and the southwestern Ontario areas.

In Nova Scotia and New Brunswick, mahogany or birch were most often combined with maple, also providing a contrast. Native wood combinations in the Maritimes, however, were both less common and usually less extensive than in Ontario. Though contrasting woods were often used in furniture structure or as veneers, the use of the darker woods was generally limited to drawer edge beading, and to thin string or keyhole inlays. On basically dark mahogany furniture, conversely, lighter woods were most popular as inlays.

Extensive contrasting mixtures of primary woods in stylized pieces are quite uncommon in Anglo-Quebec furniture. As in the Maritimes, combinations were most typically limited to inlays or drawer edge beading. The woods used with maple in Quebec, however, are most often indigenous butternut or other maple of a different grain.

To reiterate, maple, and to a lesser extent birch, are the only primary furniture native hardwoods commonly used in all areas of Canada during the Georgian period. Combinations of maple and cherry are very strongly indicative of Upper Canada origin, while mixtures including walnut are positive indications. One must be cautious in locating or attributing cherry and maple combinations, however, for they are also common to New York State, though sometimes with different treatments or in different patterns. There is also a considerable quantity of 19th-century New York State furniture in Ontario.

"Secretary and Bookcase," from Hepplewhite. See fig. 79.

Maple mixed with lesser amounts of butternut, or the reverse, is good evidence of Quebec Eastern Townships or New Brunswick origin. Maple furniture with a minor use of mahogany or birch is most likely to have come from the Maritimes, or possibly New England.

Maple inlays, or figured maple veneered surfaces incorporated into basically mahogany furniture, are another matter. Maple string or band inlays were commonly applied by Anglo-Quebec urban cabinet-makers, as in the Maritimes, and in New England and New York. Only in Ontario furniture is stringing exceptional. Some of the finest existing New England furniture, in fact, is of figured maple veneers and inlays combined with mahogany, though this was generally too opulent for the Maritimes. Maple-inlaid furniture, in the end, must really be sorted out by studying the forms of inlays, and the overall stylistic and design details.

Birch

Birch is a common primary cabinet wood only of the Maritimes, the poor man's mahogany of New Brunswick and Nova Scotia. It was probably a furniture wood of availability-necessity rather than of choice, for plain, straight-grained birch is not a handsome or rich wood when finished (except for occasional branch-crotch cuts), and is extremely susceptible to rapid decay. Though not unknown, birch was not favoured as a furniture wood in Quebec or Ontario unless there was no option. It is, of course, native there, but because of preference for other woods, was simply not often used.

Though structurally simple furniture of birch as the sole primary wood is by far the most typical in the Maritimes, mixed birch-maple and birch-mahogany pieces are commonly found as well. These combinations also appear even more frequently in northern New England, particularly Maine and New Hampshire. Simple northeastern American pieces wholly of birch are also not uncommon, and can be stylistically very similar to Maritimes birch furniture. As with Ontario vs. New York State cherry and maple, identifications here based solely on wood are always uncertain.

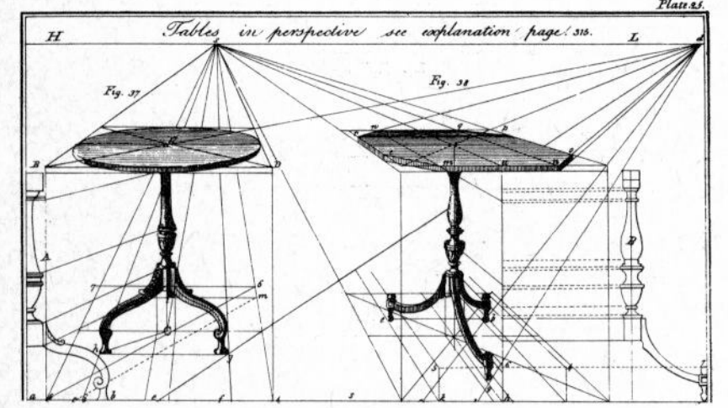

"Tables in Perspective," from Sheraton's *The Cabinetmaker and Upholsterer's Drawing-Book*, 1792.

Cherry

Black Cherry, like birch in the Maritimes, was the poor man's mahogany of Ontario and New York State. Unlike birch, it is an extremely rich and warm wood; many people prefer it to mahogany. As well as in combination with maple, of course, considerable early furniture survives that is wholly of cherry as the primary wood. In basic or generic Chippendale or Hepplewhite forms, Georgian furniture in cherry can sometimes be difficult or even impossible to differentiate absolutely as originating in Ontario, as opposed to New England-New York. Cherry is very rarely seen in Eastern Townships furniture of Quebec, or in the Maritimes. Though native, wild cherry in those areas is usually shrubby, and not of cabinet-making size or quality.

Butternut

Butternut as a cabinet wood in Canada virtually points to the Quebec Eastern Townships and the Saint John River valley of New Brunswick, as the natural range of butternut, like walnut, is rather limited. Butternut was long a favourite wood of French-Canadian traditional cabinet-makers, and French-inspired furniture is readily identified stylistically. English-Canadian butternut furniture is mostly of a higher "country" category. Butternut is a light and open-grained wood, hardly more distinguished than plain and unfigured birch. Furniture of butternut is also rarely of the highest quality in style or proportion, and was typically embellished only with simple maple stringing.

Butternut was always used as solid members, never as a veneer, and only rarely as an inlay wood, and then usually as stringing on maple furniture. Because of its lightness and less-than-rich cabinet qualities, butternut was also a furniture wood used perhaps more because of availability than aesthetic choice.

Walnut

Walnut has an even more limited natural growth range than butternut in Canada, restricted to the Niagara Peninsula and Lake Erie areas of Ontario. Walnut was also a traditional cabinet wood of the Pennsylvania Germans, who migrated into Upper Canada between the end of the American Revolution and the 1830s. Most Georgian-period walnut furniture in Ontario, because of its cultural origins, is directly derivative of the somewhat Germanized Georgian styles common, also in walnut, to southern Pennsylvania, New Jersey, Maryland, and northern Virginia.

The Germanic furniture of Ontario, in walnut as well as other woods, is usually well-proportioned in basically American late colonial and early Federal forms, but is often structurally heavier than necessary, even considering requirements of stability and durability. It is characterized by an absence of veneers, though heavy maple inlays were sometimes used. The use of the primary wood, walnut or maple, often also extends to hidden areas where a British or Anglo-American maker would more likely have used a lighter secondary wood such as pine.

Walnut was also used occasionally by English-tradition cabinet-makers, though examples of such pieces are uncommon. Much more typical was the use of walnut for contrasting details on English-derived Ontario furniture, particularly as inlaid banding and as drawer-edge beading strips.

Other Hardwoods

Ash was not generally used as a cabinet wood, and is found only in early Windsor chairs, or occasionally in later country furniture, sometimes in a curly variation. The few known pieces in curly ash, all of Ontario origin and all later than the Georgian period, are so imposing in their bright yellowish wood as to overpower any other furniture around them.

Oak and chestnut, both native woods and of similar grain, were also only rarely used in furniture during the early 19th century, and then usually as a secondary wood, or occasionally in simpler country pieces such as kitchen tables. The basic trend of fashion during the late Georgian period was to mahogany and satinwood, and its North American substitutes. Oak was long out of favour, and had been since the early 18th century, except as a secondary wood of English furniture. Oak was not to return to popularity as a cabinet wood until the 1880s.

There exists at least one early descriptive reference to chairs of beech, and its use was not uncommon in Windsor chairs. Beech was occasionally used as well in other country furniture. Beech in Canada, however, does not usually grow to large size or good saw-log diameter, and its use has not been noted in formal or stylized furniture.

Limitations of Inherent Evidence

Once whatever tentative conclusions that can be made have been determined from examination of the species and usage combinations of woods, further evidence for locating and dating furniture must come from stylistic and mechanical details. We must also consider carefully the apparent habit patterns, based on broad observation, of wood and use of other materials by cabinet-makers in different regions. Many of these craft patterns were influenced by the origins and training of makers, others by the availability of materials, and still others by markets and the preferences of customers upon whom all the specialized craftsmen depended for their livelihood.

Unfortunately, since in examining furniture we are really dealing with people and their infinite capacity for variation, there are no absolutes. Being a field where each specimen is unique, there is nothing in furniture identification even approaching the precision of scientific taxonomy, the identification and classification of natural species. There are also no absolute and dead-certain internal or inherent cabinet-making characteristics that will indicate beyond question that a particular piece of furniture was made in New Brunswick rather than Maine, or originated in upper New York State, and not Ontario. There are, instead, only subtle indications, which must be assessed both collectively and dispassionately.

Historical Information

Without any broad and absolute Canadian stylistic differences to separate the Georgian-period furniture from that of Britain, or particularly to differentiate between English Canada and the northeastern United States, to say nothing of their internal regions, we must also look at external evidence and historical information.

Historically documented examples of furniture are extremely valuable for comparative purposes. Most particularly, self-identifying, i.e., labelled or otherwise maker-marked pieces, are rare and fortunate discoveries. They alone provide the strongest possible evidence of the styles, materials usage, and workmanship of individual makers.

There were, during the Georgian period, only two makers known to have used paper labels. Thomas Nisbet of Saint John, New Brunswick (working 1814 to 1838) labelled quantities of his work before 1830 (see figs. 120, 165, 221, 283), and some forty examples are now known. An earlier Nova Scotia partnership in 1810-11, Tulles, Pallister & McDonald of Halifax, also labelled their very fine work, of which only two pieces are now known to survive. (See figs. 105, 127.) All other known maker citations are individual handwritten markings, usually in pencil.

Next in line, on the scale of reliability of evidence, is established association with a specific maker, though the furniture itself may be unmarked. One of the largest intact unified collections of furniture by a single Canadian craftsman, a group of over forty pieces made between 1835 and 1880 by John Warren Moore of St. Stephen, New Brunswick, was recently transferred by Moore's granddaughter to the Kings Landing Historical Settlement near Fredericton. She had fortunately insisted the pieces remain together. With the furniture went an accumulation of fifty years of Moore family correspondence, some describing precisely and dating many of the pieces.

Though post-Georgian, this unique collection and its documents can now serve in the future as sound evidence for reliable attribution of other pieces of furniture to John

Warren Moore. Without its preservation through generations of the Moore family, not only could none of it have otherwise been attributed to Moore, but much of it could not reliably have been located to New Brunswick, or in some cases even been established for a certainty as being Canadian.

Such preservation of evidence is rare. In certainly the vast majority of cases, where furniture has long ago been separated from its historical roots and associations, the identification goal is one of arriving essentially at a legal proof. Just from examining a piece of furniture alone, absolute identification — attribution to a specific maker in a particular place at a particular time — is clearly impossible, except in very isolated instances, without available evidence beyond that inherent in the piece of furniture itself.

Perhaps the least reliable of external evidence is unsupported and usually unsupportable word-of-mouth association. Whether a dealer says a piece was "discovered at . . . " or came from "such and such an estate," or an individual says it was a favourite of her great-great grandmother, any and all such information must be examined critically and for what it really is. Sometimes this information is accurate and helpful and matches nicely the internal or inherent evidence of the characteristics of the piece of furniture itself. However, one never knows. There have also been numerous occasions where stated family associations, in circumstances where there was no apparent motive for deception, were completely believed by informants but could not possibly have matched the furniture in question.

Every bit as unreliable as unsupported word-of-mouth history is location — where a piece was found. This must also be considered critically. Locations may correlate with other observations, in which case, well and good. They may also, however, be inconclusive in more cases than not. In this event, discovery location by itself becomes meaningless, and is no real clue to actual origin.

Consideration of Details

In isolating regional characteristics beyond the choice and usage of woods we must now consider minutiae, those small details common to all pieces of furniture, as to all antiques. Taken separately, and then compared, these details can often be indicative of origins.

Basic Austerity

One overall characteristic of earlier English-Canadian furniture, as outlined in the previous chapter, is its simplicity, and even austerity. The only exceptions are the formal work of some very few cabinet-makers-in-mahogany in Halifax, Saint John, Quebec, and Montreal. We must remember that in population and economic complexity Canada, even as late as 1830, was a small country. The coterie of people able to afford elegance, or to patronize those cabinet-makers capable of producing it, was very very small in comparison to that of older, more established American cities, and miniscule by British standards. Likewise, in a heavily first-generation colonial situation, as mentioned earlier, many of this small "establishment" looked to England both as home and the source of true elegance. Small wonder that the great balance of Canadian furniture would be considered provincial in an English view, or "country" by American definitions.

Example — Chippendale Chairs

One of the commoner generic forms and a good example of Canadian Georgian furniture is the late Chippendale chair. (See figs. 8-33.) These occur with varied eared, arched, or square back forms, and simply pierced vertical back-splats. The woods are as outlined earlier: mahogany, birch, or figured maple in the Maritimes; butternut or maple in the Eastern Townships; and maple in Upper Canada. No chairs have been observed in cherry or walnut. With uncommon plank-seated exceptions, these chairs have separate upholstered slip seats, with the seat frames invariably of white pine.

The legs of these chairs are either straight and square, or straight-square-tapered, and usually H- or box-stretchered. Seat structures were very often edge-planed in simple bead or quarter-round mouldings, as were sometimes the exposed corner edges of legs and stretchers. Very few Canadian Chippendale chairs are known with front cabriole legs. Carving is also extremely uncommon, and where it is present, is minimal and confined to chair backs. Veneers and inlays were never used, and secondary woods were limited to frame glue blocks.

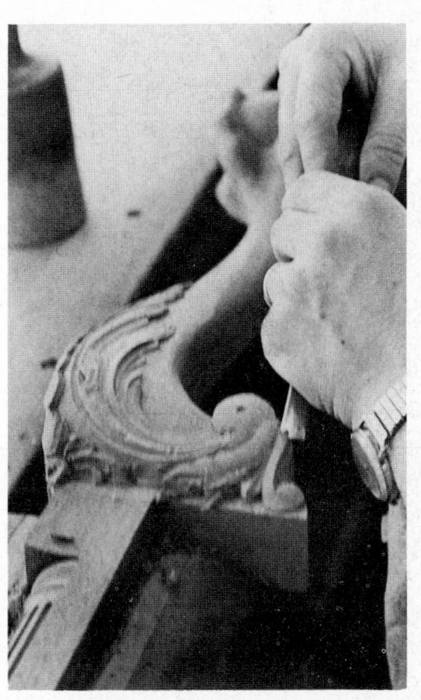

Carving the cabriole leg of a reproduction Chippendale highboy, at the Kittinger Co., Buffalo, N.Y.

Example — Chests of Drawers

The same austerity is apparent in chests of drawers. Most English-Canadian chests are flat faced, with either solid drawer fronts, or veneering of mahogany, figured maple, or birch over pine. There may, on better pieces, be cock-beaded drawer edge mouldings of a contrasting wood. Drawer fronts usually close flush with sides and cross-spacers. Bevelled or moulded overlapping drawer fronts, while very common on New England chests, are more an exception on Canadian pieces and a sign of American derivation. Drawers, internally, are invariably of white pine, with sides dovetailed into fronts and often backs.

It is not at all unusual to find two similar primary hardwoods used for chests and other case pieces. Usually the lesser wood was used for sides and possibly tops, while the better wood was reserved for facing — drawer fronts, spacers, and corner posts if any. Birch and mahogany or birch and maple combinations in chests are identified particularly with Nova Scotia and New Brunswick, with wholly mahogany furniture limited largely to Halifax, Saint John, and Fredericton.

Inlays

In chests, desks, and other drawered furniture, the English form of inlaid keyhole lozenge or diamond is very typical, especially in the Maritimes, but also to a perhaps lesser extent on the formal furniture of Quebec and Ontario. Though usually plain and of a wood contrasting with the drawer fronts, these inlays occasionally were of bone or horn.

The inlaid keyhole lozenge is less common on American furniture, which more generally had brass keyhole liners or applied brass keyhole plates. The latter, conversely, are not typical in Canada, exept on clearly American-derived furniture such as the maple and walnut Germanic pieces of the Niagara Peninsula of Ontario and New England-inspired examples of the Maritimes.

Inlay work on Canadian furniture was tasteful but minimal, rarely complex and never imposing, like that of English and some American furniture. Thin single or parallel string inlays are the types perhaps most often encountered, usually in a contrasting wood such as maple on mahogany or walnut on maple. Patterned or geometric band inlays, of several woods, are quite rare, and appear to be restricted largely to furniture of the Montreal area, with a smaller number of observed New Brunswick and Ontario examples.

Motif inlays — corner fans, rosettes, or shells — with a few known isolated exceptions, appear only on mahogany tall clock cases. Tall clock cases, correspondingly, are perhaps the most opulent single form of Canadian furniture, and that on which cabinet-makers lavished the greatest work and expense. (See figs. 123-135.) These uncommon motif inlays are not of native woods, and appear to have been imported as packaged units or in block form, to be sawed off in thin sections as needed.

Veneers

Other than mahogany, early veneers of exotic woods are most uncommon. Very infrequently, furniture had small sections veneered in satinwood or European walnut. Aside from these exceptions, however, figured veneers are invariably of native maple, birch, or walnut. Exotic veneers did not become widespread in Canada until well into the second quarter of the 19th century.

Simplifications

At times, sheets of sawed veneers appear to have been in tight supply, though the cabinet-makers, of course, made do with what they had. There are numerous examples of Canadian furniture veneered in rather strange patterns, or only on select and facing surfaces, in such a way that it is obvious the maker was eking out every scrap of material, even though the end result may have looked a bit odd. (See figs. 194, 220.)

As with veneers, the structure and treatment of even the best of English-Canadian furniture will sometimes show great short-cuts and simplifications. This is explainable, not on grounds of lack of materials, tools, or skills, but by simple economy. These short-cuts, at the same time, allow a piece of furniture to appear superficially far more sophisticated than it actually is.

Bow-front chests, for example, are uncommon, and serpentine or reverse-serpentine fronts are rare. Both seem most common to Nova Scotia and New Brunswick. (See fig. 194.) Reflecting economies of time and effort, only very slight convex bowing was accomplished by hot or steam bending and forming of drawer fronts. More extreme bows,

Bow-front Chest, from Hepplewhite. See figs. 231-233.

or serpentine fronts, were done by block-cutting and shaving, and usually only on the exterior. The wood was typically pine, to be veneered later. These block-cut but curved-fronted drawer fronts are generally flat and uncarved on the inside, and thus up to two inches thick at the extreme of exterior convex curves.

Hardware

Like veneers or good mahogany, hardware, it seems, was also often difficult to come by, or too expensive to use. The hardware of Georgian-period Canadian furniture was invariably English. Unlike the United States, cabinet hardware does not seem to have been manufactured in Canada until well into the 19th century.

Perhaps the predominant drawer hardware form was the pressed English lion's head plate holding a ring handle. Next in popularity on better pieces was the oval sheet brass "Sheraton" plate, with a bowed handle mounted between two studs. The Chippendale flat brass plate, however, is rarely seen as original hardware, because in English and American pieces it was used before the late 18th-century period of English-Canadian furniture. There are several known instances, however, of 18th-century English hardware, re-used from earlier pieces, being original to the Canadian furniture on which it was later mounted. (See nos. 198, 306.)

Castors, again English, were limited usually to the finest work, and are typically present only on mahogany furniture. In the Georgian period, castors were very uncommon, though not unknown, on pieces made of native woods.

As already mentioned, brass keyhole liners were used, of course, on finer pieces, and applied keyhole plates were limited to furniture of American derivation, given an availability of the hardware. Esoteric hardware, such as specially cast rather than manufactured drawer brasses, or cast brass ormolu work, is never seen on Canadian furniture.

However, reflecting the general austerity of design and treatment of most Canadian furniture, the majority of chests, desks, and other drawered pieces had little or no real hardware at all. Turned wooden knobs, for example, attached by dowel pins glued into position, were commonly used instead, often even on sophisticated mahogany, maple, or cherry pieces which clearly deserved better. Much early furniture has been "upgraded" in recent years with the addition of brass reproduction drawer pulls and keyhole plates replacing original wooden knobs and unornamented keyholes. It is essential, in examining English-Canadian furniture, to check closely the hardware and details and determine what has been replaced.

Proportion

Examples of Canadian Georgian furniture very often include design or proportional incongruities, which can be so covert or subtle as to be difficult to distinguish. A small table may have heavier-than-necessary or disproportionately turned legs. (Fluted, reeded, or rope-carved legs are rare on Canadian tables; plain turnings are the rule.) Chests of drawers, which in design should have extended or "Chippendale" bracket feet and skirt, may instead have plain short and turned legs, these particularly common in Nova Scotia and New Brunswick. Otherwise excellent pieces may have corners showing inexplicable exposed rather than concealed dove-tailing. Original nails may appear in joints that one would expect to see dove-tailed, or mortised and pinned. Flared "French" feet on chests of drawers may be separately made and joined, rather than integral with the sides or skirt (and structurally stronger).

Summary

All of these various points of difference in detail between Canadian and American furniture are generalities. In discussing the characteristics of furniture, and other crafts, produced by people who linguistically, historically, and culturally were far more alike than different, we simply cannot make clearly defined conclusions about national or regional differences.

In the whole procedure of English-Canadian furniture identification, we are thus in a position of first examining and considering closely wood usage and all internal details. We must then weigh in other word-of-mouth historical evidence, perhaps from unknown or unreliable sources. Finally, we must try to arrive at a conclusion and a defensible identification — one that may hardly be provable as Absolute Truth — but simply fits beyond a reasonable doubt.

The process is in fact, as mentioned earlier, similar to that of a judge or a jury trying to decide legally, from the balance of physical evidence and the verbal statements of witnesses, (possibly conflicting and of uncertain veracity), whether the defendant is guilty beyond a reasonable doubt. While there are no such black or white judgements, furniture identification can be even more difficult. A piece of early furniture is a mute witness on its own behalf. Word-of-mouth history is at best third- or fourth-hand hearsay. Originating in the distant past, it cannot be cross-examined. The furniture examiner's only strong advantage is the use of precedent — the ability to compare with other (hopefully multiple) known or reliably established examples.

The exercise is one of thinking and logic, and not of guessing or wishing to believe. The strength of the evidence must necessarily govern, and limit, the extent of the conclusions.

Because the pieces are most similar, simpler furniture of eastern Canada and the northeastern United States is certainly the most likely to resist certain differentiation and identification. In examining pieces long since detached from any known family, or historical or geographical background, it may in some instances be plainly impossible to arrive at sound and beyond-reasonable-doubt judgements even as to Canadian or American origin.

With somewhat more cases we can reasonably conclude that a piece of furniture is indeed Canadian, and often be able to locate it to a particular province or region. In the best of circumstances, given a piece of unknown origin that incorporates highly individual construction, carving, or other elaboration, and particularly if there are other similar and known pieces to compare it with, we might even be so fortunate as to come up with a well-reasoned attribution to a specific maker. That is the height, and the rare reward, of furniture identification.

Sofa, from Sheraton. See figs. 63-69.

Attributions and Makers

In any consideration of the stylized furniture of Georgian-period Canada the cabinet-makers themselves, with a few notable exceptions, remain the greatest enigma. Of the trained and skilled makers who came to British North America in the 18th and early 19th centuries, little is known beyond bare-bones chronologies. Biographical research of early cabinet-makers has been occasional and sketchy, and largely focussed on those few makers whose extant furniture can be readily identified. For the majority we know little beyond names, locations, and approximate working dates, and more often than not even this is incomplete.

Making definitive connections between surviving furniture and its makers is, in most cases, quite impossible. Except for clocks, which often have case-maker marked faces, the quantity of known existing marked or labelled Georgian-period Canadian furniture is miniscule, perhaps fewer than 200 pieces. The percentage of all known makers represented among those marked pieces is equally small.

It seems to be a fact of life that, like most craftsmen, cabinet-makers were not record keepers or self-historians. Day-book entries were single-line records of transactions, often scrawled, and not descriptive references to designs or details. Some makers were probably even illiterate. Others were undoubtedly jealous of their competitors, mistrustful of their wives or children, cheating on their taxes, concealing receipts from creditors, or had other problems. In any event, we can presume that some cabinet-makers, like other businessmen, certainly had reasons other than sloth or sloppiness not to keep precise records or mark carefully everything they made.

No Canadian makers' day-books have yet been found with descriptions of transactions that are sufficiently precise to identify the pieces recorded. Also, there are neither known diaries nor customer correspondence. No early cabinet-maker is known to have recorded his memoirs and experiences. The only cabinet-maker, in fact, to be represented today both by a large body of known furniture, and considerable documentation in family letters, is John Warren Moore of St. Stephen, New Brunswick. Moore, however, was active much later than the Georgian period. Thomas Nisbet, of Saint John, New Brunswick, is well known from a number of existing labelled pieces of his furniture, but none of his documentary records appear to have survived.

These conditions, plus the large-scale, 20th-century, removal of furniture from its original contexts, makes attributions both difficult and often tenuous. Those occasional excellent and undoubtedly Canadian, i.e., definitely not British nor American, pieces that appear without comparable known examples, or clues as to their specific makers, are always frustrating. Determination of region, and approximate dating, is about the most that can usually be accomplished. Local scholars, and university students with research projects, sometimes research individual cabinet-makers, and even get to know them down to how many chickens they kept and what their debts were. Without some lucky find, however, such as descriptive, detailed day-books or family letters, no amount of biographical research based on standard archival sources can discover what these cabinet-makers actually produced.

We know from documentation that the earliest cabinet-makers were of English, Scots, and American origin *and* often of training. Probably, judging from names alone, Scots predominated. Furthermore, we sometimes encounter, among pieces of furniture, examples which are clearly Scottish in style (see figs. 12, 33, 38, 39), or clearly English (see figs. 22, 30, 51), or obviously American in type and derivation (see figs. 3, 28, 54, 55), still without having any idea as to the actual makers. All makers setting up shops also had to adapt to local conditions, such as woods and economy, and to local preferences and taste in style and design.

The assumption that cabinet-makers trained in a certain regional tradition would continue producing in that tradition even after moving to a new land may be disputable. It is more reasonable to suspect, for example, that a Scottish cabinet-maker coming to a New Brunswick Loyalist community might switch to New England forms, not so vastly different from his own, if that was what his clientele wanted. If this were not the case, a lot of key questions must remain unanswered. Considering the preponderance of English and Scottish makers, for instance, why are even the earliest Canadian Windsor chairs all of the American rod-back rather than the British splat-back form? (See nos. 54-57.)

It is necessary, in a situation with so much early information either originally unrecorded or long lost, to be extremely careful in the matter of attribution. It is very easy otherwise to get carried away by enthusiasm for a supposition, and wind up in the trap of self-delusion.

George MacLaren, in *Antique Furniture by Nova Scotian*

Craftsmen, mentions Edward Draper, who arrived in Halifax with the Cornwallis expedition in 1749, as a maker of chairs with "rush-bottomed seats," or simple ladder-backs. It is possible that some of these chairs still survive, but still no 18th-century ladder-backs are likely to be attributed to Draper simply because of an absence of connecting information — Draper documents or marked chairs.

MacLaren also mentions, among a number of Loyalist cabinet-makers, Daniel, Henry, and Job Goddard, of the famous Rhode Island cabinet-making family. The Goddard brothers were listed for a short time as carpenters in Shelburne, Nova Scotia, and are then presumed to have moved to Halifax in 1788. Did they work there as cabinet-makers? We do not know, and no piece of remotely attributable Nova Scotia Goddard furniture has yet been found. Daniel Goddard is then known to have been a cabinet-maker in Digby in 1819, but none of his furniture has come to light either. The Goddard family style (i.e., Newport, Rhode Island), which would be quite apparent, has certainly not appeared in Nova Scotia. The Goddard style, however, might also have been too opulent and costly for immediate post-Loyalist Nova Scotia, in which case the Goddard brothers would have had little choice but to adapt their techniques downward to simpler pieces.

The point is that this is all speculation. We know the Goddards immigrated as Loyalists to Nova Scotia and presumably, cabinet-making being their craft and skill, worked at it if they could. What they may have produced is still a complete mystery, in spite of the likelihood that some of their work still survives.

Robert Chillas came as a Loyalist to Saint John, New Brunswick, in 1783, and was recorded there as a practising cabinet-maker. In 1819, some thirty-five years later, he is known to have provided some furniture for a house in Saint John. One piece (see fig. 221) from that house, and stylistically within the realm of an 1819 dating, recently went to the Kings Landing Historical Settlement, and has been attributed to Robert Chillas by Charles Foss in *Cabinetmakers of the Eastern Seaboard.* On the basis of that, yet further connections have been made. A few other similar pieces are also known (see fig. 90), most probably of New Brunswick origin. Still, the fact that Chillas supplied unspecified furniture to a house in 1819, together with the known existence of one piece of compatible date range from that house, seems insufficient for a solid Chillas attribution. Of the pieces illustrated following, figs. 90 and 221 seem certainly to have been built by the same maker; the similarities are obvious.

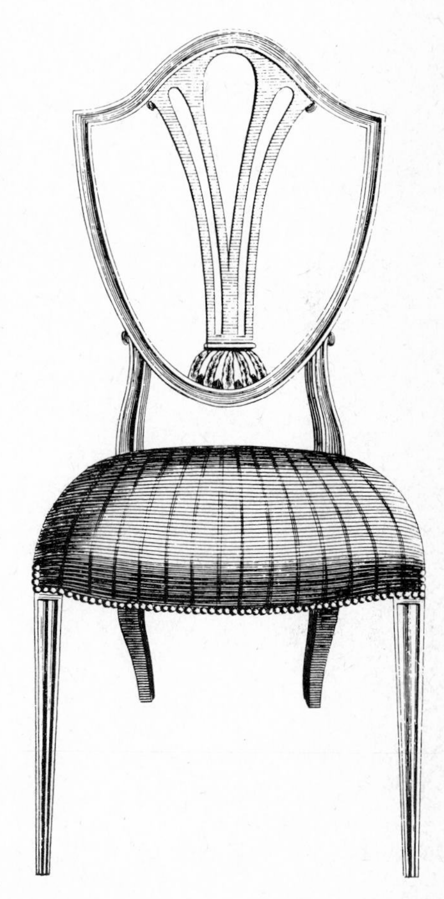

Side Chair, from George Hepplewhite, *The Cabinet-Maker and Upholsterer's Guide*, 1794. See figs. 19-21.

Whether that maker, however, based on Foss's attribution of fig. 90, was indeed Robert Chillas, is still subject to reasonable doubt.

Nothing else is known about Chillas. His wife died in 1824 at age seventy-eight, but whether he predeceased or survived her is not established. Where, then, is at least thirty-five years of Chillas's production, as presumably an independent cabinet-maker, from his arrival in Saint John to his death?

James Waddell is a somewhat better known maker, though his work was not quite of the calibre of the urban cabinet-makers' using mahogany. MacLaren has established that Waddell (1764-1851) came to Halifax about 1813 from Glasgow, moved to Truro about 1815, and later went to South Maitland, Nova Scotia. At South Maitland he is known to have worked as a ship carpenter or ship finisher. Four of his pieces are known through certain family connections (see figs. 9, 10, 215), and one other signed piece has since come to light (see fig. 232). Thus Waddell has a most unusual existing record of known and attributable furniture.

Waddell was, however, a part-time furniture maker, employed on ships when jobs were available. This was not uncommon, particularly among rural or country cabinet-makers who could never be assured of a continuous flow of new orders for furniture alone. A mixing of specialties within one's own range of talents was hardly limited to cabinet-makers. Potters, for example, usually also made brick and drainage tile, and their land and livestock holdings often indicate that they were self-sufficient farmers as well. Some potters we know produced and fired only in the winter, building up inventory to carry them through the next growing (and clay-digging) season.

Clock-makers on occasion were also silversmiths or engravers. (See figs. 139, 141.) Some 19th-century silversmiths were also pewterers. There is evidence that some chair-makers were also coopers or wheelwrights, or the reverse. In an age before unemployment insurance and welfare were even concepts, no occupation had sanctity. Thus there is no reason to doubt that urban furniture makers probably strayed from their prime crafts in slack times. Though documentary records are so far non-existent, common sense suggests that even the best of cabinet-makers on occasion took contracts for room panelling, staircase construction, or ship interiors.

There is, in fact, little other explanation for the paucity of remaining work by makers, such as Robert Chillas or even Thomas Nisbet, with known long working lives. Even fires, prevalent as they were, are unlikely to have consumed that much of their production. The most logical answer that we come to is that even the best cabinet-makers could not specialize full time in their primary craft, and therefore did not really build as much furniture as we might suppose.

The recorded lives, movements, and works of Thomas Nisbet, Alexander Lawrence, and other documented makers are recorded as well as possible in Ryder's *Antique Furniture by New Brunswick Craftsmen,* MacLaren's *Antique Furniture by Nova Scotian Craftsmen,* and Foss's *Cabinetmakers of the Eastern Seaboard.* There is no reason to repeat these brief biographies here. It is clear, however, that only in the Maritimes has direct maker attribution of stylized English-Canadian furniture become really feasible, and then subject only to the realistic limits of inadequate present knowledge.

The further west one looks the more remote are the possibilities for direct attributions, again due to a lack of the essential connecting links. Montreal, the centre of British North America, was developing a sizeable and sophisticated English-language population by 1780 to 1790. Montreal certainly produced some of the finest Georgian-period furniture known, and numerous pieces exist which date probably prior to 1800. Yet Elizabeth Collard in her checklist "Montreal cabinetmakers and chairmakers, 1800-1850," (*Antiques,* May, 1974) notes only one recorded 18th-century cabinet-maker, and only eleven makers operating before 1810.

Except for a few clocks, no labelled or otherwise maker-marked Georgian-period furniture of Montreal has yet emerged, much less descriptive early documents, and thus no specific maker attributions of Montreal pieces are presently possible. Still, if early advertisements of quantities and varieties of stock-on-hand, including considerable upholstered furniture, are valid evidence, and there is no reason to suppose they are not, then a great amount of good furniture has certainly vanished over the century and three-quarters following 1800.

Much of the furniture advertised may well have been English or American, imported to fill out inventories and to satisfy the English taste. Cabinet-makers acting as importers certainly became a growing tendency in the 19th century, but we have no real idea of relative quantities imported as opposed to home produced. Many advertised furniture categories may have been used furniture of varied origins, bought for repair and resale.

Cabinet-makers, we know, could enjoy no real security in their specialties in this new, raw land of scattered first- and second-generation populations. As well as taking other compatible jobs or contracts that might appear, all cabinet-makers developed diverse business directions, for they had no choice. Furniture repair, refinishing, and re-upholstery were clearly bread-and-butter parts of the business. So was the buying, restoring, and resale of used furniture. Thus, most cabinet-makers had to be furniture dealers, and hardly limited their stock to their own production. Some makers, as advertising indicates, were even paint and varnish retailers, and hardwood lumber dealers.

Diversity was the only way, in most areas, of staying constantly employed. As well as contract work, many cabinet-makers even advertised themselves in dual or multiple roles. Household joinery, chair-making, turning, carriage-making, and upholstering were commonly advertised secondary pursuits. Undertaking, always in demand, was virtually an automatic role of cabinet-makers, who were also the coffin makers. Decorative crafts as well — lettering and sign painting, gilding, furniture finishing, japanning, and even house painting and paper-hanging — also appear as cabinet-makers' advertised offerings.

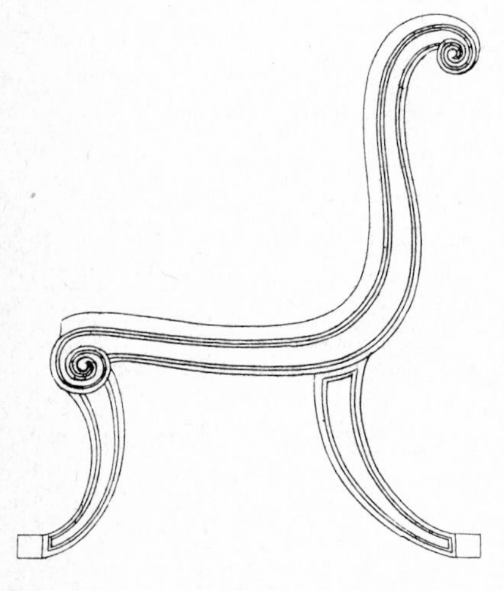

Chair form, from Hope's *Household Furniture and Interior Decoration*, 1807. See fig. 50.

While cabinet-making and its adjuncts was a full occupation and primarily a cash business in urban environments such as Montreal, this was not always true of frontier areas such as Upper Canada. While there are few extant advertisements in Ontario from before 1820, cabinet-makers there offered to take maple and walnut lumber, and "country produce," in at least partial exchange for furniture or services. The barter system was engrained in these areas, and was not entirely replaced by the common denominator of money until local production and demand became integrated with a broader economic stream than the immediate rural community. Mahogany, of course, was unavailable, and cabinet-makers instead depended on local suppliers for their woods.

Frontier areas, as well, had a far greater proportion than did the urban centres of winter-only cabinet-makers, people who farmed spring through autumn. These were the producers of "country" furniture, often good in design and proportion, but invariably simple and unornamented. Like rural potters, such cabinet-makers probably focussed on only a few utilitarian forms — chairs, tables and chests of drawers were most in demand — and then marketed locally either through direct sales or to village and cross-roads stores.

In underpopulated Upper Canada, local cabinet-makers were producing some quite sophisticated furniture possibly as early as 1800. (See figs. 89, 178, 220.) There is every reason to suspect, however, that these makers also took on every order they could get, and made considerable plainer country furniture as well.

At the same time they rarely, if ever, advertised. Advertising cost money, and like other craftsmen in rural areas of small population, their skills were already known to their immediate markets. The only real advertising need was for announcements of starting in business, or changing partners or locations. In Upper Canada, for example, Joan MacKinnon in *Kingston Cabinetmakers before 1867* established that fewer than ten per cent of the cabinet-makers in Toronto before 1865 ever advertised at all, and she estimated the percentage in Kingston was probably under twenty-five per cent.

In spite of the beginning of settlement in Upper Canada immediately following the American Revolution, the earliest known furniture maker, a chair-maker named Daniel Tiers, advertised in 1802 that he had recently set up shop in York (Toronto), and was both making chairs and importing from Quebec. In Kingston, with a population of 220 by 1784, the first known cabinet-maker was Abia Sayre, who was established before 1810. (Kingston had no newspaper as an advertising medium before then.) Sayre at least announced that he was prepared to make a full range of apparently sophisticated furniture types. Whether he did or could we do not know. Sayre was followed shortly after by Greno and Sawyer, Samuel Howe, and William Baker, all in 1811.

None of these earlier Upper Canada cabinet-makers, or the others, are known to have marked their work in any way, any more than did most makers elsewhere. Not from before about 1830 do we begin to find more than a handful of attributable pieces, and those few are largely among the Pennsylvania-German-derived furniture. Numerous students have done some very solid work in locating and recording early makers in specific areas, establishing generically what they made by studying advertisements or daybooks, and in a few cases have even traced careers. Still, in considering surviving furniture, this work unfortunately cannot bring us much closer to establishing who made what, where and when.

Thus we are left with enigmas that may never be capable of solution, the connection of specific cabinet-makers to specific surviving pieces. The past casualty rate among furniture on one hand, and of records and written first-hand documentation on the other, has simply been too great over a century and three-quarters for the establishment of a full picture at this remove. In this sense Canadian decorative arts studies have not only begun late, but perhaps too late.

Research on cabinet-makers will continue for a long time to come, and their range of activity, their capabilities, and their problems in a new society will become further clarified. Still, both to judge and to identify their remaining works, we will never get away from reliance on current analytical abilities and technology. Though we can always wish for large representations of labelled pieces backed up by copious descriptive letters and diaries, this appears to be fantasy. We must instead look to patterns of wood usage, forms and styles, comparisons of examples, and common sense and rationality to be able to isolate the earlier English-Canadian furniture that is the best of the Canadian decorative arts.

Sofa, from Hepplewhite's *The Cabinet-Maker and Upholsterer's Guide,* 1794. See figs. 59, 61.

English-Canadian Furniture of the Georgian Period

1.
Wing Chair
Sheffield, New Brunswick, c. 1790-1810

A characteristic of many New Brunswick armchairs is this chair's rather short arms, while the cabriole front legs with ball and claw feet indicate an earlier and probably American derivation. The legs and turned stretcher rungs are mahogany and the upper frame is pine. The stretcher rungs are similar to those on figs. 17, 43, and 44. These turned stretchers, also English and northeastern American in inspiration, in Canada have been observed only on New Brunswick chairs.

Height: 122.5 cm (48¼ in.); *Width:* 80.0 cm (31½ in.)
Kings Landing Historical Settlement

2.
Wing Chair
New Brunswick, c. 1800-10

This chair, with extremely short arms, also has ogee or cabriole front legs, but is unstretchered. The legs are mahogany, and the upholstery frame is of pine.

The very existence of numbers of late Chippendale and Regency wing-back upholstered chairs in New Brunswick is indicative of the heavy American Loyalist migration in the 1780s, and of their preferences. Such chairs are not commonly found from more predominantly English- and Scottish-settled areas.

Height: 116.0 cm (41 3/4 in.);
Width: 72.0 cm (28 3/8 in.)
Kings Landing Historical Settlement

3.
Wing Chair
New Brunswick, c. 1790-1810

With square, tapered front legs and rectangular stretchers, this chair also has short arms, with the arm frame sloped back from the front of the seat. The base is of mahogany, and the upper frame of pine. (Similar example, cf. Shackleton, no. 3.)

The mahogany footstool, of the 1840s, is attributed to Alexander Lawrence.

Chair, *Height:* 124.5 cm (49 in.);
Width: 64.0 cm (25 1/8 in.)
Stool, *Height:* 41.0 cm (16 1/8 in.);
Width: 54.0 cm (21 1/4in.)
Kings Landing Historical Settlement

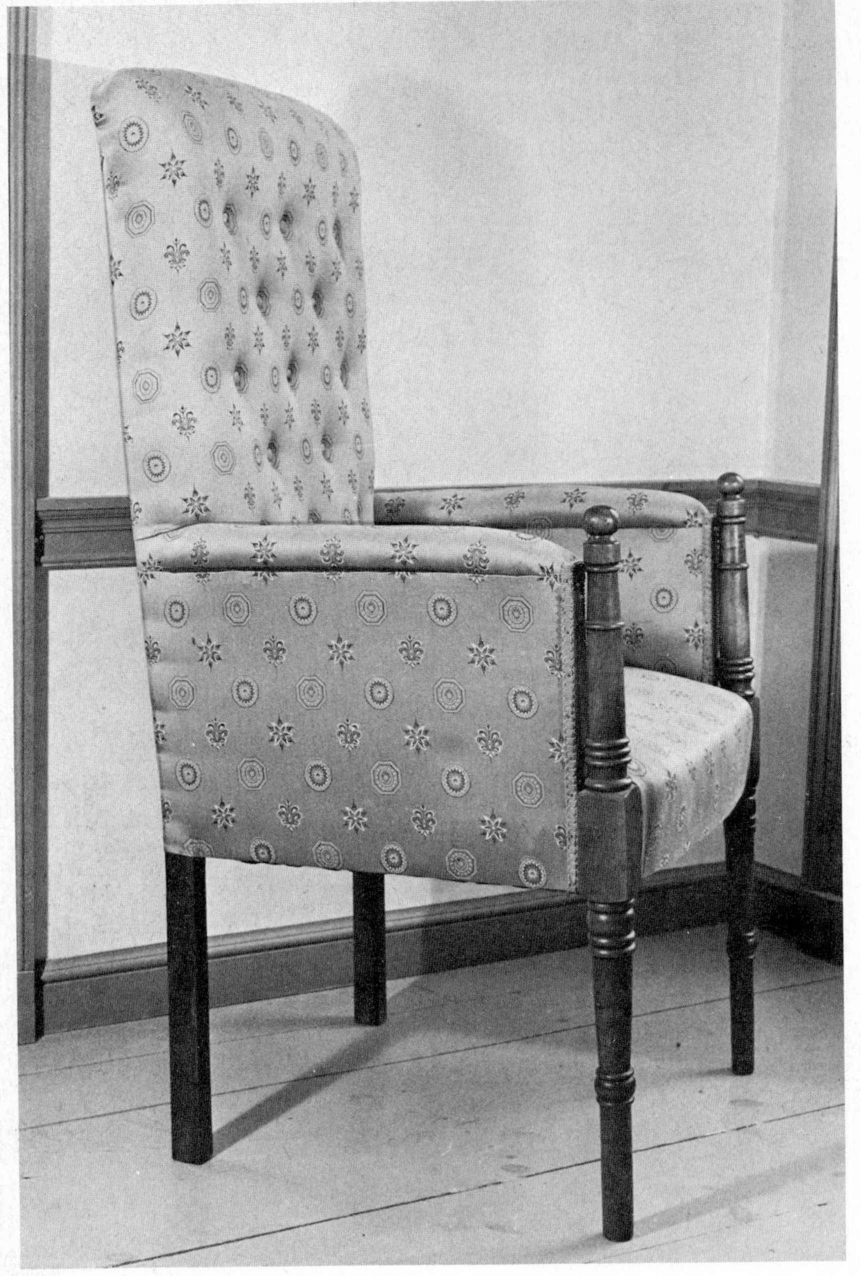

4.
Armchair
Sussex, New Brunswick, c. 1810; marked by P. McKay

In a very unusual Sheraton-derivative style, this baronial chair with its turned front legs and ball-finialed posts is of mahogany, with secondary pine in the upholstery frame. The mark *P. McKAY / SUSSEX* is stamped in two places on the pine seat frame. McKay is not recorded as a chair- or cabinet-maker, nor are other marked examples of his chairs presently known.

Height: 122.5 cm (48¼ in.);
Width: 69.0 cm (27⅛ in.)
Kings Landing Historical Settlement

5.
Wing Chair
New Brunswick, c. 1810-25

As a simplified version of American-derived wing chairs, this piece has plain-turned front legs, of the type often found on Maritimes chests of drawers. The legs are mahogany and the upper frame of pine. The side wings of the chair are unusually deep while the arms are correspondingly very short. (Similar example, cf. Pain no. 334.)

Height: 117.0 cm (46 in.);
Width: 69.0 cm (27⅛ in.)
Loyalist House, Saint John

6.
Wing Chair
New Brunswick, c. 1810-25; found in Sussex

With a curved rather than fully winged back, this chair has four turned legs of birch rather than the more usual square back legs. The upholstery frame is pine. The straight castors are English.

Height: 128.0 cm (50$^{3}/_{8}$ in.);
Width: 70.0 cm (27$^{1}/_{2}$ in.)
Kings Landing Historical Settlement

7.
Wing Chair
Montreal, c. 1820-30

With a mahogany lower frame and turned and reeded front legs, this chair has unusual wings which overhang the lower frame. The upholstery frame is pine. The wings are somewhat shorter, and the arms a little longer, than is typically the case on wing chairs of Maritimes origin. The legs, combining ring turning with reeding, dictate a later than usual date for this chair.

Height: 116 cm (45$^{5}/_{8}$ in.);
Width: 67.5 cm (26$^{1}/_{2}$ in.)
Private Collection

8.
Armchair
Quebec, Eastern Townships, c. 1790-1810

Chippendale chairs in Quebec, except for cultural mixtures (see figs. 18, 34) occur only from English-speaking areas. With its simple pierced back-splat, this slip-seated piece is of mixed birch and butternut, not a typical combination. The bead moulding on the seat rail and leg fronts is common on Canadian Chippendale-derivative chairs from all areas.

Height: 94.6 cm (37¼ in.);
Width: 52.2 cm (20¾ in.)
Canadiana, Royal Ontario Museum

9.
Side Chair
Truro or South Maitland, Nova Scotia, c. 1810-20; attributed to James Waddell

With square legs and pinned frame and without bead moulding, this chair is of unfigured maple. The separate slip seat overlaps its side rails.

Chippendale country chairs of this type were still being produced in Nova Scotia certainly as late as 1820, and possibly as late as 1825-30. (Similar example, cf. Dobson, no 101.)

Height: 94 cm (37 in.);
Width: 50.2 cm (19¾ in.)
Nova Scotia Museum

10.
Side Chair and Armchair
Truro, Nova Scotia, c. 1810-20; by James Waddell

Both of these chairs, like fig. 9, are of straight-grained maple. Though not part of a set, the structure and framing and the piercing of the back-splats of the chairs is very similar. The seats are now upholstered, but the chairs may originally have had slip seats.

Waddell is known to have made furniture at least as late as 1825. As known family pieces, these chairs were given to the Nova Scotia Museum by James Waddell's great grandneice. (See also figs. 215, 232.)

Left, *Height:* 95.8 cm (37¾ in.); *Width:* 50.8 cm (20 in.)
Right, *Height:* 97.1 cm (38¼ in.); *Width:* 54 cm (21¼ in.)
Nova Scotia Museum

11.
Side Chair
Quebec, probably Montreal area, c. 1790-1810

Very simple in form and construction, this chair with beaded front leg and seat rail edges is of mahogany, generally not available far from ports of landing. The piercing of the back-splat is very similar to that of fig. 8.

Height: 95.3 cm (37½ in.); *Width:* 55.6 cm (21⅞ in.)
Canadiana, Royal Ontario Museum

12.
Side Chair
New Brunswick, c. 1800-10

The rather ecclesiastical-Gothic design of the pierced back-panel is very unusual in an otherwise country-Chippendale chair. The wood is entirely mahogany, and the square legs and the seat rails are bead moulded on the outer edges.

Height: 97.8 cm (38½ in.); *Width:* 54 cm (21¼ in.)
New Brunswick Museum

13.
Side Chair
Probably Nova Scotia, c. 1815-25

Though wholly of birch, a common Maritimes cabinet wood, this chair is unusual in that it is assembled with original round dowel pins, rather than square pegs, holding the mortise and tenioned joints together. (See also fig. 9.) The slip seat has a pine frame. (Similar example, cf. Dobson, no. 101.)

Height: 95.5 cm (37⅝ in.); *Width:* 52.3 cm (20⅝ in.)
Private Collection

14.
Side Chair
Montreal, c. 1800-15

This rather simple chair is of mahogany, with the usual bead-moulded seat frame and leg edges. The top rail has odd sharply pointed tips, and the centre stretcher is inletted only into the lower edges of the side stretchers.

Height: 92.5 cm (36$^3/_8$ in.);
Width: 53 cm (20$^7/_8$ in.)
Private Collection

15.
Side Chair
Montreal, c. 1800-15

With an unusual scroll-carved back-splat, this chair with its bead-moulded front leg and seat frame edges (see also figs. 163, 173) is wholly of mahogany. The back rail has spiral-carved tips. (See also figs 16, 17, following.) The pronounced centre concavity in the top rail is a stylistic throw-back to the early 18th century, and not typical of these chairs.

Height: 93 cm (36$^5/_8$ in.);
Width: 53 cm (20$^7/_8$ in.)
Private Collection

16.
Armchair
Eastern Ontario or Quebec, c. 1800-1820

The pierced and woven-circle carved back-splat of this chair is an unusual form, as are the scroll-carved tips of the top rail. The chair is entirely of curly and bird's-eye maple, with bead-moulded seat rails and outer edges of the square-tapered front legs. The piece is oddly proportioned, with a back somewhat small for the frame. The arms and arm posts of straight-grained maple are either early replacements or, more likely, later additions.

Height: 91.5 cm (36 in.);
Width: 70 cm (27½ in.)
Canadiana, Royal Ontario Museum

17.
Side Chair
New Brunswick, c. 1795-1810

This chair, with its scroll-carved top rail ends and matching carvings in the thinly pierced back-splat, is of mahogany except for the stretchers, which are birch. The turned stretchers are somewhat similar to those on the armchair in fig. 1. Though finely pierced, the back side of the back-splat is roughly finished, still showing saw and plane marks. The rounded seat frame to front leg corners, and the front braces, are derivative of the Chinese Chippendale fashion in the United States in the late 18th century.

The Chinese Chippendale influence, however, had a negligible impact on Canadian cabinet-making, and those uncommon pieces which appear are usually from heavily American-settled areas.

Height: 95.9 cm (37¾ in.);
Width: 52.6 cm (20¾ in.)
Kings Landing Historical Settlement

18.
Commode Chair
Quebec, c. 1790-1820

Considerable furniture in mixed French-traditional and English styles was produced in Quebec between 1780 and about 1830, all by French-Canadian makers. This commode chair, of maple with a pine seat, combines traditionally French arms and structure with a clearly Chippendale-derived back with pierced splat. The piece has its original blue paint.

Height: 101.6 cm (40 in.);
Width: 57.8 cm (22¾ in.)
Canadiana Royal Ontario Museum

19.
Armchair
Eastern Ontario or Quebec, Eastern Townships, c. 1810-20

The base and pierced back-splat of this chair are of bird's-eye maple, and the back legs, top rail, and arms are of straight-grained maple. The design and structure are rather lighter than is usual. Bird's-eye and curly maple came into fashion and general use as cabinet woods only in the 19th century, and are the exception in Hepplewhite-derived furniture. Such pieces as this transitional chair thus usually date later than the conventional Chippendale period.

Height: 91.4 cm (36 in);
Width: 55.5 cm (21 7/8 in.)
Canadiana, Royal Ontario Museum

20.
Side Chair
Nova Scotia, c. 1810-20

In mixed birch and unfigured maple, a common Nova Scotia combination, this slip-seated chair with its arched back is very simple, though well designed and constructed. It may originally have been one of a set of dining chairs. The centre joins of the pierced back panel are convex carved, and the seat is unusually narrow. Mixed Chippendale-Hepplewhite chairs such as this, as well as figs. 19 and 21, are Canadian cabinetmakers' closest approach to the English and American Hepplewhite "shield-back" form. (Similar example, cf. Dobson, no. 103.)

Height: 95.2 cm (37½ in.);
Width: 44.5 cm (17½ in.)
Canadiana, Royal Ontario Museum

21.
Armchair
New Brunswick, c. 1810

As a well-proportioned country piece, wholly of birch, this chair has a pierced back-splat with central carved joins very similar to those of fig. 20. The arms, with posts rather crudely attached to the front legs, are either original to the piece or very early additions.

Height: 91.5 cm (36 in.);
Width: 60 cm (25⅝ in.)
Kings Landing Historical Settlement

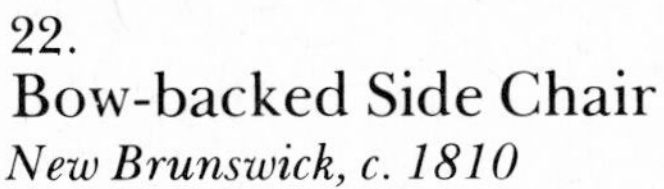

22.
Bow-backed Side Chair
New Brunswick, c. 1810

Except for later 19th-century Windsor chairs, stylistically mixed but English manner bow-backed forms are most unusual as earlier Canadian chairs. The wood is mahogany, with birch stretchers. The back-splat is pierced as intersecting arches, with a small floral carving at the intersection. The usual bead moulding surrounds the seat rails, and thin beading outlines the back frame.

Height: 83.8 cm (33 in.);
Width: 53.3 cm (21 in.)
New Brunswick Museum

23.
Side Chairs
Quebec, Montreal area or Eastern Townships, c. 1800-10

This pair of chairs, probably from a larger set, are unusual in a Canadian context in having straight rather than arched or serpentine back rails. Entirely of birch, the legs, seat rails, and the back frames are bead moulded. Chairs of this austere square-backed form have not occurred in sufficient numbers to really be considered a regional type, but have been found so far only in the Montreal-Eastern Townships area.

Height: 91.4 cm (36 in.);
Width: 50.8 cm (20 in.)
Canadiana, Royal Ontario Museum

24.
Side Chair
Montreal area, c. 1800-10

Though not identical to or of the same set as the preceding pieces, this chair is the same type. The chair is of mahogany, with bead moulding also carried around the back, and the present upholstery probably replaces an original slip seat.

Height: 92 cm (36 1/4 in.);
Width: 52 cm (20 1/2 in.)
Private Collection

25.
Side Chairs
Port Hope, Ontario, c. 1810-20

Sheraton- and Chippendale-derivative chairs in Ontario are not commonly found from contexts west of the St. Lawrence River Valley or Kingston. This pair, of straight-grained maple, have atypical pierced back-splats, and round-cornered slip seats. The seat frames are quarter-round moulded, rather than with the usual edge bead moulding.

Height: 94.5 cm (37 1/4 in.);
Width: 48.7 cm (19 1/8 in.)
Private Collection

26.
Side Chairs
Newfoundland, c. 1800-20

Early Newfoundland furniture is quite basic and relatively unstylized compared to that of Nova Scotia and New Brunswick, and is typically of birch mixed with pine or spruce. (See also fig. 31.) With slightly arched back rails and reeded back-rods, these chairs show Hepplewhite and Sheraton roots, but with no real adherence to the styles. Probably from two separate sets, the chairs are of birch, with original spruce plank seats. (Similar examples, cf. Dobson nos. 105, 107.)

Height: 86 cm (34 in.);
Width: 36 cm (14 in.)
Canadiana, Royal Ontario Museum

27.
Side Chairs
Nova Scotia, c. 1800-20

In Canada, pierced-slat or so-called "ribbon-back" Chippendale chairs, as a ladder-back form, seem unique to Nova Scotia. This simple pair, with slip seats, are of mahogany without edge moulding, and were probably part of a larger set. The plain square legs are heavily stretchered. While a common English type, pierced serpentine-slated ladder-back chairs did not seem to achieve great popularity in Canada, and have been found only in Nova Scotia.

Height: 92.1 cm (36¼ in.);
Width: 51.4 cm (20¼ in.)
Private Collection

28.
Side Chair
Nova Scotia, c. 1800-20

Typical of such "ribbon-back" pieces, this ladder-backed chair is rush seated. The legs and pierced top rail are of mahogany, while the stretchers and back-slats are birch. The legs and seat frame are centrally joined into front corner-blocks. The outer edges of legs, stretchers, and back posts are bead moulded.

Height: 97.8 cm (38½ in.);
Width: 50.2 cm (19¾ in.)
Nova Scotia Museum

29.
Side Chair
Nova Scotia, c. 1800-20; found in Truro

Very similar to the preceding chair, this piece may be by the same maker, but has most unusual chamfered legs and stretchers, an archaic characteristic. The legs, back posts, and stretchers are of mahogany, while the top rail and back-slats are maple. This seat design, with seat rails and legs separately joined into front corner-blocks, is a construction form probably of New England origin, where early examples are known in the William and Mary, and Queen Anne styles. In Canada the type seems peculiar to Nova Scotia, where it is fairly common in this late form. The seat structure is inherently weak, and becomes loose if subjected to horizontal or diagonal stresses.

Height: 95.2 cm (37½ in.);
Width: 50.8 cm (20 in.)
Nova Scotia Museum

30.
Side Chair
Fredericton, New Brunswick, c. 1800; attributed to Hunter & Ross (1788-1804)

With separate slip seat, this piece has mahogany bead-moulded legs, seat rails, and top rail. The stretchers and serpentine back-slats are of maple. Such plain serpentine-slated ladder-backed chairs are uncommon. This chair was certainly one of a set, and an identical mate is known in a private collection.

Height: 97.8 cm (38½ in.);
Width: 54 cm (21¼ in.)
New Brunswick Museum

31.
Side Chair
Newfoundland, probably Conception Bay area, c. 1800

As a rare early Newfoundland example (any Newfoundland furniture earlier than c. 1850 is scarce), this plank-seated chair is of white pine, with simple beaded-edge moulding, and a reeded fan carving in the back top rail. The chair shows a Chippendale influence, but is a wholly Newfoundland form. Like the chairs in fig. 26, the seats of such pieces are generally very narrow.

Height: 91.5 cm (36 in.);
Width: 45.1 cm (17¾ in.)
Canadiana, Royal Ontario Museum

32.
Corner Chair
Nova Scotia, possibly Amherst, c. 1785-1800

English-Canadian corner chairs appear to be extremely rare; they were probably too specialized a form to gain widespread usage in small houses. This chair is wholly of birch, with an original dark stain. The cabriole front leg is unusual in Canadian furniture. The bead-moulded cross-stretchers are joined in the centre by a large hand-forged nail, clinched over on the underside. The curved back is joined in the centre, and the back posts project through, with the back rail then retained by wedges. This chair came from the original furnishings of the Black house in Amherst, N.S.

Height: 79.1 cm (31 1/8 in.);
Width: 48.9 cm (19 1/4 in.)
Canadiana, Royal Ontario Museum

33.
Corner Chair
Probably New Brunswick, c. 1800-10

This chair is also entirely of birch, originally stained, and combines particularly English-patterned back-splats with light-turned and cross-stretchered legs. The upholstery is early, but probably replaces an original slip seat. This chair had been considered as an American piece brought to New Brunswick by Edward Winslow. The wood, back-splats, and legs, however, suggest both non-New England origin and a later-than-Loyalist-period dating. The chair is more likely of New Brunswick origin, and later acquired by Winslow.

Height: 81.9 cm (32 1/4 in.);
Seat side width: 47.7 cm (18 3/4 in.)
New Brunswick Museum

34.
Child's Commode Chair
Quebec, c. 1790-1810

As another good example of the often archaic French-English stylistic mixtures (see also fig. 18) that appeared in French cabinetmaking in Quebec in the later 18th century, this commode chair shows both Louis XV design influences and a Queen Anne-Chippendale derivation. The chair is of mixed maple, birch, and pine, and has much of its original red paint.

Height: 74.9 cm (29 1/2 in.);
Width: 34.3 cm (13 1/2 in.)
Canadiana, Royal Ontario Museum

35.
Armchair
New Brunswick, c. 1800-20

This chair, showing inspiration as well as good proportion and construction, has a carefully bowed and slightly flared back combined with well-shaped sweeping arms, with the arm supports moulded on the front edges. The chair is wholly of mahogany, with an upholstered seat. Chairs of this square-backed and square or rectangular back-rod type (see figs. 36-38 following) seem in Canada to be a largely New Brunswick mixed form, and numerous examples are known there. (Similar example, cf. Pain, no. 344.)

Height: 86.4 cm (34 in.);
Width: 58 cm (22.9 in.)
History Division, Museum of Man, National Museums of Canada

36.
Side Chair
Probably New Brunswick, c. 1810

Stylistically mixed but Sheraton-backed as are the following pieces, this chair also has reed-moulded back rods. Otherwise it follows the frame and stretcher form of other Canadian late Chippendale-Hepplewhite chairs. The wood is mahogany, and small fan carvings decorate the inner corners of the top rail. The chair has a long family history in Saint John, N.B.

Height: 95.9 cm (37¾ in.);
Width: 54 cm (21¼ in.)
Canadiana, Royal Ontario Museum

37.
Side Chair
New Brunswick, c. 1810

As a chair very similar but not identical to the preceding piece, this example may be by the same maker. The chair is of mahogany, and the back rods are reed moulded on the edges, with the same reed moulding around the inner and outer edges of the back frame. The legs of this chair have been cut down by perhaps 10 cm.

Present Height: 85 cm (33½ in.);
Width: 54.6 cm (21½ in.)
Private Collection

38.
Side Chair
New Brunswick, c. 1800-20

A simpler chair of the same type as those preceding, this piece has the abrupt concave back post reduction that appears to be a general Scottish-Sheraton-Canadian characteristic.

The chair is wholly of mahogany, with tapered legs and slip seat, and only the back rods and inner edges of the back posts are reed moulded.

Height: 86.4 cm (34 in); *Width:* 50 cm (19 5/8 in.)
History Division, Museum of Man, National Museums of Canada

39.
Armchair and Side Chair
Ontario, Fergus-Elora area, c. 1815-30

Made as a group of two armchairs and four side chairs, this set came from an Ontario-Scottish community, and the chairs were almost certainly fabricated by a Scots immigrant cabinet-maker.

Like the previous piece, these chairs also have back posts reduced from a concave cut above the seat line. The open backs have laddered cross-slats. The chairs are wholly of cherry, including the original plank seats with quarter-round moulded edges.

Armchair — *Height:* 88 cm (34 5/8 in.); *Width:* 53.3 cm (21 in.)
Side Chair — *Height:* 88.6 cm (34 7/8 in.); *Width:* 48.3 cm (19 in.)
Private Collection

40.
Armchair
New Brunswick, c. 1820-35

Essentially a late Regency type, this chair includes mixed English and French styles. This occurred often, as French-Canadian cabinet-makers emulated basically English forms in the late 18th and early 19th centuries. The chair is of mahogany, with the upholstery frame of pine. The arm posts and cabriole legs are well carved, with a turned centre stretcher. The side stretchers, however, show a French derivation. The plain turned and blocked back legs and back posts, slightly curved back at seat level, are a traditional Quebec form of a century and more earlier, and indicate that the chair was probably fabricated by a French-Canadian maker.

Height: 85.1 cm ($33^1/_2$ in.);
Width: 57.1 cm ($22^1/_2$ in.)
Kings Landing Historical Settlement

41.
Armchair
Quebec, Eastern Townships, c. 1820-35

Another but simpler late Regency chair, but with good conformation, this piece has only surface upholstery of the seat and back. The front legs and arm posts, the front skirt, and the back legs and uprights are of maple, while the side seat-rails, arms, and crest rail are birch. The secondary wood of underseat glue-blocks is not known. Chairs of this type became very popular in the late 1820s and continued to be made in many variations into the 1860s.

Height: 88.9 cm (35 in.);
Width: 59.4 cm ($23^3/_8$ in.)
Private Collection

42.
Side Chair
Montreal, c. 1810-20

With reeded legs, back posts, and inlaid back cross-rail, this square-backed mahogany Sheraton chair was probably part of a set. Canadian Sheraton furniture with close adherence to the style is the exception. The X-stretchered back-splat is a basically English type, not typical of Canadian chairs. (See also figs. 45, 46.) The oval inlay and broken line geometric banding in the top rail are of maple.

Height: 91.5 cm (36 in.);
Width: 48.3 cm (19 in.)
Canadiana, Royal Ontario Museum

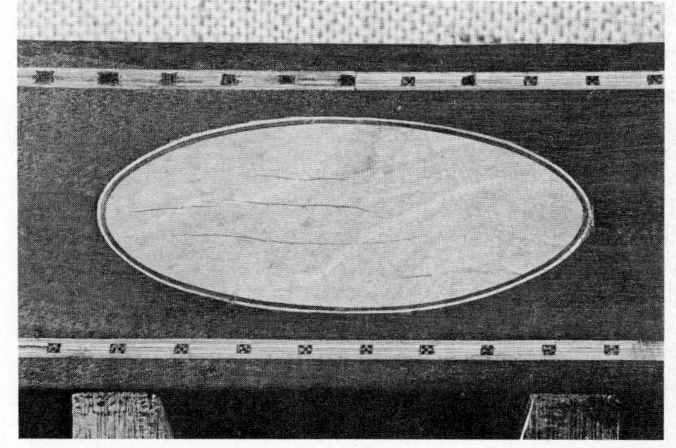

43.
Armchair and Side Chair
New Brunswick, c. 1810-25

Sheraton chairs and sofas of the type with classically curved backs and arms curving into turned arm supports became a popular and widespread style as the Chippendale period declined. With reeded arms and back posts, these mahogany chairs with slip seats are from a set of six. The turned X stretchers are an American-derived type found only in New Brunswick and Nova Scotia. (See also figs. 17, 44.) The arm supports of the armchair are unusual in being connected to the seat frame rather than as extensions of the front legs. (See also fig 52.) The back-slats and front corners are reeded, and the top rails panel carved. (Similar example, cf. Foss, pg. 40.)

Height: 84.2 cm (33 1/8 in.);
Width: 52 cm (20 1/2 in.)
Loyalist House, Saint John

44.
Armchair and Side Chair
New Brunswick, c. 1820-1830

With reeding and stretchering very similar to that of the preceding chairs, these later pieces may be by the same maker. The backs and heavier legs suggest a somewhat later date. The chairs, part of a set, are of mahogany with slip seats. The back centre carvings were done as separate pieces, and attached between the cross-rods with small vertical pins.

Height: 87.5 cm (34 1/2 in.);
Width: 52 cm (20 1/2 in.)
Kings Landing Historical Settlement

45.
Armchair
New Brunswick, Robert Parker shipyard, Tynemouth Creek, c.1820-30

The Sheraton chair form, like the Chippendale, in its later period was carried into the realm of country furniture, so that many design variants and mixtures appear. This well-proportioned chair, wholly of birch, was made by a ship-finisher rather than a specialist cabinet-maker. The square-tapered legs are a departure from the usual form, as is the English-derivative X-stretchered and panel cross-slat in the back. (cf. Ryder, pp. 61-2.) (Similar example, cf. Foss, pg. 40.)

Height: 87 cm (34$^1/_4$ in.);
Width: 53.3 cm (21 in.)
New Brunswick Museum

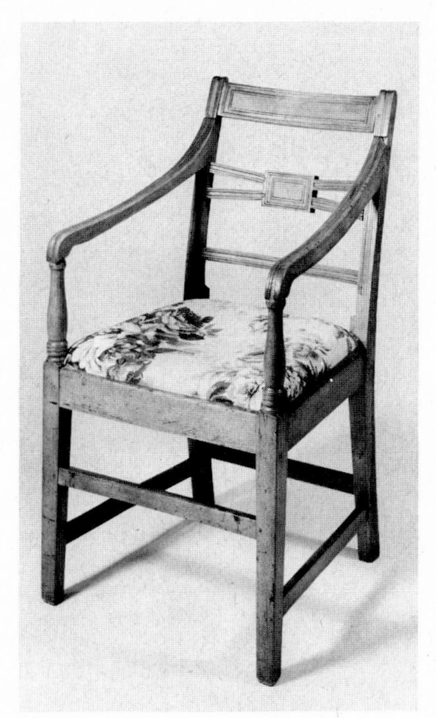

46.
Armchair
Ontario, Ottawa Valley, c. 1820-30

Though very similar to the preceding piece, this chair is of butternut, and originates from a French-speaking area. Other than the square-tapered front legs, the chair is basically Sheraton in design origin, except for the extreme and concave downward slope of the arms (see also fig. 18), a traditionally French characteristic indicating a French-Canadian maker.

Height: 82.6 cm (32$^1/_2$ in.);
Width: 47 cm (18$^1/_2$ in.)
Canadiana, Royal Ontario Museum

47.
Armchair
New Brunswick, c. 1815-25

With an upholstered rather than slip seat, this square-legged chair has upper back posts reduced in the same manner as the two previous New Brunswick pieces and the Scottish-Ontario chairs, figs. 39. The wood is mahogany. The extended top rail, as on this and the two chairs following, is another stylistic adaptation. (Similar example, cf. Pain, no. 340.)

Height: 90.2 cm (35½ in.); *Width:* 51.4 cm (20¼ in.)
Canadiana, Royal Ontario Museum

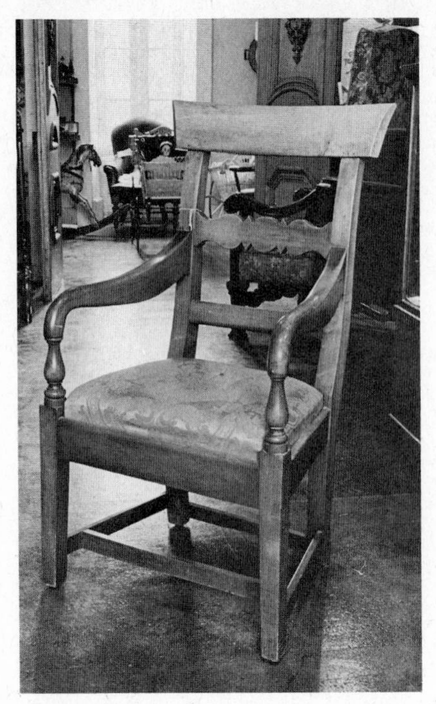

48.
Armchair
Ontario, Waterloo County, c. 1830-40

This somewhat later piece, very mixed and derivative, includes a scroll-cut back-slat and a heavy top rail. The chair is wholly of maple, and originates from a heavily Pennsylvania-German-settled area.

Height: 87.6 cm (34½ in.)
Wellington Country Historical Museum, Fergus, Ontario

49.
Armchair
Ontario, Niagara Peninsula, c. 1815-30

Showing its Ontario-German influence, this vestigial Sheraton-Hepplewhite chair is of straight-grained maple, and was found in St. Catharines, Ontario. The reeded edges of the upper section, back, and arms were hand chiselled, not planed. The plank seat, with quarter-round moulded eges, is original.

Dimensions unavailable
Private Collection

50.
Side Chair
Montreal, c. 1810-20

The straight "Grecian" or "sabre-leg" chair is an English type which became extremely popular in North America after about 1805, and seemed to gain popularity with time. The form continued to be made by factories into the 1850s in myriad variation, later often of bird's-eye maple with full stretchering and turned front legs. Chairs such as this, in a pure early form with both back and front legs without stretchers, and the back itself outcurving in clean lines, are rare in Canada. The chair is of maple, stained black, with small brass stars applied, perhaps later, to the top rail. (Similar example, cf. Pain, no. 358.)

Height: 79.7 cm (31 5/8 in.);
Width: 45.4 cm (17 7/8 in.)
Canadiana, Royal Ontario Museum

51.
Armchair
New Brunswick, c. 1810-15

Scroll-armed chairs of this type are also a distinctly English-Regency form, widely copied in Canada and the United States. Though appearing in Canada perhaps as early as 1810, the scroll arm, often extreme, was also included in later Empire chairs of the 1830s and later. This piece, of mahogany, is also a so-called sabre-legged chair, in pure form without stretchers. The back rod and top rail are reeded. (Similar examples, cf. Pain, nos. 357-58.)

Height: 84.5 cm (33 1/4 in.);
Width: 49.5 cm (19 1/2 in.)
Kings Landing Historical Settlement

52.
Armchair
Quebec City area, c. 1820-35

A late Regency-Sheraton type, with a panel pinned between the back cross-rods, this chair is of mahogany with an upholstery frame of pine. The front legs and separate arm supports are simply turned, and there are no inlays. The pinning of arm support posts to seat frame sides was an uncommon (see also fig. 43) but not regionally isolated technique.

Height: 85.1 cm (33½ in.);
Width: 57.1 cm (22½ in.).
Canadiana, Royal Ontario Museum

53.
Armchair
New Brunswick, c. 1820-40

As a stylistic mixture, this chair combines Sheraton and Regency elements, and adds adaptations as well. All four legs are turned; the top rail extends beyond the back posts and the slightly curled-over arms extend forward of their supports. The back posts are reduced above seat level and the two crossroads are without a centre panel. The turning and treatment of the front legs and arm supports are somewhat similar to that of the McKay armchair, fig. 4. The chair is completely of birch, without carving or moulding.

Height: 96.5 cm (38 in.);
Width: 53.3 cm (21 in.)
Kings Landing Historical Settlement

54.
Armchair
Halifax, c. 1780-90; marked by Joseph DeGant

The DeGant Windsor chair factory, opened in Halifax in 1780, was the earliest known English-Canadian chair factory and produced the earliest marked and identifiable furniture. Many DeGant chairs are hot-branded *DEGANT/WAR*[*ranted*] · *HAL*-[*ifax*] on the bottoms of the shaped single-plank seats. This marked square-backed armchair, with bamboo turnings, is of maple under its original dark green paint. The DeGant factory also made straight chairs and a bamboo-turned arrow-backed type. (cf. MacLaren, no. 26.) (Similar example, cf. Pain, no. 242.)

Height: 81.3 cm (32 in.);
Width: 44.5 cm ($17^1/_2$ in.)
Canadiana, Royal Ontario Museum

55.
Armchair
Halifax, c. 1805-15; marked by J. Humeston

Another representative early Windsor chair-maker was Joy Humeston of Halifax, working from 1805 to c. 1815. Humeston is known for square-backed chairs and short settees, very similar to the DeGant and others' pieces, branded *J. HUMESTON/ HALIFAX* on the seat bottoms. This bamboo-turned chair is of mixed maple and birch, and painted black. As on American chairs of the same type, the top rails of these chairs are laid on pins formed at the tops of the side posts, and the central rods are inserted and held in holes drilled in the top rails and seats. (Similar example, cf. Dobson no. 81.)

Height: 84 cm (33 in.)
Nova Scotia Museum

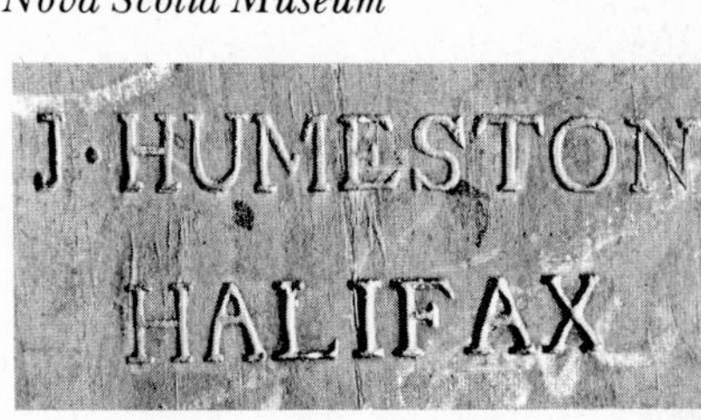

56.
Armchair
Probably Nova Scotia, c. 1780-1800

Windsor chairs of the continuous back and arm type are a distinctly New England form, and in Canada are of Loyalist derivation. With its deep saddle-carved seat, this chair is typical of the Canadian form of earlier bow-backed Windsor pieces in that the back is nearly flat because of the seat being rectangular with the rear only slightly curved. The pine seat is also very shallow in relation to width. The turned legs, front arm supports, and side stretchers are maple, while the bow back, spindles, and centre stretcher are of ash. The legs project through the seat and are retained by wedges. (Similar examples, cf. Dobson nos. 79, 81.)

Height: 88.3 cm (34¾ in);
Width: 42.8 cm (16 ⅞ in.)
Canadiana, Royal Ontario Museum

57.
Side Chair
Probably Nova Scotia, c. 1780-1800

Bow-backed Windsor chairs, also on a New England pattern, continued in production with little change at least into the 1860s. This chair, with leg turnings nearly identical to the preceding piece, also has a seat very shallow in relation to width. The grain of the pine seat, dished in the centre, runs across rather than front to back, making the seat front liable to splitting, which has in fact occurred. The legs project through the seat and are wedged. The back bow, spindles, and central stretcher are of ash, while the legs and side stretchers are maple. (Similar example, cf. Pain, no. 265.)

Height: 84.5 cm (33¼ in.)
Width: 39.7 cm (15⅝ in.)
Canadiana, Royal Ontario Museum

58.
Side Chair
Quebec, St. Joachim area, c. 1800-20

The mixed French-English furniture types (see also figs. 18, 34, 40, 46) of the 1780-1830 period were built solely by French-tradition makers, often in archaic English styles. There is no indication that English or Scottish makers adopted French characteristics. This slip-seated chair, in a Queen Anne derivative form, is basically English in its back and seat frame, excepting the straight crest centre section. The base, however, is traditionally French, with rounded and toed cabriole front legs, heavy turned stretchers, and Louis XIII-derived back legs. The piece is wholly of pine, most unusual for a stylized chair. Because of the French characteristics, the chair is probably an original piece, rather than a direct copy or replacement of a chair from an English set.

Height: 98.2 cm (38⅝ in.);
Width: 50.2 cm (19¾ in.)
Montreal Museum of Fine Arts

59.
Sofa
Montreal area, c. 1790-1810

Like tall clocks, Canadian sofas in the Georgian period appear to have been limited to households of some wealth. Particularly as stretcher-based forms, sofas are rare dating from the period before about 1820. This piece has its lower frame, of eight legs with reeded facing and full stretchers, of cherry, with a pine upper frame. The sofa suggests an American Loyalist influence and is from the original furnishings (though dating earlier) of a house built in 1820 at Maitland, Ontario, on the St. Lawrence River.

Height: 90 cm ($35^1/_2$ in.);
Length: 168.0 cm (66 in.)
Canadiana, Royal Ontario Museum

60.
Sofa
Montreal, c. 1800-15

With rolled arms and an arched back, this six-legged sofa has plain square-tapered legs and full lower stretchering, all of mahogany, with a pine upholstery frame. Square-legged stretcher-based sofas do not seem to appear in Canada from other than the Montreal area.

Height: 92.7 cm (36½ in.);
Length: 215.9 cm (85 in.)
Private Collection

61.
Sofa
Montreal area, c. 1800-1815

Also of mahogany, the six tapered legs of this straight-backed sofa are without stretcher supports and are pinned into a pine upholstery frame. Like the previous piece, the legs are without moulding or other embellishment. (Similar example, cf. Pain, no. 381.)

Dimensions unavailable
Private Collection

62.
Sofa-Bed
New Brunswick, c. 1810-20

Though often imaginative and useful in design, combination or dual-purpose furniture surviving from the Georgian period is extremely rare. A rather angular and uncomfortable piece, this sofa is of mahogany and mahogany veneer over pine. The arms are slightly rolled, with turned face caps. When unhooked behind, the back hinges down to form a flat bed and is supported by two hinged wooden legs which drop down as the back is lowered. The seat frame and arms are rigid, and the plain heavy-turned mahogany legs are of a type often found on Maritimes furniture.

Height: 74.6 cm (29^3/8 in.);
Length: 198.1 cm (78 in.)
Kings Landing Historical Settlement

63.
Sofa
Nova Scotia, c. 1805-20

The form of Georgian-period Canadian sofa most often encountered is the Sheraton-Regency type with exposed or partially exposed arms joined to the seat frame by turned supports. In Canada such sofas most generally originate from Nova Scotia. This fine piece, wholly of mahogany with secondary pine in the under structure, includes three rectangular bird's-eye maple inlays and stringing in the seat rail and leg blocks, and three parallel line inlays in the curved arm fronts. The front legs are turnings, while the rear legs are square.

Dimensions unknown
Private Collection

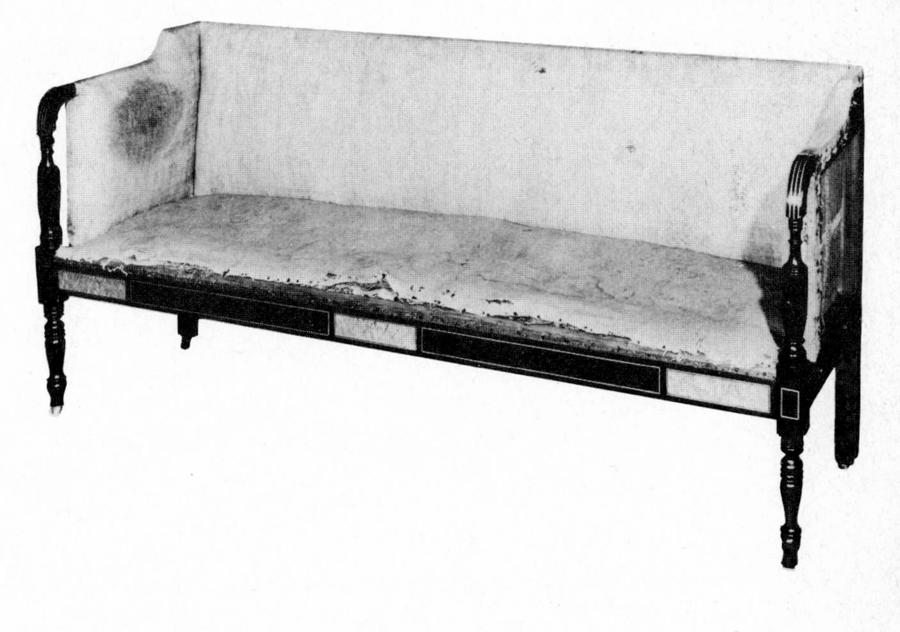

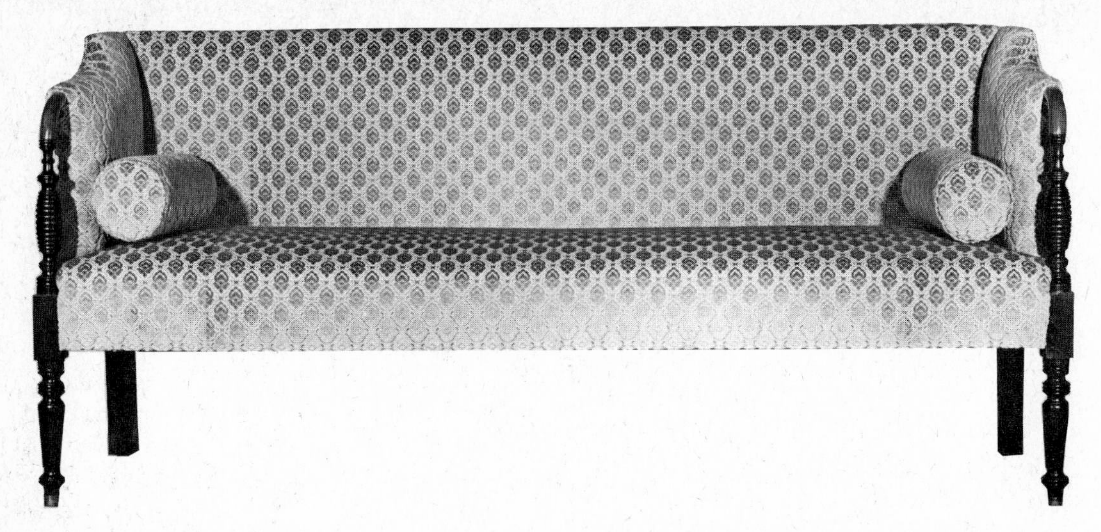

64.
Sofa
Nova Scotia, c. 1820-30

This sofa, of mahogany with the upholstery frame of pine, has simple rectangular bird's-eye maple inlays in the upper leg blocks. The tight multiple ring turning of the bulbous arm support posts is typical treatment on Nova Scotia and New Brunswick furniture (precise dating of this manner of turning is uncertain), and may date this sofa to the later end of its style range.

Height: 84.4 cm (33¼ in.);
Length 189.2 cm (74½ in.)
Private Collection

65.
Sofa
Probably Montreal, c. 1820-30

Partly because of a long family history, this sofa is presently considered a Montreal piece, though the tight ring turnings of the legs and arm supports are more typical of the Maritimes. All exposed wood is mahogany, with a mixed pine and butternut upholstery frame. The exposed reeded upper arms and back rail are exceptional; usually these areas are upholstered over. The centre leg is also much more in keeping with Montreal than with Maritimes style.

Height: 86.3 cm (34 in.);
Length: 183.5 cm (72¼ in.)
Canadiana, Royal Ontario Museum

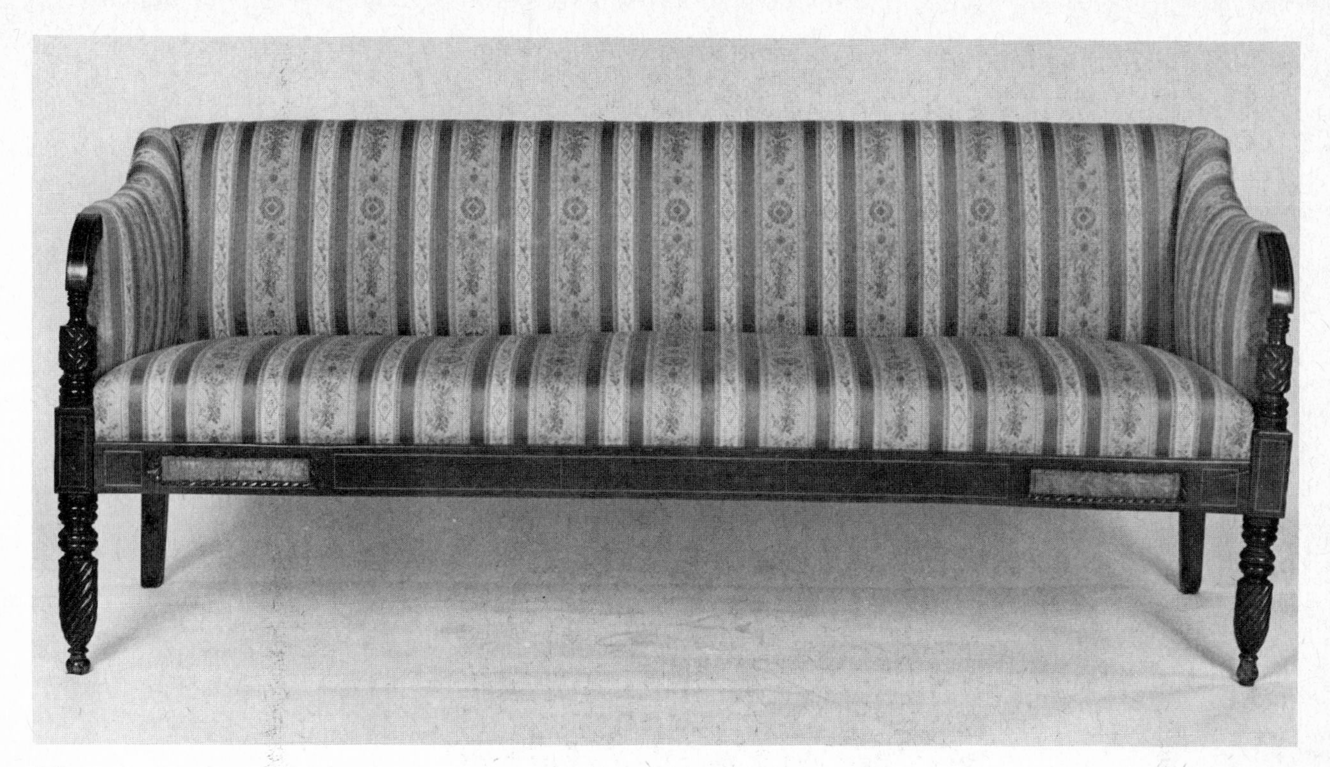

66.
Sofa
Probably Nova Scotia, c. 1825-1835

The late Regency or Empire turnings, the rope and cross-hatched carving of the legs, and the arm-support pillars of this sofa indicate that it is considerably later in date than most such pieces. The sofa is of mahogany; the secondary wood is pine. The arms, leg blocks, and seat rails are outlined with maple string inlays. The bird's-eye maple rectangles are separate panels, retained in recesses in the seat rail by applied rope-carved quarter-round mouldings.

Height: 76.5 cm (30¹/₈ in.);
Length: 184.0 cm (72³/₈ in.)
History Division, National Museum of Canada

67.
Sofa
Ontario, c. 1820-30

Though exposed-arm Sheraton sofas are not a usual Ontario form, and are found more frequently in the Maritimes, this sofa was found in Farmersville, Ontario. The piece is of walnut, with small bird's-eye maple rectangular panels inserted in the front leg blocks. In spite of the vase-turned arm supports, the heavily turned legs and the applied semi-round moulding on the seat rail suggest a dating for this piece toward the end of its style range. (Similar examples, cf. Shackleton, no. 182; Pain, no. 382.)

Length: 193 cm (76 in.)
Private Collection

68.
Sofa
Nova Scotia, c. 1820

A characteristic of many Nova Scotia Sheraton sofas is a strong vase turning in the arm support. This sofa is of mahogany, with a pine underframe and simple rectangular maple inlays in the leg blocks. The arms are reeded, but there is no stringing.

Height: 82.5 cm (32½ in.);
Length: 162 cm (63¾ in.)
Canadiana, Royal Ontario Museum

69.
Sofa
Nova Scotia, c. 1820-30

Though most Maritimes sofas are formal pieces and of mahogany, occasional country examples are found in native woods. With heavy turnings in the legs and lighter vase turnings in the arm supports, this sofa is wholly of birch and secondary pine. The lozenge inlays and thin stringing in the leg blocks are of maple.

Height: 80.5 cm (31¾ in.);
Length: 143.5 cm (56½ in.)
Nova Scotia Museum

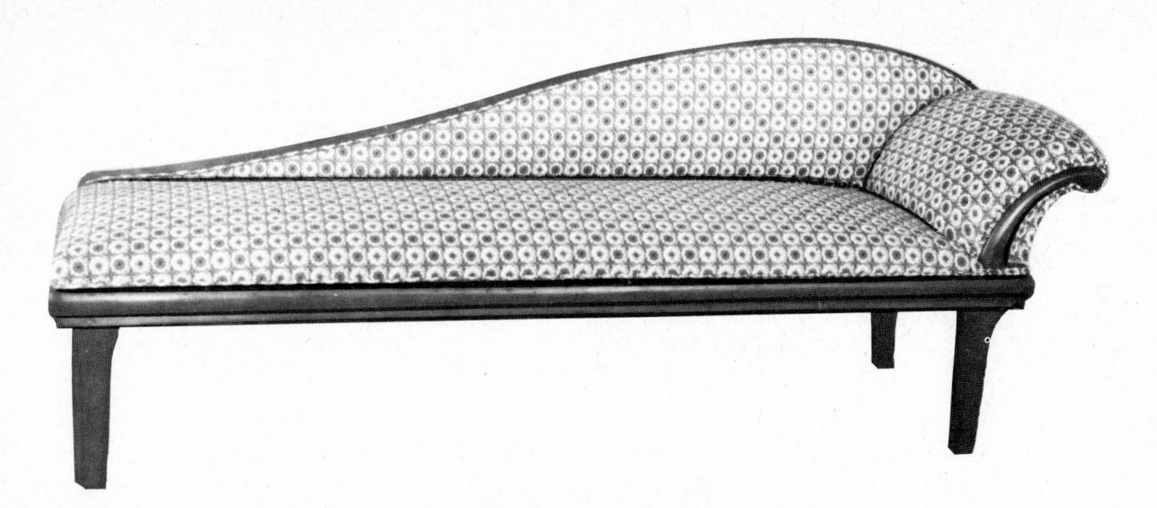

70.
Sofa — Daybed
New Brunswick, c. 1810-20

So-called "Grecian" or "Recamier" daybeds did not become widespread in Canada until the late Empire period of the 1830s. This simple but delicate piece is an exception. The daybed is wholly of pine, without a secondary wood. The arm and back are structurally separate from the base frame and its plain square legs. The sofa belonged originally to Moses Picard of Maugerville, who had come from Rowley, Massachusetts, in 1763.

Height: 67.9 cm ($26^{3}/_{4}$ in.);
Base Length: 170.2 cm (67 in.)
New Brunswick Museum

71.
Sofa
Saint John, New Brunswick, c. 1820-25; attributed to Alexander Lawrence

Though early Empire furniture in the style of Duncan Phyfe of New York was not common in Canada, certainly the form had an impact on a few Canadian cabinetmakers. (See also figs. 72, 105, 182.) With gracefully scrolled arms and a continuous line of arms and seat rail, the sofa is of mahogany, with secondary pine in the frame. The arm facings, seat rails, and the front legs are reeded. The seat rail has three leaf-carved inset panels and the rectangular centre panel is repeated in the crest rail. The attribution to Lawrence is based on a nearly identical piece still in the possession of the Lawrence family. Alexander Lawrence, born in Scotland in 1788, immigrated to New Brunswick and worked as an independent cabinet-maker from 1817 until his death in 1843. (cf. Ryder, pp. 31, 32.) He is not known to have marked his furniture.

Height: 87.6 cm ($34^{1}/_{2}$ in.);
Length: 216.5 cm ($85^{1}/_{4}$ in.)
New Brunswick Museum

72.
Window Seat
New Brunswick, c. 1820-25; possibly by Alexander Lawrence or Thomas Nisbet

Window seats, as special-purpose pieces, are a very uncommon Canadian form. This piece, with scrolled arms and reeded arm and seat facings in a continuous line, is treated very similarly to the preceding sofa. The heavy straight legs are incongruous to the style, but incorporate the multiple tight ring turnings so common to Nova Scotia and New Brunswick legged furniture. The window seat is of mahogany, with secondary pine in the upholstery frame.

Length: 167.6 cm (66 in.)
Private Collection

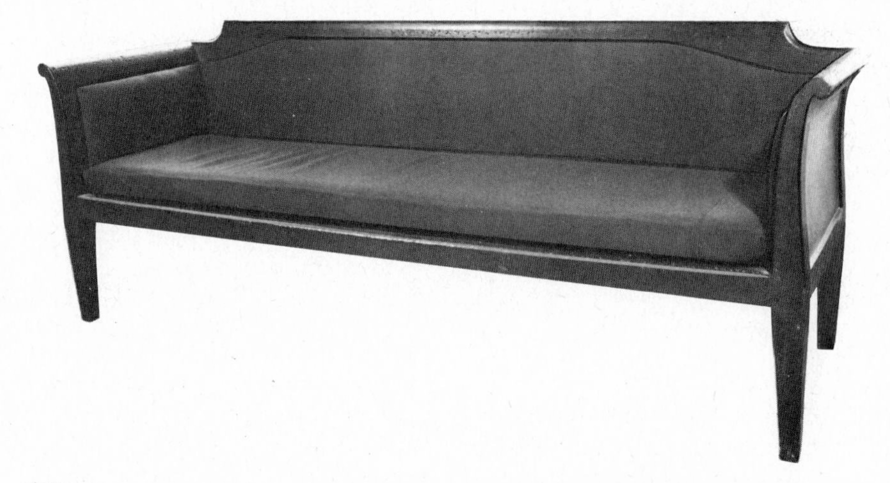

73.
Sofa
Ontario, Niagara Peninsula, c. 1820-40

Very few Georgian-period sofas are found from Ontario; early Upper Canada was, during that period, in a first-settlement stage which usually precluded such comforts. Sofas which do occur are most likely to be refined country pieces. This sofa, with panelled ends and slightly rolled arms, is of walnut with secondary pine in the underframe, and clearly of Pennsylvania-German derivation.

Height: 73 cm (28¾ in.);
Length: 197.7 cm (77½ in.)
Private Collection

74.
Sofa Table
Probably Montreal area, c. 1810-20

With a very high round stretcher just beneath the case, this free-standing Regency table is a particularly English form, with mahogany top, leaves, and base, and mahogany veneering over pine in the frame and drawer fronts. The drawers are matched with false drawer fronts on the opposite side. The operative drawer fronts, both on the same side, are outlined with maple string inlays, though not the false fronts, and flanked on each end by lozenge line inlays. The concave legs are faced with triple string inlays, also of maple. The top and leaf edges are reeded, and the leaves have double wooden-hinged wing supports. The brass feet and castors are original, but the drawer knobs are replacements. This table has a long Toronto family history, but in all its characteristics it is of Montreal origin.

Height: 72.1 cm (28 3/8 in.); *Length, leaves down:* 98.1 cm (38 5/8 in.)
Canadiana, Royal Ontario Museum

75.
Sofa Table
Montreal, c. 1810-20

As a four-columned Regency example, this table is of mahogany with mahogany veneer over secondary pine in the upper frame. An inlaid three-quarter-inch band of curly maple surrounds the top and leaf edges. The two long drawers open one on each side, and are matched by opposing false drawer fronts. Maple string inlays outline the case corner blocks, the drawer and false drawer fronts, and the upper surfaces of the legs.

Height: 79.3 cm (31¼ in.);
Length, leaves extended:
153.7 cm (60½ in.)
Canadiana, Royal Ontario Museum

76.
Sofa Table
Ontario, Napanee area, c. 1810-20

With its concave and bowed legs and central stretcher, this handsome table is stylistically a New York form, and a similar example is illustrated in Montgomery, no. 333. The table is of cherry, with drawer and false drawer fronts of bird's-eye maple. The secondary wood is pine. The triple-elliptic end leaves are extremely unusual in Canadian furniture. All hardware is original. The table was collected years ago in Napanee, Ontario, and is perfectly consistent with the woods and design influences of that area

Height: 77.5 cm (30½ in.); *Length, leaves extended:* 152.4 cm (60 in.)
Canadiana, Royal Ontario Museum

77.
Sofa Table
Ontario, Niagara Peninsula, c. 1820-30

In a particularly English-Regency rather than Niagara American-Germanic style, this table is of well figured curly maple, with secondary pine in the drawer structure. The drawer edge beading is walnut. The string inlays of the legs, vertical supports, and drawer fronts are all of dark horn (see also fig. 225), only occasionally employed as an inlay material. The lion's paw feet are original, but the drawer pulls are replacements.

Height: 71.5 cm (28 1/8 in.); *Length, leaves down:* 82.5 cm (32 1/2 in.)
Private Collection

78.
Secretary-Desk
Quebec, c. 1790-1800

Truly opulent Canadian furniture, in an English sense, is rare and was always specially commissioned. This secretary, of well selected mahogany, has carved upper door mouldings and claw feet. The interior, quite simple, is also of mahogany. There are no inlays. The secondary woods are pine and, most uncommonly, poplar. The piece was made in Quebec, by an unknown English cabinet-maker, for Edward Augustus, Duke of Kent and Strathern (and Queen Victoria's father) during his stationing there, either during 1791-93 or 1796-98. The original brass hardware is English.

Height: 213.4 cm (84 in.);
Width: 111.8 cm (44 in.)
Canadiana, Royal Ontario Museum

79.
Secretary-Desk
Montreal, c. 1800-10

With a drop-front, this desk is of mahogany with secondary pine. The string inlays are all of maple, as is the inlaid oval in the skirt. The interior includes eight small drawers, all with turned bone knobs. The back of the bookcase section is lined with early wall-paper. The English hardware is original to the piece.

Height: 229.6 cm (90 3/8 in.); *Width:* 118.8 cm (46 3/4 in.)
Canadiana, Royal Ontario Museum

80.
Secretary-Desk
Aurora, Ontario, c. 1835; by John Doane

With rope-carved quarter columns in the upper section and plain quarter columns below, this desk is characteristic of Doane's use of specially selected and densely figured bird's-eye maple. (See also fig. 236.) The well shaped ogee bracket feet, with pads, extend fully from the edges of the bracket moulding, rather than being slightly set back as in many Niagara Peninsula pieces. (See figs. 87, 238.) The lower drawers, overlapping the frame, have brass keyhole liners and interior structures of pine. The upper section, with flat door panels, has pull-out candle or lamp slides, and is a separate unit, detachable from the base. The lower drawer knobs are replacements. (Similar example, cf. Shackleton, nos. 319-20.)

Height: 181.6 cm (71½ in.);
Width: 102.8 cm (40½ in.)
Private Collection

81.
Secretary-Desk
Probably Montreal, 1805; signed by Jacob Gober

Low secretary desks typically had two hinged doors closing the upper section; no identified Canadian examples have been located with tambour shutters. This desk is of mahogany and mahogany veneers over secondary pine. The skirt and sides are surrounded with a maple and mahogany geometric band inlay, interrupted at the butting of the sides and front. The classical column inlays in the upper section were probably English as, like hardware, motif inlays were often imported. The drawer pulls and keyhole plates are original. The right upper door is signed on the inner side, faintly in chalk, *Jacob Gober, 1805,* not necessarily the maker.

Height: 141.3 cm (55⁵/₈ inches); *Width:* 104.4 cm (41¹/₈ in.)
Canadiana, Royal Ontario Museum

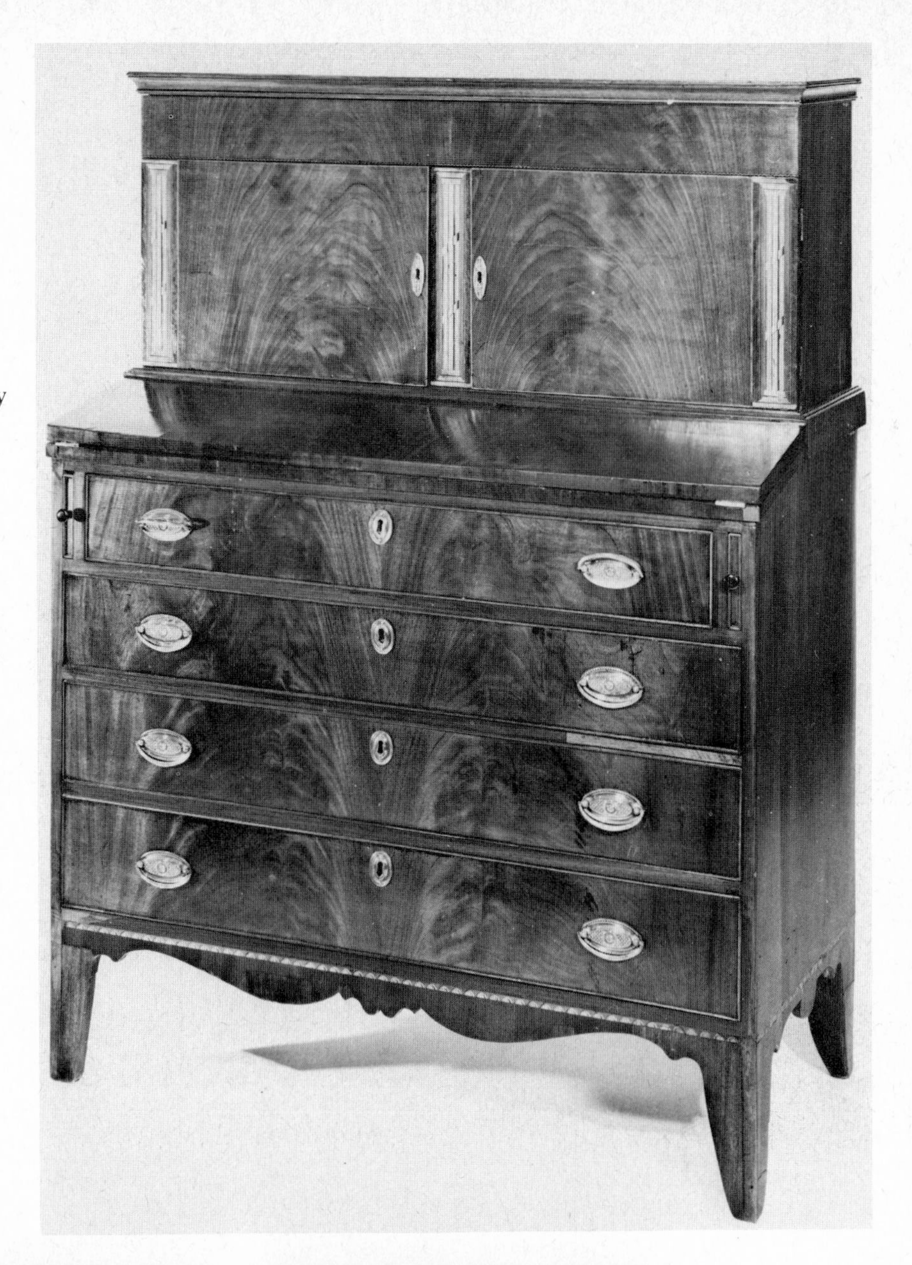

82.
Secretary-Desk
New Brunswick, c. 1810-20

Furniture of the Maritimes often included original turned wooden drawer knobs and unstyled turned legs on pieces which, in design and configuration, would appear to deserve better. This desk is of mahogany and mahogany veneering over pine, with separate mahogany inlaid bands around the drawers and top. The drawer fronts and upper doors are also outlined with maple and mahogany interrupted string inlays. The flush-fitting drawers are edged with beading strips. This desk was purchased in 1820, perhaps but not necessarily new, by Tristram Moore in Moore's Mills, New Brunswick. It was repaired by John Warren Moore in 1884, and is referred to in a letter of that year. (Similar example, cf. Dobson, no. 134; Foss, p. 24.)

Height: 127 cm (50 in.);
Width: 100.4 cm (39½ in.)
Private Collection

83.
Secretary-Desk
Nova Scotia, c. 1810-20

With reeded upper section door panels, in imitation of sliding tambour shutters, this desk is a particularly New England form, probably built by a Loyalist maker. The flared and footed legs are attached to a bracketed, traditionally Chippendale, base, an unusual stylistic mixture. The desk is wholly of birch, with interior secondary pine, and the brass drawer knobs and pulls appear original. The top section is a separate detachable unit. The writing surface supports slide out horizontally, as on the two preceding pieces, but then tilt down slightly when extended to match the angle of the folding writing surface. Though the lower drawers are edge beaded, there are no inlays. This desk was found in Argyle, Nova Scotia, and probably originates from that area.

Height: 138.4 cm (54½ in.);
Width: 95.9 cm (37¾ in.)
Henry and Barbara Dobson

84.
Secretary-Desk
Nova Scotia, c. 1820-30

In a very typical Maritimes combination of woods, this simpler desk has a structure of birch, with bird's-eye maple drawer fronts and upper door panels, mahogany band inlays around the drawer fronts, and with pine as the secondary wood. As on all such desks, the upper drawer is short to allow space for the pull-out slides. (Similar example, cf. Pain, no. 670.)

Height: 141 cm (55½ in.);
Width: 101 cm (39¾ in.)
Nova Scotia Museum

85.
Secretary-Desk
New Brunswick, c. 1820-30

Though the knee-hole desk, as a form, is uncommon in Canada during the Georgian period, pieces such as this, as well as table desks and small lowboys, are found in New Brunswick. Occasionally these pieces have reeded legs; more often they are undistinguished turnings. All, however, have some manner of fan carving at the corners of the knee-hole. (See also figs. 86, 263.) This desk, with a folding writing surface supported by sliding arms, has a sliding cover for the upper unit, retracted under the top. The piece is wholly of butternut, with secondary pine. The drawer knobs are original. The desk has been attributed to Thomas Beatty of Carleton, New Brunswick.

Height: 117.5 cm (46¼ in.);
Width: 106 cm (41¾ in.)
New Brunswick Museum

86.
Flat-top Desk
New Brunswick, c. 1815-20

Flat-surfaced table desks did not become a popular type until the second half of the 19th century, but they do occasionally appear much earlier, usually as country pieces in pine. With reeded legs and an arched knee-opening with scroll-carved border and reeded fan carvings in the corners, this desk is of mahogany, with pine as the secondary wood. The drawer knobs are original, while the drawers never had locks. The solid top is edge reeded. Numbers of examples of this type, often with plain turned legs (see figs. 85, 263) have been observed in New Brunswick. There is sufficient variation to suggest that such pieces seem to be a regional type, rather than a product of any single maker. (Similar examples, cf. Foss, pp. 29-30.)

Height: 72.3 cm (28$^{1}/_{2}$ in);
Length: 106.7 cm (42 in.)
Private Collection

87.
Secretary-Desk
Ontario, Niagara Peninsula, c. 1830-40; possibly by John Grobb

With three large drawers above, this two-section slant-front desk has its cover and writing surface supported by folding brackets rather than by the usual wooden pull-out slides. The desk is of cherry and secondary pine, with the interior cupboard door and drawer fronts of bird's-eye maple. The piece was found in Camborough, Ontario, and has been attributed to a maker named Fulton. However, the ogee bracket feet are set back slightly from the base moulding, and combined with plain quarter columns, are characteristic of known work of John Grobb (1800-1885) of Clinton Township, an American-born Mennonite. (Similar example, cf. Pain, no. 1156.)

Height: 142 cm (55⁷/₈ in.);
Width: 106.3 cm (41⁷/₈ in.)
Private Collection

88.
Bureau-Desk
New Brunswick, c. 1800-10

Bureau desks with square bracket feet, unlike slant-front desks, are not a common Canadian form. Of solid mahogany, without veneering or inlays, this austere but handsome desk has a very simple interior with seven small drawers and adjacent upper letter slots, also in mahogany. The secondary wood and drawer structures are of pine. The brasses are early and appear original.

Height: 116.7 cm (46 in.);
Width: 107 cm (42¹/₈ in.)
History Division, Museum of Man, National Museum of Canada

89.
Bureau-Desk
Ontario, Niagara Peninsula, c. 1800-1810

As a drop-front or bureau-desk, with tapered "French" feet and English lion's-head ring drawer pulls, this desk follows a Niagara-area English, rather than Pennsylvania-German, tradition. The desk is wholly of curly maple, with secondary pine, including the pigeon-hole separators and walnut drawer-edge inlays. The piece is very similar in design and construction to the chest of drawers, fig. 220, and may be by the same maker.

Height: 122 cm (48 in.);
Width: 114.3 cm (45 in.)
Canadiana, Royal Ontario Museum

90.
Bureau-Desk
New Brunswick, c. 1810-20; possibly by Robert Chillas, Saint John

With exterior maple string inlaying remarkably similar to that on the chest of drawers, fig. 221, this desk is also of mahogany, with the face and drawer fronts of mahogany veneer over secondary pine. The interior, of mixed mahogany and bird's-eye maple, is string inlaid in mahogany, with a standard arrangement of small drawers under letter-slots, and a central cupboard. The mahogany knobs are original. The desk was found in Ontario, but has no traceable associations there. (Similar example, cf. Foss, p. 24.)

Height: 121 cm (47 5/8 in.);
Width: 102.7 cm (40 3/8 in.)
History Division, Museum of Man, National Museum of Canada

Bureau-Desk
New Brunswick, c. 1800-10
See fig. 92

Clock
Quebec, c. 1830
See fig. 140

Slant-front Desk
Montreal area, c. 1800-15
See fig. 94

91.
Bureau-Desk
Probably New Brunswick, c. 1800-10

This bureau-desk is most unusual as a Canadian example in having oak sides and backs in the lower drawers, generally characteristic only of English furniture. The sides and top are of plank mahogany, while the drawer fronts are mahogany veneer over pine, with parallel maple string inlays, both rectangular and oval. The base inlay does not carry around the sides. The interior small drawers have bird's-eye maple fronts with bone pulls, and mahogany sides with pine bases.

In spite of the use of oak and the fact that both North American pine and maple were available to English cabinet-makers, the form of this desk with its simple splayed feet and plain drawer knobs, and the combination of wood usage, is so typically New Brunswick that English origin is unlikely. The desk was, of course, probably the work of an emigrant English rather than American-Loyalist maker.

Height: 112.5 cm (44¼ in.);
Width: 107.8 cm (42½ in.)
Kings Landing Historical Settlement

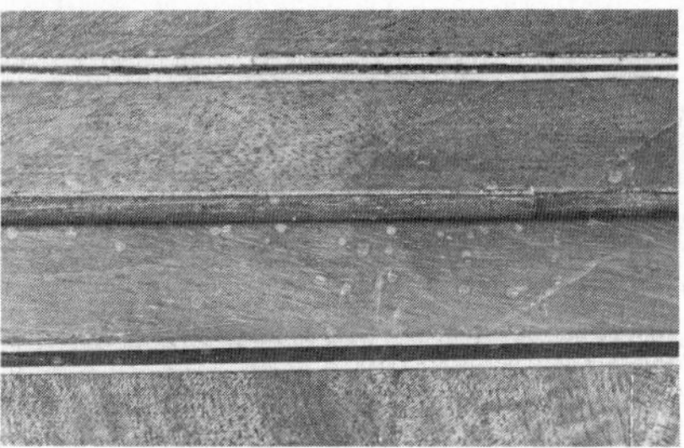

92.
Bureau-Desk
New Brunswick, c. 1800-10

Long in a Halifax, Nova Scotia, collection, this desk has maple parallel string inlays very similar, though here with cove corners, to those on the preceding piece. The sides, top, and interior drawer fronts are of solid mahogany, and the drop-front and large drawers are mahogany veneered over pine. The large drawer sides and backs are of poplar, uncommon though not unknown as a Canadian secondary wood, with pine bases. The interior cupboard door inlays are also maple, as are the strange feathered inlays in the flanking vertical drawers. The small interior drawer pivoted pulls appear original, though the oval plate pulls are replacements of similar originals.

Height: 110.5 cm ($43^{1}/_{2}$ in.);
Width: 120.7 cm ($47^{1}/_{2}$ in.)
Canadiana, Royal Ontario Museum

93.
Slant-front Desk
Quebec, c. 1786-96

This relatively austere desk with plain square bracket feet is of mahogany, with secondary pine in the case and drawer structure. The interior contains the usual arrangement of letter-slots and a central small cupboard. There are no inlays. The cover, supported by pull-out slides, suggests wood scarcity, for it is of a knotted piece of mahogany that would probably not have been used if the maker had had sufficient wood available for selection.

The desk was made in Quebec for Sir Guy Carleton, Lord Dorchester, during his second term from 1786 to 1796 as Governor-in-Chief of British North America.

Height: 108.8 cm (42⁷/₈ in.);
Width: 105.1 cm (41³/₈ in.)
History Division, Museum of Man, National Museum of Canada

94.
Slant-front Desk
Montreal area, c. 1800-15

As an uncommonly sophisticated example, the hinged cover of this desk uses the same forms of imported English inlays, the shell and corner fan motifs, that were employed on better Quebec clocks. The desk is of cherry, with secondary pine. The lower drawers are outlined with curly maple inlaid banding, and the string inlays in the cover and the keyhole lozenges are also of maple. The interior is of curly maple, with mahogany string inlays, spacers, and applied beading and mouldings. The central interior section is slightly extended and block carved. The interior drawer knobs are original, and the lower pulls partially replaced. The desk has a long Montreal family history.

Height: 108.1 cm (46¹/₂ in.);
Width: 107 cm (42¹/₈ in.)
Private Collection

95.
Slant-front Desk
Nova Scotia, Annapolis Valley, c. 1790-1810

An early New England derivative desk typical of those found in the Maritimes, this piece is well proportioned but very simple and basic. The desk is wholly of birch, with the interior and drawer structure of pine. The original paint is a dark red on the exterior with a dark green interior. The square bracketed feet, the originals rotted, are replacements as are the drawer pulls, the latter inserted in the originally bored holes. (Similar example, cf. Pain, no. 661.)

Height: 107.3 cm ($42^1/_4$ in.); *Width:* 95.2 cm ($27^1/_2$ in.)
Robert O'Neill

96.
Slant-front Desk
Eastern Ontario, c. 1800-20

With a sloped cover as the writing surface, supported by pull-out wooden slides on either side of the top drawer, slant-front desks in Canada are usually more American than English derivative and, as such, are most typically found in areas of American settlement. This desk, of curly maple with secondary pine, has extra sections joined to provide the flared legs. The sides are joined to the top with exposed rather than concealed dove-tailing. The widely spaced double string inlays of the drawer fronts and cover are also of maple, and the shell inlay is probably imported. The interior sections are of maple, containing inner drawers with birch sides, pine bottoms, and mahogany fronts with small bone knobs, a most unusual combination. The brasses are replacements, but with plates similar to the originals.

Height: 104.5 cm ($41^1/_8$ in.); *Width:* 105.4 cm ($41^1/_2$ in.)
Private Collection

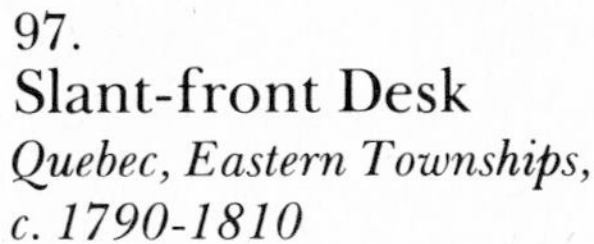

97.
Slant-front Desk
Quebec, Eastern Townships,
c. 1790-1810

This desk, with a sound family association, has its case and drawer fronts of a mixture of bird's-eye and straight-grained maple. The plain extended bracket feet are typical of both English- and American-inspired furniture of the turn-of-the-century period. The secondary wood is pine, as are the simple interior spaces and drawers. Unlike the plain plank covers of some lesser quality desks, end pieces have been included to prevent possible curling. The sides and top are joined with exposed dovetailing. The hardware is replacement.

The desk was made for Dr. Nathaniel Jenks of Barnston Corners, Quebec, on his premises, from wood he provided.

Length: 108.2 cm (42⁵/₈ in.);
Width: 91.5 cm (36 in.)
Private Collection

98.
Slant-front Desk
New Brunswick, c. 1790-1810

This desk, of curly birch with secondary pine, is somewhat unusual in that its bracket base is extended only half a board width and is topped with a thin moulding; the case is on top of, rather than mounted inside, the base section. The interior spacers and drawer fronts are of mahogany. The brasses appear to be original.

The desk belonged originally to Moses Pickard of Maugerville, New Brunswick, who came from Rowley, Massachusetts, in 1763.

Height: 109.8 cm (43¹/₄ in.);
Width: 106.7 cm (42 in.)
New Brunswick Museum

99.
Slant-front Desk
Nova Scotia, c. 1800-25

Taller than usual, this desk has an extra row of three drawers below the cover, and was probably a store-keeper's or clerk's desk. The case and drawer fronts are of curly birch, while the secondary wood is pine. The interior has birch separators and small birch-fronted drawers. The turned birch knobs are original. The extended bracket feet appear to have been shortened at some point, by approximately 10 cm.

Present Height: 120 cm (47¼ in.); *Width:* 111.1 cm (43¾ cm.)
Nova Scotia Museum

100.
Slant-front Desk
Nova Scotia, c. 1815-25

This desk is a good example of extreme mixing of woods and very individual stylistic anomalies. The structure of the desk is straight-grained birch, with a cover centre panel of curly birch. The drawer fronts are of bird's-eye maple, with extremely thin mahogany string inlays and stained maple edge-beading strips. The interior is of mixed maple, mahogany, and birch. The secondary wood is pine. While the drawers have brass keyhole liners, the lid keyhole has a most unusual surrounding bone inlay in an outer mahogany inlay. The extreme Empire lower skirt scalloping appears to be a later addition and may have been recut in the 1840s or '50s from an originally more simple bowing. The brass and wooden knobs are original.

Height: 104.8 cm (41¼ in.); *Width:* 109.6 cm (43⅛ in.)
Private Collection

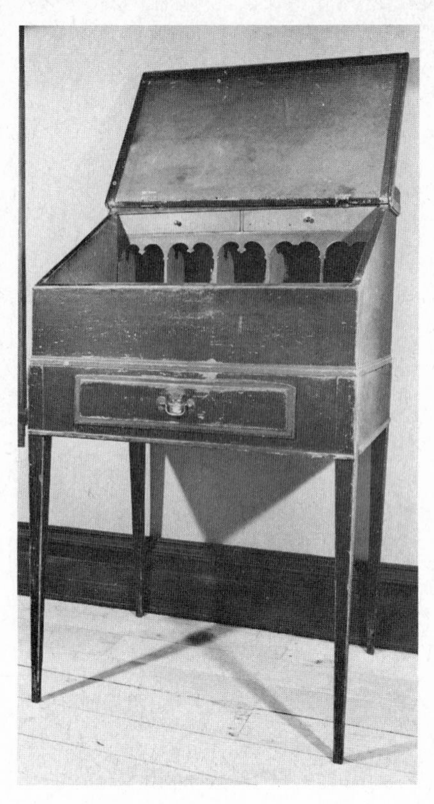

101.
Slant-front Desk
Ontario c. 1815-30

Clerk's, shop-, or store-keeper's standing desks are usually simple country forms and essentially unstylized. This example, with its thin square-tapered legs, arched interior letter spaces, and single moulding-edged drawer, is more elaborate and finely made than most. The desk is wholly of pine, and painted. The upper section and base are separate units. The drawer pull and interior drawer knobs seem original. (Similar examples, cf. Pain, nos. 681-82, 684-88.)

Height: 132.1 cm (52 in.); *Width:* 79.3 cm (31¼ in.)
Private Collection

102.
Cylinder-fall Desk
Probably New Brunswick or Nova Scotia, c. 1815-25

Cylinder or drum-cover desks in Canada usually appear only as later 19th-century roll-top types, despite the form being an early 19th-century development. This piece is an exception. The desk is of mahogany, constructed in separate upper and lower sections, with a solid surface on the lower unit. (See also fig. 244.) The interior drawer faces, lower drawer fronts, side posts, and short square-tapered legs are faced with maple rectangular string inlays. The extended writing surface is a pull-out slide, containing a lock in its under-bar which secures to the lowered quarter-cylindrical cover. In later roll-top desks the lock is typically in the cover itself. The keyhole inlays are also of maple, and the secondary wood is pine. This desk was found in Toronto, having a long history there, but its characteristics are clearly more of the Maritimes.

Height: 112.4 cm (44¼ in.);
Width: 118.1 cm (46½ in.)
Private Collection

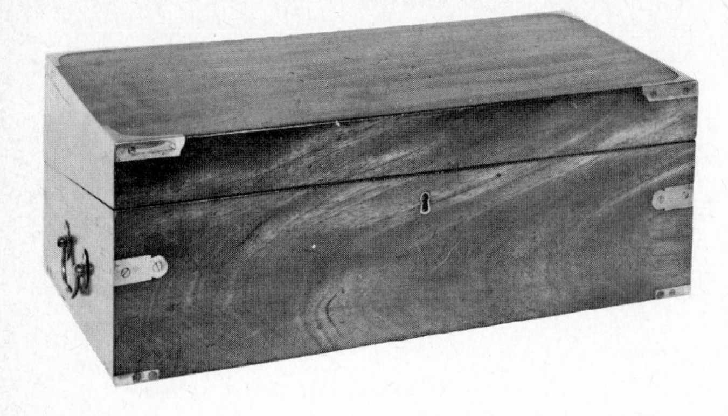

103.
Travelling Desk
St. Stephen, New Brunswick,
c. 1833-35; by John Warren Moore

Lap or travelling desks are rare as Canadian cabinet-work, and most of those found are of English origin. With its flush brass-bound corners and edges, this desk is of mahogany, with the top surface mahogany veneered over pine. The base is also of pine. The interior is compartmentalized under a folding baize-covered writing surface in mahogany and pine. A most unusual internal secret drawer opens by depressing a wooden spring with a thin pin from the outside. This desk had been in the Moore family since its making.

Height: 18.5 cm ($7^{1}/_{4}$ in.);
Length: 53.3 cm (21 in.)
Kings Landing Historical Settlement

104.
Bookcase
Nova Scotia, c. 1820-30

Free-standing bookcases are virtually unknown in the range of earlier Canadian furniture types, since the population enjoyed few books. This bookcase, of well figured bird's-eye maple with mahogany string inlays, has two drawers below. The drawers have mahogany beaded edges, keyhole inlays, and original pulls. The secondary wood is pine. As one of an identical pair, the bookcase has attached to its back a partial inventory label of the Liverpool Insurance Co. of Halifax, for which the pieces were probably made.

Height: 103.5 cm ($40^{3}/_{4}$ in.);
Width: 92.7 cm ($36^{1}/_{2}$ in.)
Private Collection

105.
Drum Table
Halifax, Nova Scotia, c. 1810-11; with labels of Tulles, Pallister & McDonald

Drum tables, patterned directly after English "rent" tables, are a rare form in Canada — only a few examples are known. This piece, with its Phyfe base, has the top, pedestal, and legs of mahogany, and the frame is mahogany veneered over pine. The piece has four actual drawers alternated with four false drawer fronts, these lacking keyholes. The edge of the top is reeded, as are the column and legs. The table is labelled in two of the drawers by the short-lived partnership (1810-11) of Tulles, Pallister & McDonald, and is one of only two known labelled pieces by them. (See also fig. 127, and cf. MacLaren, pp. 43, 131.)

Height: 73.7 cm (29 in.);
Diameter: 86.3 cm (34 in.)
Location Unknown

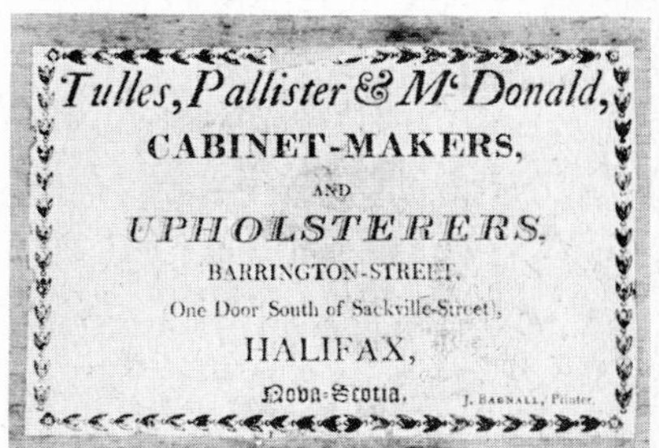
Tulles, Pallister & Mc Donald,
CABINET-MAKERS,
AND
UPHOLSTERERS.
BARRINGTON-STREET,
One Door South of Sackville-Street),
HALIFAX,
Nova-Scotia.
J. Bagnall, Printer.

106.
Drum Table
Ontario, c. 1820

A simpler version of a drum table, this piece includes four drawers, but without alternating false drawer fronts. The table is of cherry with four reeded legs, a plain turned column, and reeded edged top. The drawer structure and underframe are of pine. The drawer fronts and skirt sections are bowed solid cherry, not veneering, and the knobs seem original. (Similar example; cf. Shackleton no. 482.)

Height: 72.4 cm (28½ in.);
Diameter: 104.1 cm (41 in.)
Canadiana, Royal Ontario Museum

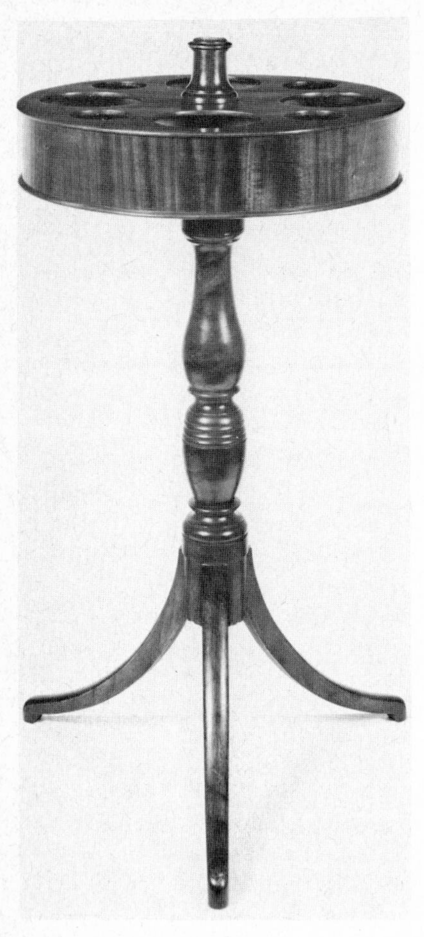

107.
Drinking Stand
Attributed as American, but possibly from Nova Scotia, c. 1810

The mahogany top of this unusual specialized stand has openings for four bottles and four glasses. The heavy turned pedestal and pin-footed concave legs are of birch. Montgomery, in *American Furniture: The Federal Period,* describes the piece as having been found in Salem, Massachusetts, and attributes it (uncertainly) only as American. The odd partially ring-turned bulbous pedestal, with many Maritimes similarities, and the legs, similar to figs. 276 and 278, as well as the combination of woods, raise questions and suggest Canadian Maritimes origin.

Height: 79.7 cm (31 3/9 in.);
Diameter: 42.5 cm (16 3/4 in.)
Henry Francis DuPont Winterthur Museum

108.
Pedestal Table
New Brunswick, c. 1810-15

With a rope-carved heavy bulbous pedestal and four reeded concave legs, this classically designed table has a tilting top, hinged on a wooden rod running through a pedestal-top block and two parallel struts mounted cross-grain on the underside of the top. The table is wholly of mahogany, with the large, framed top-supporting block of maple. The castors are English.

Height: 75.9 cm (29 7/8 in.);
Diameter: 119.4 cm (47 in.)
Canadiana, Royal Ontario Museum

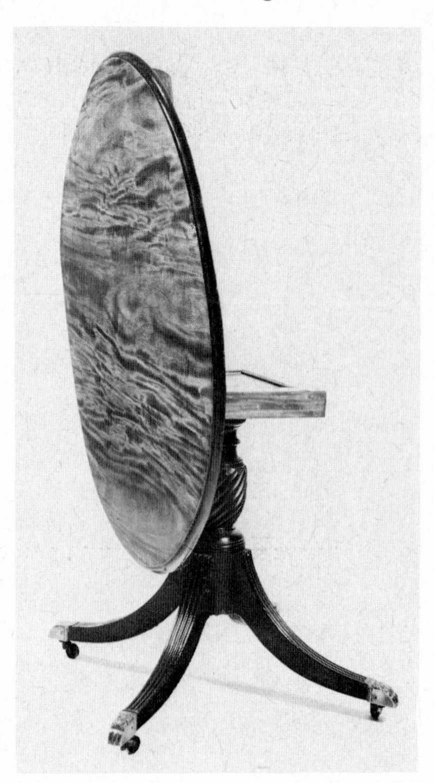

109.
Pedestal Table
New Brunswick, c. 1790-1800

Of darkly stained mahogany, this tilt-top table is pinned through a column block and two struts in the same manner as figs. 108 and 111. Solid, stable cabriole legs ending in "snake" feet are quite typical of these earlier pedestal tables. The straight column with its abruptly terminated rope-carved urn turning is somewhat clumsy. (Similar example, cf. Shackleton, no. 467.)

Height: 71.7 cm (28¼ in.);
Diameter: 72.4 cm (28½ in.)
Kings Landing Historical Settlement

110.
Pedestal Table
Montreal, c. 1790-1800

One of an identical pair, this mahogany tilt-top table is equipped with an English brass top hinge and latch. The pedestal, legs, and padded feet are more finely formed than on the preceding piece, and the legs suggest an English emigrant cabinet-maker.

Height: 71.1 cm (28 in.);
Diameter: 77.8 cm (30¼ in.)
Canadiana, Royal Ontario Museum

111.
Pedestal Table
Nova Scotia, c. 1800-10

The tilting top of this table is pin hinged in the same manner as figs. 108 and 109. With a top and snake-footed legs of mahogany, the pedestal is birch, with a reeded rather than rope-carved urn turning. Straight but slightly tapered upper pedestal sections, usually above an urn or bulbous turning, as on this table, are very common on English-Canadian pedestal tables and candle-stands of the earlier 19th century. (Similar example, cf. Pain, no. 58.)

Height: 71.1 cm (28 in.);
Diameter: 85.7 cm ($33^3/_4$ in.)
Private Collection

112.
Pedestal Table
New Brunswick, c. 1800-1820

With a fixed rather than tilting top, this table has a tapered urn pedestal and somewhat ungainly cabriole snake-footed legs. The table is wholly of birch, darkly stained to emulate mahogany.

Height: 73 cm ($28^3/_4$ in.);
Diameter: 79 cm ($31^1/_8$ in.)
Kings Landing Historical Settlement

113.
Pedestal Table
New Brunswick, c. 1800-20

Dished-top pedestal tables and candle-stands of Canadian origin are extremely rare. (See also fig. 266.) This piece also has its top formed of two sections, butted together and retained by underside strips. The table is wholly of butternut, with a dark stain. The bulbous turning of the pedestal is a common form. (Similar example, cf. Shackleton, no. 465; Pain, no. 88.)
Height: 69 cm ($27^1/_8$ in.);
Diameter: 75.5 cm ($29^3/_4$ in.)
Kings Landing Historical Settlement

114.
Pedestal Table
Quebec, Eastern Townships, c. 1815-25

With very widely flaring concave legs and a heavy turned central column (see also figs. 106, 166), this unusually large table has an oval tilt-top, hingeing the long axis vertically. The top is mounted on a wooden bar between cross-grain struts, and held with a brass latch. The entire table is of densely figured curly maple; there is no secondary wood.

Height: 69.8 cm (27½ in.);
Length: 151.1 cm (59½ in.)
Canadiana, Royal Ontario Museum

115.
Pedestal Table
Ontario, c. 1830-40

Still in a basically 18th-century form, this table is a good example of adaptations in the direction of simplicity that occurred as standard forms were produced in the country furniture tradition long after their periods of prime fashion. With a tilt-top of curly birch pinned through a pedestal block (see figs. 108, 109, 111), the pedestal and cabriole legs are also of birch, while the top underside struts and pedestal block are pine.

Height: 71 cm (28 in.);
Diameter: 81.3 cm (32 in.)
Canadiana, Royal Ontario Museum

116.
Card Table
Montreal, c. 1810

With an extra swing leg, this ovolo-cornered table has a skirt and top of mahogany veneering over pine, and mahogany legs. The hinged top is felt covered. The string inlays surrounding the lower edge of the top and skirt, and in the faces of the four fixed legs, are of maple. This table was made for Sir James Monk (1745-1826), Chief Justice of the Court of King's Bench at Montreal from 1794 to 1824.

Height: 73.7 cm (29 in.);
Width: 91.5 cm (36 in.)
Canadiana, Royal Ontario Museum

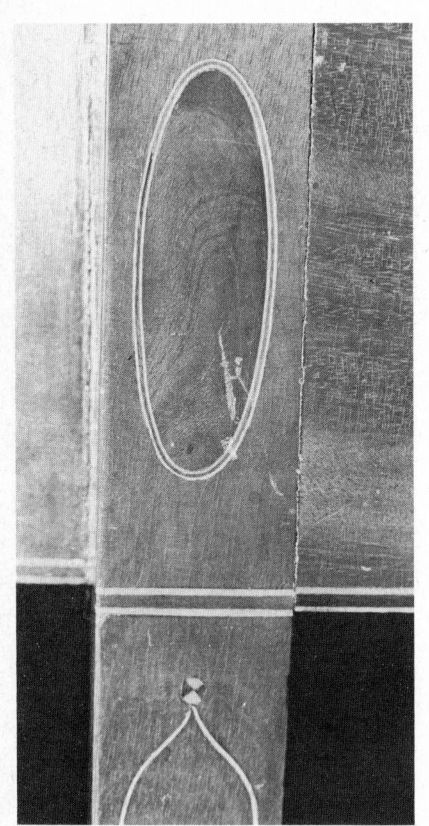

117.
Card Table
Montreal, c. 1810

The legs and unfelted top of this table are of solid mahogany, while the skirt and drawer front are of mahogany veneer over pine. The two front legs and the skirt are outlined with simple maple string inlays. The original castors and drawer pulls are English. The plain rounded corners of the top are the most unusual form on Canadian card tables, while complex corners are rare.

Height: 74.7 cm (29 3/8 in.);
Width: 90.7 cm (35 3/4 in.)
Private Collection

118.
Card Table
Montreal, c. 1810-25

With a mahogany top and lightly turned legs, this table has maple string inlays around the top edges and outlining the skirt side and corner panels. The frame and drawer are of pine with mahogany veneer facing, and a separate mahogany inlaid band surrounds the lower edge of the skirt. The right rear leg is a swing leg. The keyhole inlay is maple, and the ring drawer pulls and the castors are original. This table is one of a known identical pair; the mate is in a private collection.

Height: 73.7 cm (29 in.);
Width: 88.9 cm (35 in.)
Canadiana, Royal Ontario Museum

119.
Card Table
New Brunswick, c. 1820-30; attributed to Thomas Nisbet, Saint John

Though unlabelled, this table in its leg turnings and carving and construction characteristics is very similar to other identified Nisbet work. The top is rotated a quarter turn on an off-center pin, which then allows the folded leaf to lie flat on the frame. The reed-moulded top, the rope, and acanthus carved legs are mahogany, and the skirt is of mahogany veneers over pine. There are no inlays. The heavy double-flared turning, low on the legs, is sufficiently similar to that on the labelled tables (figs. 120, 165, 187) and on the unlabelled dining table (fig. 164) to be considered a Nisbet characteristic.

Height: 74.6 cm (29 3/8 in.);
Width: 92.1 cm (36 1/4 in.)
Kings Landing Historical Settlement

120.
Card Table
Saint John, New Brunswick, c. 1820-30; labelled by Thomas Nisbet

This table, although it is somewhat simpler than the preceding piece, is virtually identical in its treatment. The top is rotated on an off-center pin before opening. The legs and top are of mahogany, and the frame is of pine with mahogany veneers. The label of Thomas Nisbet is on the underside of the top.

Height: 75.5 cm (29¾ in.);
Width: 91.5 cm (36 in.)
New Brunswick Museum

121.
Card Table
Quebec, Eastern Townships, c. 1800-20

This handsome but simple table is a departure from the typical form in having a round rather than square top when opened. The top is supported by an extra swing leg. The table is wholly of curly maple, except for a pine inner drawer structure. The brass pulls are replacements, and the legs may have been shortened slightly. (Similar examples, cf. Pain, nos. 69, 70; Shackleton nos. 455, 498.)

Height: 70.2 cm (27⅝ in.);
Width: 84.8 cm (33⅜ in.)
Private Collection

122.
Two-sectioned Card Table
New Brunswick, c. 1820-40

Rather than the usual fold-over-top pattern, this card or library table is in two separate units, which attach together or which otherwise can serve as small side tables. The tops are half circular while the skirt frames are triangular, and the construction is quite similar to that of the dining table, fig. 167. The table is wholly of birch, without a secondary wood.

Height: 72.5 cm (28½ in.);
Diameter: 103.9 cm (40⅞ in.)
Kings Landing Historical Settlement

Drop-Leaf Pedestal Table
Montreal, c. 1810
See fig. 182

Tall Clock
Trois-Rivières, *Quebec, c. 1800-20*
See fig. 129

Drop-Leaf Table
Montreal, c. 1790-1810
See fig. 173

123.
Tall Clock
Quebec, possibly Quebec City, c. 1800-1815

With reeded upper case columns and brass-stopped fluted quarter columns in the pendulum case, this clock is of mahogany and mahogany veneering over butternut, uncommon as a secondary wood. Imported fan inlays decorate the pendulum case, and floral inlays the door and base. A small portrait of General James Wolfe is painted in an inset above the face, and the brass English works, from an earlier clock, are marked *W. Nicholas, London.* Though the case-maker is presently unknown, this clock has a long history of ownership near Quebec City.

Height: 214.3 cm (84$^{3}/_{8}$ in.);
Width: 45.1 cm (17$^{3}/_{4}$ in.)
Canadiana, Royal Ontario Museum

124.
Tall Clock
Quebec, c. 1785-1800; marked by James Orkney

James Orkney is one of the better-known early "clock-makers," working at three successive locations in Quebec from about 1780 to after 1820. His actual working dates are uncertain. (cf. Burrows pp. 157-9.) This clock, of mahogany with imported fan inlays in the pendulum case and base, has fluted brass-stopped quarter columns and bracketed base and feet.

Orkney may have been a New England Loyalist as this clock and the one following, with open fretwork above an arched hood and with three brass finials, are New England types. (cf. Montgomery p. 192.) The brass face is engraved *James Orkney/ QUEBEC* while the works are English.

Height: 230.9 cm (92$^{1}/_{2}$ in.);
Width: 52.1 cm (20$^{1}/_{2}$ in.)
Canadiana, Royal Ontario Museum

125.
Tall Clock
Quebec, c. 1800-1815; marked by James Orkney

Although with different inlays, this clock is of the same stylistic type, and in design is very similar to the preceding piece. The case is wholly of mahogany, and mahogany veneers over secondary pine. The framed and glazed pendulum door is an anomaly, and if original, as it appears to be, is unique among Canadian tall clocks. The motif inlays, as on the previous piece, are imported. On the face of the clock is painted *ORKNEY . . . Quebec.* James Orkney would appear to have been a case-maker rather than a clock-maker, as the works in all Orkney clocks observed are English, including this piece.

Height: 229 cm (90 in.);
Width: 52.7 cm (20¾ in.)
History Division, Museum of Man, National Museum of Canada

126.
Tall Clock
Quebec, c. 1800-20; marked by James Orkney

Stylistically different, with its broken arch cornice and flared feet, and somewhat later than the preceding pieces, this clock has maple and mahogany fan and oval inlays clearly made by Orkney rather than imported. Only the lower case central inlay is an English type. The case is of mahogany with secondary pine, and maple round and oval string inlays are set into the lower case and pendulum door, with a string-bordered rope inlay across the skirt. The works are English, and the face is painted *Jas. Orkney / Quebec.*

Height: 231.5 cm (91⅛ in.);
Width: 45.3 cm (17⅞ in.)
Private Collection

127.
Tall Clock
Halifax, Nova Scotia, c. 1810-11; labelled by Tulles, Pallister, & McDonald

With reeded quarter columns and a broken arch cornice, this fine clock is of mahogany, with interior secondary pine. The clock stands on thin "French" feet (see also figs. 126, 133, 136) rather than the more typical bracket base. Maple string inlays form an oval in the mahogany-veneered door and a circle in the base. The works are English. The label of Tulles, Pallister, & McDonald is inside the pendulum case. This partnership, on Barrington Street in Halifax, is known to have worked only from 1810 to 1811. Of their obviously excellent work, only two labelled examples are known, this clock and the drum table, fig. 105. (cf. MacLaren, pp. 43, 131.)

Height: 231.1 cm (91 in.);
Width: 50.8 cm (20 in.)
Nova Scotia Museum

128.
Tall Clock
Trois Rivières, Quebec, c. 1800-20; marked by G. & H. Bellerose.

This well-inlaid piece is of mahogany, with mahogany veneering over secondary pine. The shell, rosette, and corner fan inlays were certainly imported. The top also has a geometric band inlay across the frieze, and the pendulum door and base are edged in curly maple. Though the works are English, the face is painted *G. & H Bellerose / Three Rivers.* The Bellerose brothers worked in Trois Rivières around 1800 to 1820, and are known only for mahogany clock cases, of which several excellent examples are shown.

Height: 228.8 cm (89⁷/₈ in.);
Width: 45.7 cm (18 in.)
Canadiana, Royal Ontario Museum

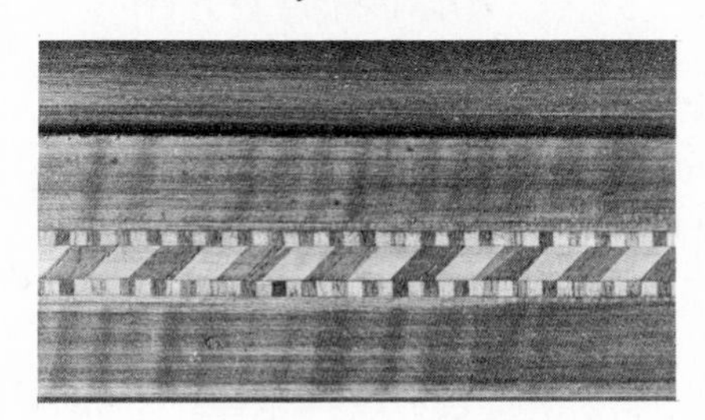

129.
Tall Clock
Trois Rivières, Quebec, c. 1800-20; marked by G. & H. Bellerose.

A very similar example to fig. 128 by the Bellerose brothers, this clock case is also of mahogany and mahogany veneering, with secondary pine. The inlaid banding and motif work, with minor differences, is nearly identical to that on the preceding piece, excepting the very ornate and unusual classical urn inlay in the base. The face is identically marked. The English works in this piece include a painted lion above the face, with eyes that flick with each one-second tick.

Height: 227.3 cm ($89^{1}/_{2}$ in.); *Width:* 46 cm ($18^{1}/_{8}$ in.)
Private Collection

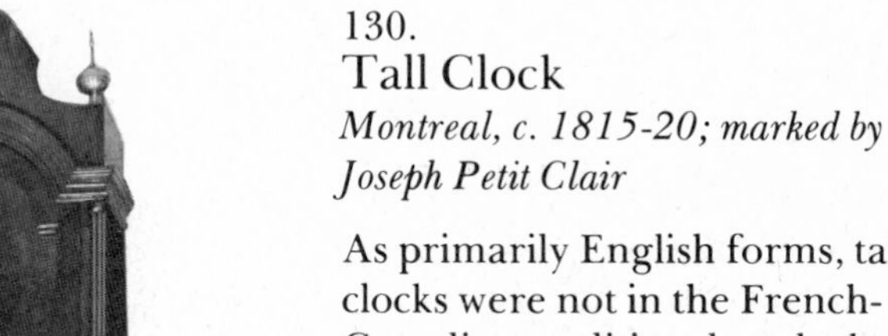

130.
Tall Clock
Montreal, c. 1815-20; marked by Joseph Petit Clair

As primarily English forms, tall clocks were not in the French-Canadian tradition, but clocks in an English manner produced by Québecois makers are not uncommon. (See also figs. 131, 132.) As a well proportioned but quite simple clock, this example is wholly of mahogany with secondary pine. The pendulum door is shaped from a single board and there are no case quarter columns or inlays. The brass face is engraved in script *Joseph Petit Clair / Montreal.* The lower case, as indicated by the cove-cornered applied moulding, was reduced in the 19th century by about 7 to 10 cm, to fit under a lower ceiling. Joseph Petit Clair is recorded working in Montreal only in 1791. (cf. Burrows, p. 178.)

Height: 227.3 cm ($89^{1}/_{2}$ in.); *Width:* 46 cm ($18^{1}/_{8}$ in.)
Private Collection

131.
Tall Clock
Quebec, probably Eastern Townships, c. 1820

With an English brass face inscribed *John Davidge / London,* this clock is wholly of butternut, with internal secondary pine. The reeded upper case columns, pendulum case quarter columns, and applied lower case and pendulum door mouldings are the only decorative treatments. The flat base, without feet, appears to be original; there is no indication of earlier feet.

Height: 232.3 cm (87½ in.);
Width: 53.3 cm (21 in.)
Canadiana, Royal Ontario Museum

132.
Tall Clock
Quebec, probably Eastern Townships, c. 1820

Very similar to the preceding piece but with square bracketed feet, this butternut-cased clock also has an English brass face and works, the face inscribed *J. Davidson, LONDON.* The secondary wood is pine. This and the previous clock are certainly by the same maker.

Height: 219 cm (86¼ in.);
Width: 50.2 cm (19¾ in.)
Private Collection

133.
Tall Clock
Halifax, Nova Scotia, c. 1815-25; marked by Alexander Troup

With a typical serpentine broken-arched cornice, this clock is of mahogany, with mahogany veneering over pine in the upper door frame. The secondary wood is pine. Though simple, with short flared feet, the clock is decorated with maple string inlays and block inserts, with a double stringing across the base. The painted clock face is marked *Alex. Troup — Halifax.* Alexander Troup (1776-1856) and his son, Alexander, Jr. (1806-1873), were both clock-makers and silversmiths. (cf. MacLaren, p. 82.)

Dimensions unavailable
Present Location Unknown

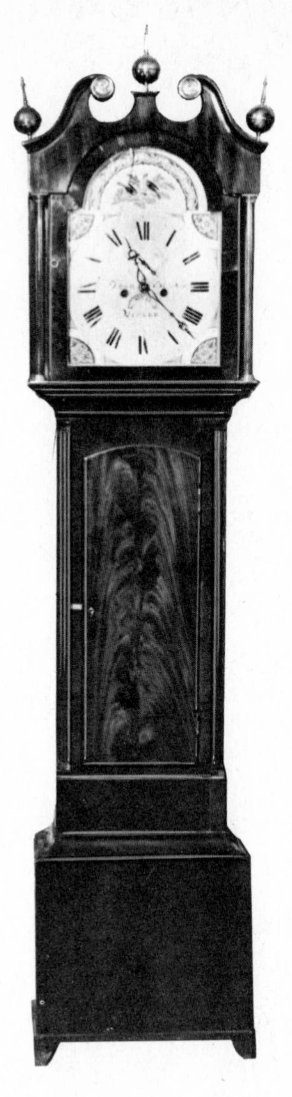

134.
Tall Clock
Pictou, Nova Scotia, c. 1820-30; marked by John Geddie

With square bracket feet, this broken-arched clock is also simply ornamented, though well proportioned. The case is of mahogany with maple string inlays, while the secondary wood is pine. The painted face is inscribed *JOHN GEDDIE / PICTOU,* though the works are English. John Geddie (working 1817-c. 1843), though a recorded clock-maker, was primarily a case-maker. A number of his pieces are known, in pine as well as mahogany. (cf. MacLaren, pp. 82-4.)

Height: 210 cm (82¾ in.);
Width: 46.5 cm (18¼ in.)
Nova Scotia Museum

135.
Tall Clock
Ontario, probably Niagara Peninsula, c. 1830

Tall clocks in the Ontario-German tradition are usually rather crude or ill-proportioned pieces. This superb and handsome example, however, is an exception. Of walnut with secondary pine, the clock incorporates the same relief cove-cornered lower panel and short ogee bracket feet of many cabinet pieces. (See figs. 159-61.) The broken arch cornice and the urn finials are well carved. Small star-flower inlays, in maple and walnut, are set into the arch roundels. The painted face is unmarked.

Height: 245.8 cm (96¾ in.);
Width: 53.3 cm (21 in.)
Private Collection

136.
Tall Clock
Ontario, Brantford area, c. 1840

Though somewhat late in date, this still-Georgian clock combines the typical Ontario mixing of curly maple and cherry, with an inlaid band of walnut across the skirt. Only the glue blocks and back are of secondary pine. The clock-works and face are English, unmarked, and considerably earlier than the case. The case may possibly be by Robert Leeming of Brantford, who is known to have built other sophisticated cherry and maple furniture.

Height: 217.2 cm (85½ in.);
Width: 43.2 cm (17 in.)
Canadiana, Royal Ontario Museum

137.
Tall Clock
Montreal, c. 1830; marked by J.B. & R. Twiss

Toward the lower end of the scale of tall clocks are those variously marked by the Twiss family of Montreal, who specialized in clock manufacturing. (cf. Burrows, pp. 135-48.) Many Twiss examples are known. All of these clocks, produced between 1821 and 1837, are wholly of pine, without secondary wood, and though well proportioned, are usually roughly constructed. The clocks originally were completely grain painted (though many have been stripped) to simulate fine and exotic woods. The ball finials are gilded wood-turnings as well.

Height: 212.7 cm (83³/4 in.);
Width: 45.1 cm (17³/4 in.)
Canadiana, Royal Ontario Museum

138.
Bracket Clock
Montreal, c. 1785-1800; marked by François Doumoulin

Canadian bracket clocks are among the rarest of all forms, far less common even than fine, tall clocks. This clock, with earlier English works, is fully mahogany veneered over secondary pine, with all its original brass hardware. There are no separate inlays. The brass face of the clock is engraved in script *Fra.[nçois] Doumoulin a Montreal,* about whom little is known. It would appear, however, that Doumoulin was a French-Canadian cabinet-maker rather than a clock-maker, and clearly working in an English manner.

Height: 46.3 cm (18¹/4 in.);
Width: 27.3 cm (10³/4 in.)
Canadiana, Royal Ontario Museum

139.
Bracket Clock
Montreal, c. 1790-1800; marked by James Grant

With an arched top and a hinged left side, as well as front doors, this clock is wholly of mahogany veneered over butternut, uncommon as a secondary wood. Only the works base is of pine. The case was further "ebonized," perhaps later, with polished black stain. The handle and keyhole plate are original. The square applied feet may be additions to a plain bracket base. The brass clock-works are engraved in script on the backplate *Jam.'s Grant/Montreal.* Grant advertised in Montreal as a clock-maker and engraver between 1792 and 1799.

Height: 37.5 cm (14³/4 in.);
Width: 26.5 cm (10³/8 in.)
Canadiana, Royal Ontario Museum

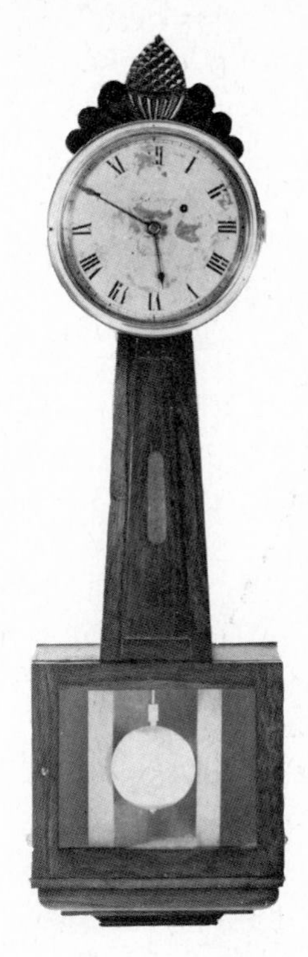

140.
Shelf Clock
Quebec, c. 1830; marked by C.J.R. Ardouin

This rather simple clock, with turned ball feet, is of mahogany, with mahogany veneer over pine on the arched top. Below the face cover the door is outlined with a narrow string-bordered rope inlay. The keyhole inlay is white bone. The works are English. Along with its numerals, the brass face is engraved *C.J.R. ARDOUIN* and *QUEBEC*. Identified Canadian shelf clocks dating earlier than the 1840s, even as simple forms, are rare. Ardouin is listed (cf. Burrows, p. 175) as working at various Quebec City locations from 1822 to 1865.

Height: 43.3 cm (17 in.);
Width: 25.4 cm (10 in.)
Canadiana, Royal Ontario Museum

141.
Banjo Clock
Montreal, c. 1815-20; marked by Martin Cheney

Presently unique as a known Canadian banjo clock, this piece is also evidence of the occasional early importation of exotic woods other than mahogany. The case is wholly of rosewood, without veneering, and with secondary pine in the back and inner frame. The tapered elongated inlay in the removable centre panel is satinwood. The original pendulum-case glass was probably reverse painted and the more Empire-style carved mahogany acorn pediment and finial may be a somewhat later addition. Martin Cheney, who moved to Montreal from Vermont in 1807, was active as a Montreal clock-maker until his death in the late 1820s. (cf. Burrows, pp. 161-2.) Also a silversmith, Cheney stamped the brass works of this clock *CHENEY* in two places with his silver punch. (cf. Langdon, p. 58.)

Height: 90.5 cm (35 5/8 in.);
Width: 24.5 cm (9 5/8 in.)
Canadiana, Royal Ontario Museum

142.
Barometer
Montreal, c. 1850-60; marked by H. Sanders

Though perhaps not furniture in a strict sense, barometers, like clocks, were wooden-cased instruments, often cased by other than the actual instrument makers. This aneroid barometer is included because of its early neo-Regency case form, but the instrument is clearly later than the Georgian period (the aneroid barometer was apparently first patented in France by Lucien Vidie in 1845). The barometer case is constructed somewhat in the manner of a guitar, with the sides mahogany veneered over formed pine and the face a thin mahogany sheet glued down. The rough and removable back is pine. While the barometer is English, its face is engraved *H. Sanders/141/Great St. James Street/Montreal.* Early Canadian instruments or cases are most uncommon in any form.

Height: 94.3 cm (37 1/8 in.)
Canadiana, Royal Ontario Museum

143.
Corner Cupboard
Northumberland Co., New Brunswick, c. 1800; attributed to William Murray

With latticed window mullions and bracket feet, this unusually small two-sectioned cupboard was built as a free-standing piece. The primary wood is mahogany, with the shelves and back of pine. The hardware is original. This cupboard is known to have belonged to John M. Johnson of Newcastle, New Brunswick, about 1800. (cf. Ryder, pp. 124-26.)

Height: 235 cm (92½ in.);
Width: 108 cm (42½ in.)
New Brunswick Museum

144.
Corner Cupboard
New Brunswick, c. 1800-10

This unusual design, with a triangular drawer between the upper and lower cupboard units, includes a window mullion arrangement similar to that on the previous piece. The cupboard is of mahogany, with simple maple string inlays and keyhole inlays, while the back is pine. (Similar examples; cf. Shackleton nos. 340, 341; Ryder pp. 124-26.)

Height: 221.5 cm (87¼ in.);
Width: 71 cm (28 in.)
Loyalist House, Saint John

145.
Corner Cupboard
Kingston area, Ontario, c. 1810-20

Like fig. 146 following, this cupboard combines half-domed doors and latticed mullions. The lower doors have hexagonal panels, framed with dentil moulding and fan-carved corners. The well-carved ovoid and square medallions in the frieze are nearly identical to those on fig. 146. The structure is wholly of pine and was originally painted. This cupboard was found, as a built-in piece, in a house off Highway 2, ten miles from Kingston. (Similar examples, cf. Pain, nos. 447, 48.)

Height: 259.1 cm (102 in.);
Width: 152.4 cm (60 in.)
Private Collection

146.
Corner Cupboard
Kingston area, Ontario, c. 1810-20

As a far simpler version of the preceding piece, but by the same maker, this cupboard has the same double-reeded half columns, but with slightly different top and base turnings. The carved medallions and fans of the previous piece are lacking. This cupboard, wholly of pine and painted, was also originally a built-in piece.

Height: 241.3 cm (95 in.);
Width: 121.9 cm (48 in.)
Upper Canada Village

147.
Corner Cupboard
Kingston area, Ontario, c. 1820-30

This cupboard, of pine and painted, has sectionally fluted and rope-carved single half columns, with urn finials. The ovoid and square medallion carvings are essentially the same as those of fig. 145. Though originally a built-in piece, the turned lower legs and bun feet are original, and incongruous with the otherwise Adamesque style. This and the two preceding pieces were unquestionably done by the same maker, though this stylistically mixed cupboard is somewhat later in date.

Height: 223.6 cm (88 in.);
Width: 127 cm (50 in.)
Canadiana, Royal Ontario Museum

148.
Corner Cupboard
Ontario, probably Peterborough area, c. 1815-30

Though stylistically similar to the preceding cupboards, including the simple oval and ovoid carved medallions, the flat-moulded pilasters and raised-panelled lower doors are a departure. The integral raised panels in the doors, more typical of later Quebec armoires, are probably a French influence, and likely indicate a French-Canadian builder. Originally a built-in piece, the cupboard is of pine, once painted but now cleaned.

Height; 262.2 cm (103¼ in.);
Width: 140 cm (55⅛ in.)
Canadiana, Royal Ontario Museum

150.
Corner Cupboard
Nova Scotia, southwest coast, c. 1820

This pine cupboard, originally a built-in unit and now missing its cornice moulding, is typical of early cupboards of southwestern Nova Scotia. Like all such pieces, the cupboard was originally painted. The flat pilaster panels are reeded, separately applied, and attached to other separate appliques forming the panel bases and cornices. The lower doors are simply panelled; the upper arched doors are solid, wide pine boards, and all mouldings are also applied. The chair is fig. 10, left.

Height: 215.9 cm (85 in.);
Width: 102.9 cm (40½ in.)
Nova Scotia Museum

149.
Corner Cupboard
Westmorland Co., New Brunswick, c. 1800-20

Curly birch, as in this cupboard, is a striking wood not commonly used during the Georgian period. As a free-standing rather than built-in piece, the cupboard has extended bracket feet, and the carved cornice moulding is unusual, as are the door panels. The thinly beaded panel moulding is integral with the door frames, in the manner of 18th-century Quebec armoires, rather than separately applied. The hardware appears original, and the secondary wood of the shelves and back is pine. (cf. Ryder, pp. 149, 151-2.)

Height: 203 cm (80 in.);
Width: 96.5 cm (38 in.)
Private Collection

151.
Corner Cupboard
Nova Scotia, southwest coast, c. 1820

As a similar but more elaborate pine cupboard, this piece has a single, wide glazed upper door, with Gothic arched mullions. The separately applied and reeded pilaster panels are treated much the same as those on the preceding piece. This, and the similarity of the keyed upper door arches, suggest that the cupboards were probably by the same maker. Also originally a built-in piece, this cupboard has its original cornice moulding. (Similar example; cf. Dobson, no. 65.)

Height: 219.7 cm (86½ in.);
Width: 138.4 cm (54½ in.)
Nova Scotia Museum

152.
Corner Cupboard
Quebec, Eastern Townships, c. 1820-35

In having a slightly bow-fronted lower section, with the door framing and panels also bowed, this cupboard is not a typical piece in spite of its relatively simple appearance. The top section, flat faced, is also unusual in that the window framings and mullions are bevelled, including the upper scalloping. Both the frieze and skirt are crossed by parallel thin maple string inlays, which continue around the corners. The inset corner blocks are not quarter rounded, but carry the same angle as the structure. The cupboard is wholly of curly and bird's-eye maple, with secondary pine. The knobs are original.

Height: 215.3 cm (84¾ in.);
Width: 128.3 cm (50½ in.)
Private Collection

153.
Corner Cupboard
Eastern Ontario, c. 1820

Except for its unusual bowed and semi-circular window mullions, this wholly-pine cupboard is of very basic construction, though well proportioned, with an original dark stain. It was never painted. The small, brass door latches and handles appear original to the piece.

Height: 200.7 cm (79 in.);
Width: 99.1 cm (39 in.)
Canadiana, Royal Ontario Museum

154.
Corner Cupboard
New Brunswick, c. 1820-30

Another simple piece, this cupboard is ornamented only by reeding cut into the frieze and the curved corners of the upper section. Originally a built-in unit, the cupboard is of pine, with its original paint.

Height: 218.5 cm (86 in.);
Width: 120 cm (47¼ in.)
Kings Landing Historical Settlement

155.
Bookcase Cupboard
New Brunswick, c. 1810-20

Formal cupboards or bookcase breakfronts are all but unknown as Canadian forms, particularly during this period, and most such pieces were intended as dish or linen cupboards. With handsome, oval-bowed upper-door mullions, this cupboard is of mahogany, with the upper and lower door frames and the frieze face mahogany veneered over pine. Other secondary areas, including the back, are pine as well. The interwoven circular and oval parallel-line maple string inlays along the frieze seem unique, and have not been observed on other Canadian pieces. Maple inset blocks form a dentil band inlay in the cornice. The lower section door panels are edged with cross-grain inlaid mahogany bands, set off by maple stringing. The plain flat bracketed base is also outlined with a rectangular maple string inlay.

Height: 199.4 cm (78½ in.);
Width: 144.1 cm (56¾ in.)
New Brunswick Museum

156.
Cupboard
New Brunswick, c. 1800-20

Of a wholly different sort, this painted pine wall cupboard was built as two separate units, the lattice-windowed upper section connected only by careful positioning and its own weight. The top has, as a cornice, only a half-round moulding matching that of the side corners. The heavy ball feet, heavier than usual, even considering the resurgence of ball feet in the 1830s, can only be considered an archaic characteristic. (See also fig. 244.)

Height: 230.5 cm (90³/₄ in.);
Width: 123.5 cm (48⁵/₈ in.)
Kings Landing Historical Settlement

157.
Cupboard
Ontario, Peel County, c. 1830

Also in two sections, this cupboard with diamond-patterned and reeded-mullioned upper doors is entirely of painted pine, except for a back of butternut planks, a reversal of the usual pattern of wood usage. The reeded dentil band around the frieze is a very common Ontario-German characteristic, observed on many cupboards. The upper section is held in place in a typical manner, by quarter-round moulding attached to the base section surface. The straight base moulding is original; this cupboard seems never to have had feet.

Height: 237 cm (93¹/₄ in.);
Width: 121.5 cm (47⁷/₈ in.)
Private Collection

158.
Sectional Wardrobe
New Brunswick, c. 1810

This very simple and lightly structured pine wardrobe was the precursor of the modern built-in closet. Even standing wardrobes, however, were rare in an age of limited personal clothing, easily kept in chests of drawers or on pegs. With flat and thinly panelled doors, archaic bun feet, and heavy cornice, this piece was built as dismountable sections, with the sides and two back panels keyed, top and bottom, into the base and secured by the cornice, in the manner of an iron six-plate stove. The wardrobe is marked inside as belonging to Lt. Henry Lodge, serving in Canada in the 104th Regiment in 1810.

Dimensions unknown
Private Collection

159.
Cupboard
Ontario, Niagara Peninsula, c. 1810-20

Ontario-German cupboards, like box chests, are very often combined with drawers. This large two-sectioned cupboard, with doors above and three deep drawers below, combines square-bracket feet with reeded corner quarter columns. The raised upper door panels have cove corners, a very typical Ontario-German treatment, while the drawer-edge bead mouldings are applied to the frame rather than the drawer fronts. (See also figs. 254, 255.) The piece is wholly of walnut, with secondary pine in the back, shelves, and drawer structures. The hardware is replacement. (Similar examples, cf. Pain nos. 1012-18.)

Height: 202 cm (79½ in.);
Width: 125 cm (49¼ in.)
Private Collection

160.
Cupboard
Ontario, Niagara Peninsula, c. 1820-30

A somewhat similar cupboard, with more usual lower cove-cornered, raised-panelled doors below three shallow drawers, this piece is also of walnut with secondary pine. The short, rounded ogee bracket feet, common on Pennsylvania furniture of the mid-18th century, became traditional, and are common on Ontario-German furniture of the late 1820s and '30s. In Canada, however, the ogee bracket foot, in spite of being an earlier form, is generally later in date on Ontario-German furniture than is the square-bracket foot. The brass knobs on this piece are replacements. (Similar examples, cf. Pain, nos. 938, 40, 41, 43.)

Height: 217 cm (85 3/8 in.);
Width: 152.5 cm (60 in.)
Private Collection

161.
Cupboard
Ontario, Niagara Peninsula, c. 1828

This unusual cupboard is the only Ontario-German piece observed with decoration by cord burning, a technique widely used in 18th-century Pennsylvania for artificially graining gunstocks, but not generally on furniture. With two upper glazed doors flanking a fixed centre section, the cupboard has shallow drawers in both upper and lower sections, and the traditional ogee bracket feet. The cupboard is of cherry, with secondary pine. Tarred cords, laid parallel on the various sections before assembly, were burned slowly, charring the wood beneath into a heavy curly maple appearance which can be felt by hand even after finishing. The upper section brass knobs are original; those below are replacements.

This cupboard came from the Fry House at Grimsby, Ontario, built in 1828, and may have been a present for the Fry-Grobb wedding that year.

Height: 228 cm (89 3/4 in.);
Width: 154.5 cm (60 7/8 in.)
Private Collection

162.
Cupboard
Markham, Ontario, c. 1830

More wholly Germanic in style than the anglicized Pennsylvania-derived furniture of Ontario, this externally simple cupboard has flat-panelled lower doors and sides, and glazed upper doors. The inner framing, partially concealed when the doors are closed, has an arched top, reeded pilasters, and heart cut-outs in each upper corner. The cupboard, long in the Switzer family in the Markham, Ontario, area, was originally painted and has been cleaned.

Height: 205.7 cm (81 in.);
Width: 137.2 cm (54 in.)
Canadiana, Royal Ontario Museum

163.
Dining Table
Prince Edward Island or Nova Scotia, c. 1800-15

Eighteenth- and very early 19th-century full dining tables are rare. This table also has a most unusual leaf-support system, with all four central section legs swinging out from the frame. When the leaves are extended, the frame is thus suspended rather than supported.

The table is wholly of mahogany, with square "Marlborough" legs reeded on the outer sides. (See also figs. 15, 173.) The separate *demi-lune* banquet ends fit against brass pins in the leaf edges.

Height: 69.8 cm (27½ in.);
Full Length: 271.8 cm (107 in.)
Sir William Campbell House, Toronto

164.
Dining Table
Saint John, New Brunswick, c. 1820-30; attributed to Thomas Nisbet

As a very similar but somewhat more elaborate piece than the following table, the leg turnings here are slightly heavier and include typically Nisbet leaf carving. (See also fig. 185.) The leaf, swing leg, and banquet-end arrangement are identical. The top and leaves are of mahogany, and the skirts are mahogany veneered over pine with applied reeded skirt-edge strips.

Height: 71.1 cm (28 in.);
Full Length; 241 cm (94⁷/₈ in.)
Kings Landing Historical Settlement

165.
Dining Table
Saint John, New Brunswick, c. 1820-30; with labels of Thomas Nisbet

As a drop-leaf table, the centre section of this piece has two fixed legs on opposite corners, and two swing legs which extend to support the leaves. The separate banquet or D end tables attach to the ends of the extended leaves, though the table would most often be used in its shorter form, with the ends placed as side or serving tables. The table has a mahogany top, and round legs showing characteristic Nisbet turnings. The skirts are mahogany veneered over pine, with reeded strips around the lower edges. A Nisbet label is attached on the undersides of the centre section and of each end.

Height: 71.1 cm (28 in.);
Full Length: 248.9 cm (98 in.)
Private Collection

166.
Dining Table
New Brunswick, c. 1815-25

Pedestal-based Regency or "Phyfe" dining tables with separate ends are far less common than multiple straight-legged types. With its four-legged central section and separate tripod-based ends, this table also has two extra leaves which can be inserted and held by brass stops, when needed. The plain turned and heavy support columns, while incongruous with the rest of the table, are not uncommon on Canadian pieces of this period. (See also figs. 106, 114.) The edges of the top and of the convex legs are reeded. The table is wholly of mahogany, without a secondary wood. The banquet-end bases seem reversed.

This table belonged to the Hon. Sir Leonard Tilley (1818-96), Premier of New Brunswick (1860-65), and Lieutenant-Governor (1873-78) and (1885-93). It was probably from the estate of his father, Samuel, who came as a Loyalist to Saint John in 1783.

Extreme Length: 262.9 cm (103 1/2 in.); *Width:* 138.4 cm (54 1/2 in.)
History Division, Museum of Man, National Museums of Canada

167.
Dining Table
New Brunswick, c. 1810-30

As a simpler country table, this piece consists of two four-legged end sections. One section then has a single, wide drop leaf, to be raised as a centre section and supported by an extra swing leg. While the end tops are half-circular, the skirt frames are trapezoidal. The top of this table is of curly birch, the frame and legs of maple, and the secondary wood is pine. Some legs of the table include knots, an indication that the maker used wood that was already available rather than selecting it especially. The construction is very similar to that of fig. 122.

Height: 69.8 cm (27 1/2 in.);
Full Length: 151.5 cm (59 5/8 in.)
Kings Landing Historical Settlement

168.
Dining Table
Nova Scotia, c. 1820-30; found on Cape Breton Island

As a very small dining table with separate banquet ends, the centre section has drop leaves supported by an extra swing leg on each side. The skirt structure of the end units is of heavy sections of birch laminated together. The legs of these banquet ends are retained by heavy bolts and are dismountable. The top and legs are of mahogany, with mahogany veneer over birch in the skirts. The lower edges of the skirts have inlaid bands of curly maple, and the secondary wood is bird's-eye maple. In spite of the strange wood mixture, furniture of this quality is not peculiar to Cape Breton Island, and this table may have been brought there from mainland Nova Scotia at an early date.

Height: 72.2 cm (28½ in.);
Full Length: 252.3 cm (99⅜ in.)
Private Collection

169.
Dining Table
New Brunswick, c. 1820-30

With wide drop leaves, this table has two swing legs supporting each leaf when extended. There is no indication that separate ends were ever used. The skirt of the centre section has exposed dove-tailing at its corners. The top is mahogany, the legs of maple, and the swing leg bars are pine. The table was found in Queen's County, New Brunswick.

Height: 69 cm (27⅛ in.); *Full Length:* 160.6 cm (63¼ in.)
Kings Landing Historical Settlement

170.
Dining Table
Ontario, Niagara Peninsula, c. 1830-40

This simple table, with fixed legs and separate banquet ends, is wholly of cherry, with secondary pine. Strangely, the centre section may be used only with the ends, for its leaves have no self-supporting arrangement. The leaves are held in position by two small tenions on their outer edge, which are fitted into mortised slots in the straight edges of the end sections. (Similar examples, cf. Stewart, p. 101; Pain, no. 31.)

Height: 73 cm (28³/₄ in.); *Full Length:* 257 cm (101¹/₈ in.)
History Division, Museum of Man, National Museum of Canada

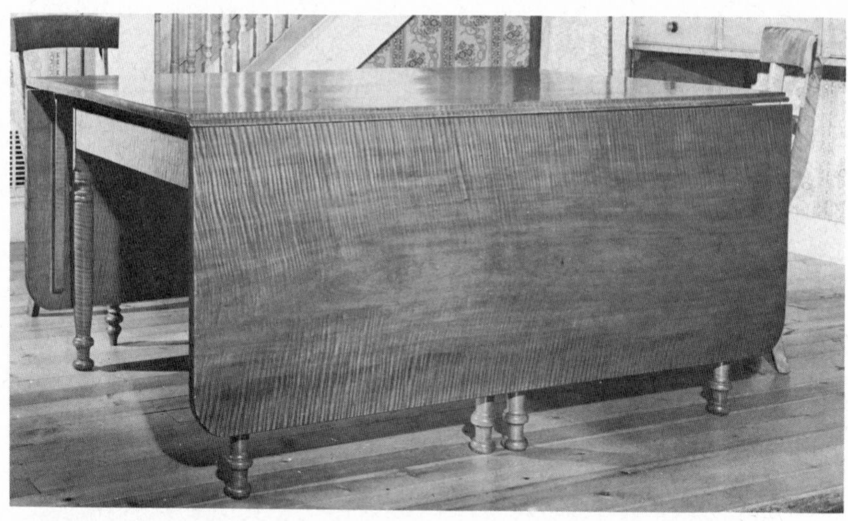

171.
Dining Table
Ontario, c. 1840, possibly by William Thompson, Agincourt

With extremely wide planks of curly maple forming the top and leaves, this table has two extra swing legs to support each leaf when raised. The table is wholly of maple, with no secondary wood. William "Sawmill Willie" Thompson ran a sawmill in the 1830-60 period, and is known to have made a few pieces of furniture each year, noted for their quality and the monumental use of curly maple. Though numbers of such pieces exist, none can be absolutely attributed to Thompson.

Height: 74.3 cm (29¹/₄ in.); *Full Length:* 210.2 cm (82³/₄ in.)
Canadiana, Royal Ontario Museum

172.
Drop-Leaf Table
Quebec, Eastern Townships, c. 1780-1800, or New Hampshire, c. 1730

The Queen Anne style is generally too early for the chronological range of English-Canadian furniture, and is not found except in stylistically archaic examples, which are not that uncommon. This drop-leaf, swing-leg table, with birch legs and maple frame and top, has club-footed cabriole legs and extended scalloped-end aprons typical of the Queen Anne period in northern New England. The combination of woods, however, is very common to the Eastern Townships of Quebec, where the table was found, as is the more English form of wooden hinge attachment of the swing legs to the frame. Two other very similar Queen Anne tables are known from the same area, suggesting a local maker simply producing in an earlier design form.

Height: 71.7 cm (28¼ in.);
Diameter: 116.8 cm (46 in.)
Canadiana, Royal Ontario Museum

173.
Drop-Leaf Table
Montreal, c. 1790-1810

Tables and chairs with somewhat heavy square and untapered late-Chippendale "Marlborough" legs are found in all areas of English-Canadian settlement, though they are uncommon. This piece, with scalloped leaves and end skirts, also has legs which are moulded on the outer edges. (See also figs. 15, 163.) The table is wholly of mahogany, except for pine glue blocks. The leaves are supported by wooden-hinged arms folding into the frame. The table is shorter than its original height, and the legs have been shortened by about 5 cm. (Similar examples; cf. Dobson no. 41; Shackleton no. 450.)

Present Height: 67.6 cm (26⅝ in.);
Length: 107.3 cm (42¼ in.)
Canadiana, Royal Ontario Museum

174.
Drop-Leaf Table
Ontario, c. 1810-30

In a very ingenious manner, but for reasons unknown, this deep-leaved table was designed with only one leaf dropping, mounted with the usual underside strap hinges. The other leaf folds up on brass end hinges to overlie the top in the manner of a card table. Each leaf, when extended, is supported by a separate swing leg. With plain square-tapered legs, the table is of curly maple, with secondary cherry and pine in the frame.

Width, leaves folded: 50.1 cm (19¾ in.); *Length:* 109.2 cm (43 in.)
Private Collection

175.
Drop-Leaf Table
Probably Ontario, c. 1815-25

Tables with square-tapered legs are, in general, both earlier than turned-legged types, and also scarcer. Simple Canadian maple or cherry country tables, however, have no clear characteristics by which to differentiate them positively from northeastern American tables. This piece, with a long Ontario association, is wholly of curly maple, and without drawers. The leaf supports are the wooden-hinged swinging arm type, much more common in Ontario than on similar New York State tables. (Similar example, cf. Pain, no. 53.)

Height: 72.4 cm (28½ in.); *Length:* 104.2 cm (41 in.)
Canadiana, Royal Ontario Museum

176.
Drop-Leaf Table
Probably Nova Scotia, c. 1815-30

Another table of the same type as the preceding piece, this example is wholly of curly birch, and also without drawers. In an unusual treatment, the square-tapered legs are flared slightly outwards at the ends. (See also fig. 286.) The leaf supports, like the previous piece, are wooden-hinged arms. The cast-iron offset castors are a later 19th-century addition, and the legs have been cut down slightly to accomodate them.

Height: 71.1 cm (28 in.);
Length: 115.5 cm (45½ in.)
Canadiana, Royal Ontario Museum

177.
Drop-Leaf Table
Probably Montreal, c. 1810-20

The Pembroke or small general-purpose, drop-leaf table, usually defined by very narrow leaves, appears to have been made in all areas of eastern Canada. To judge by comparing surviving examples, however, it was not as popular or as common as larger and wider-leaved tables.

Wholly of mahogany, with secondary pine in the drawer structure, this table has a long drawer at one end and a plain panel rather than a matching false-drawer front at the other. Maple string inlays outline the sides of the square-tapered legs and the entire top surface.

Height: 75.5 cm (29¾ in.);
Length: 72 cm (28⅜ in.)
History Division, Museum of Man, National Museum of Canada

178.
Drop-Leaf Table
Ontario, Niagara Peninsula,
c. 1800-20

With a scalloped X-stretcher mortised and pinned into chamfered flats of the inside corners of the legs, this Pembroke table is wholly of cherry, with secondary pine. The beaded-edge drawer, on one end only, has its original pull. The leaves are supported by wooden-hinged pine arms folding into the frame. (Similar example, cf. Stewart, p. 143.)

Height: 71.1 cm (28 in.);
Length: 81.3 cm (32 in.)
Canadiana, Royal Ontario Museum

179.
Drop-Leaf Table
Ontario, Niagara Peninsula,
c. 1815-30

A simpler and perhaps later version of the Ontario Pembroke table form, this piece has square, finely tapered legs, without stretchers, and is wholly of walnut with no secondary wood. There is no drawer. The leaves, extended, are supported by crossing pull-out slides mounted in the frame.

Height: 71.1 cm (28 in.);
Length: 81.3 cm (32 in.)
Canadiana, Royal Ontario Museum

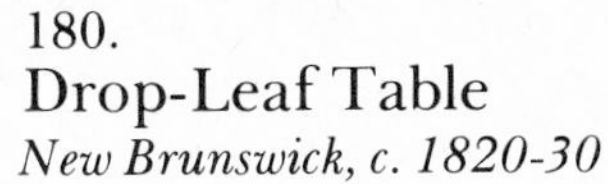

180.
Drop-Leaf Table
New Brunswick, c. 1820-30

This fine, small Pembroke table is wholly of bird's-eye maple, with a drawer in one end, and secondary pine only in the drawer structure. The heavy ball-footed legs are fluted in the manner of Classical Revival building columns, an extremely unusual treatment in Canadian furniture. The drawer has an apparently original plain wooden knob.

Height: 71.1 cm (28 in.);
Length: 72.8 in ($28^5/_8$ in.)
Kings Landing Historical Settlement

181.
Drop-Leaf Table
New Brunswick, c. 1820-40

Round-topped drop-leaf tables are not common as a Canadian type, compared to square- or rectangular-topped examples. This table, with long leg tapers broken by single rings, is wholly of mahogany. The leaf supports are pull-out sliding bars mounted in the frame. There is no drawer. (Similar examples, cf. Pain, no. 54; Shackleton, no. 498.)

Height: 68.6 cm (27 in.);
Length: 105.4 cm ($41^1/_2$ in.)
New Brunswick Museum

182.
Drop-Leaf Pedestal Table
Montreal, c. 1810

As a good example of adherence to American fashion, this table is purely a Duncan Phyfe type, though not a Phyfe piece. The table is of mahogany, and mahogany veneering over pine in the upper structure and drawer front. The drawer front is outlined with a fine dentil string inlay, and the frame skirt is bordered with a multi-coloured, diagonal-patterned inlay. The legs and vase-turned pedestal are well reeded; the pedestal reeding twists slightly, probably unintentionally. The table is complete with corner turned drop-finials, typical of Phyfe tables of the 1800-10 period. The original hardware is English.

Height: 68 cm (27½ in.);
Length: 91 cm (35⅞ in.)
Canadiana, Royal Ontario Museum

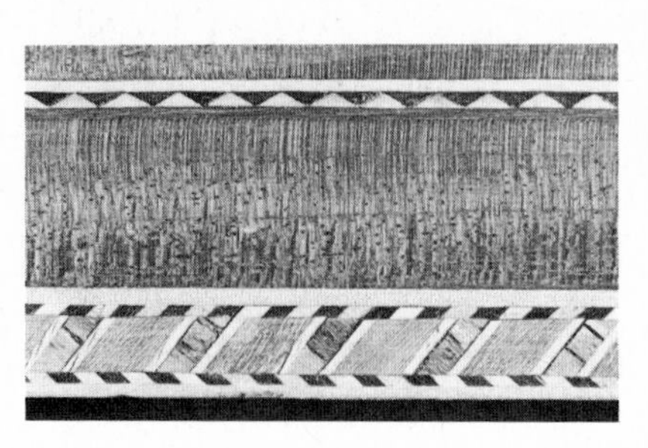

183.
Drop-Leaf Table
Ontario, Niagara Peninsula, c. 1820-35

Rope-carved or reeded legs are very much the exception on Ontario furniture, compared to plain turnings, and more typical of the Maritimes. This table, with a long family history in Grimsby, Ontario, is of cherry, with end panels of curly maple outlined with figured cherry inlays. The double-elliptic leaves are a New York influence. The rope-carved legs, with upper and lower ring turnings, have the small ball feet which became common on Ontario and New York State tables of this period. (Similar example, cf. Minhinnick; p. 201.)

Height: 72.8 cm (28⅝ in.); *Length:* 91.4 cm (36 in.)
Private Collection

184.
Drop-Leaf Table
Ontario, Niagara Peninsula, c. 1815-20

One of the finest examples of Ontario tables, this piece is lightly proportioned. The table is wholly of cherry, with deep leaves supported by swing legs. A walnut band inlay borders the frame-end skirts. The rope carving of the legs has, from the top, a left-hand twist at one end, and a right-hand twist at the other. This change of leg twists, usually between sides or ends, but sometimes corner to corner as on the preceding and following examples, is the rule on Canadian tables and other pieces with rope-carved legs.

Length: 126.4 cm (49¾ in.); *Width, leaves down*: 50.7 cm (20 in.)
Private Collection

185.
Drop-Leaf Table
New Brunswick, c. 1820-30; attributed to Thomas Nisbet

Of mahogany with secondary pine, this table has the upper leg carving (see also fig. 164) and turnings typical of Nisbet work. The twist of the rope-carved legs is right and left, corner to corner. The extremely long drawer is backed on the opposite end with a false drawer front. The wooden knobs appear to be replacements, but are correct.

Height: 72.1 cm (28 3/8 in.);
Length: 99 cm (39 in.)
Kings Landing Historical Settlement

186.
Drop-Leaf Table
Saint John, New Brunswick, c. 1820-30; attributed to Thomas Nisbet

A similar table, but without the upper leg carving, this piece also incorporates the lower double ring leg turnings that are so common to Nisbet work. Wholly of mahogany, with secondary pine only in the wooden-hinged leaf supports, there is no drawer. The twist of the rope-carved legs switches side to side.

Height: 72 cm (28 1/4 in.);
Length: 105 cm (41 1/4 in.)
History Division, Museum of Man, National Museums of Canada

187.
Drop-Leaf Table
Saint John, New Brunswick, c. 1820-30; labelled by Thomas Nisbet

Simpler than the preceding pieces, this table has a half-length, wooden-knobbed drawer stopped by the crossing pull-out slides which support the leaves. A false drawer front is at the opposite end. The Nisbet label is on the inside bottom of the drawer. The table is of mahogany, with secondary pine.

Width, leaves down: 52.1 cm (20½ in.); *Length:* 98.5 cm (38¾ in.)
York-Sunbury Historical Society, Fredericton

188.
Drop-Leaf Table
New Brunswick, c. 1825-40

Though the ring turning is a Nisbet style, this table is not attributable as a Nisbet piece. The legs have the long scallion-stalk turning (see also figs. 190, 191, 302) most typical of the second quarter of the 19th century. The single end drawer has its front surrounded by a maple string inlay, and there is no opposing-end, false-drawer front. The table is of mahogany, with secondary pine.

Length: 91.2 cm (35⅞ in.); *Width, leaves extended:* 95.8 cm (37¾ in.)
Kings Landing Historical Settlement

189.
Drop-Leaf Table
New Brunswick, c. 1825-40

Wholly of mahogany and with unusually fine leaves of curly or "fiddle-back" mahogany, this table has heavy-turned legs ending in straight castors. The single drawer has its original wooden knob. The secondary wood is pine.

Height: 71.4 cm (28¹/₈ in.);
Length; 106.4 cm (41⁷/₈ in.)
Kings Landing Historical Settlement

190.
Drop-Leaf Table
Ontario, c. 1825-40

A good, later Ontario country piece, this table has a long history in the Grafton area. It is basically of cherry except for curly maple frame-end panels, and secondary pine. The legs have double-bulbous or "scallion-stem" tapered turnings, separated by rings, and ending in the small ball feet which seem to have become universally popular after about 1830. There is no drawer.

Length: 106.5 cm (41⁷/₈ in.); *Width, leaves down:* 49 cm (19¹/₄ in.)
Private Collection

191.
Drop-Leaf Table
New Brunswick, c. 1825-40

With the same form of double-bulbous leg turnings as the preceding piece, this table is wholly of mahogany, with a wooden-knobbed drawer in one end, and a false drawer front on the other. The thin mahogany inlaid bands on the lower edges of each skirt also bisect the upper leg blocks.

It might be noted again here that, while not an absolute characteristic, rounded-cornered leaves are by far more common on Maritimes tables, and square-cornered leaves most typical on earlier Ontario tables.

Height: 75 cm (29½ in.);
Length: 86.7 cm (34⅛ in.)
Kings Landing Historical Settlement

192.
Sideboard
Eastern Ontario, c. 1800-1820

With plain square-tapered legs, this small bow-fronted, curly maple sideboard is an unusually elaborate piece for Ontario in this period. The drawer fronts are outlined with inlaid mahogany bands, inside of which are string-outlined, chevron-patterned band inlays of maple and cherry. The drawer pulls with their odd plates are original. The apparent string inlays of the kneehole-arch corners and legs are actually shallow grooves, coloured with a dark stain. These may have been added later in the 19th century. The secondary wood is pine.

Height: 91.4 cm (36 in.);
Length: 132.1 cm (52 in.)
Government House, Ottawa

193.
Sideboard
Eastern Ontario, c. 1800-1820

As a similar but far simpler bow-fronted maple sideboard, this example is possibly by the same maker as that preceding. The keyhole inlays are cherry, and the secondary wood is pine. The English castors are original, and the drawer pulls may also be. Originally a single, deep drawer, the left drawer was divided into two sometime in the 19th century. A third example of these maple bow-fronted sideboards, with simple cherry string inlays, is known in a private collection.

Height: 79.3 cm (31¼ in.);
Length: 139.7 cm (55 in.)
Canadiana, Royal Ontario Museum

194.
Sideboard
New Brunswick, c. 1800-1815

Many Georgian-period Maritimes pieces show construction adaptations indicating labour economies and material shortages. This sideboard, with a mahogany top and mahogany veneered pine drawer fronts, has birch sides and legs. The serpentine drawer fronts are block-carved, not bowed, and are quite thick, and flat on the inner sides. The birch legs are mahogany veneered only on the facing side of the front legs, and each of the legs is tapered only on two sides. The string inlays and intersected keyhole inlays are of maple.

Height: 109.2 cm (43 in.);
Length: 167.6 cm (66 in.)
Canadiana, Royal Ontario Museum

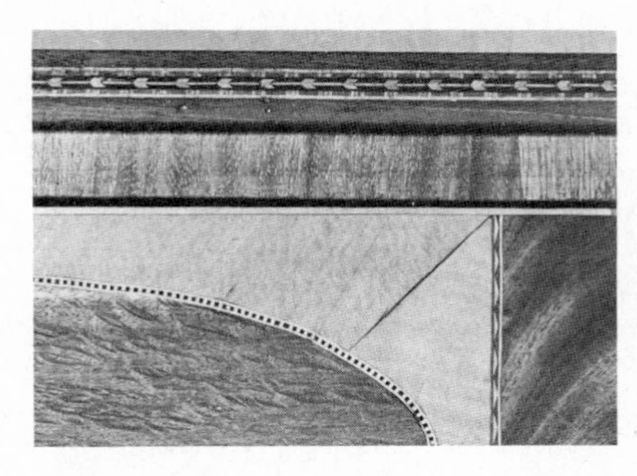

195.
Sideboard
Montreal, c. 1800-1820

With light reeded legs, this mahogany and mahogany veneered sideboard is one of those uncommon pieces which serves as an indicator of the range of exotic woods being imported as bundled-sheet veneers very early in the 19th century. The centre inlaid oval is of satinwood, in a rectangle of maple. The top and lower case edges are surrounded by geometric band inlays, which in a lighter form also outline the central inlaid rectangle and the edge of the cupboard doors. The keyhole inlays are maple. While early, the brass knobs are probably replacements. (Similar example, cf. Pain, no. 538.)

Height: 100.3 cm (39½ in.);
Length: 171.5 cm (67½ in.)
Canadiana, Royal Ontario Museum

196.
Sideboard
Montreal, c. 1820-30

This late Regency sideboard, though with earlier characteristics,is among the more opulent examples of Georgian-Canadian furniture. The piece is of mahogany and mahogany veneerings over secondary pine, with a typically Montreal geometric inlaid band around the lower edge of the case. The string inlays in the drawer fronts and the keyhole inlays are of maple. The English hardware is original. Later Regency furniture in Canada commonly combines reeding and rope carving in multi-segmented legs and pillars. Multi-segmented turned members are also characteristic of the later American Empire style, but the Regency furniture is generally much lighter in its proportions.

Height: 98.8 cm (38⁷/₈ in.);
Length: 182.2 cm (71³/₄ in.)
Canadiana, Royal Ontario Museum

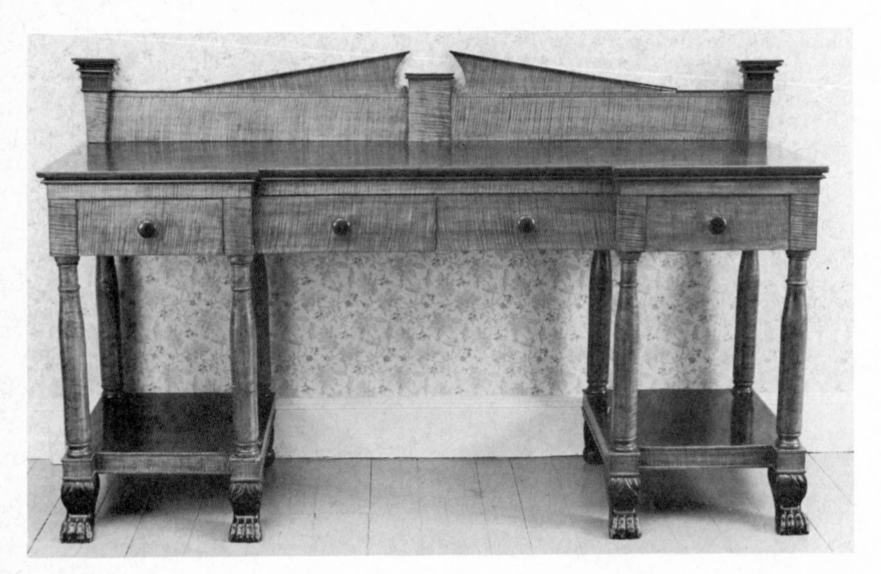

197.
Sideboard
Probably Toronto, c. 1825-35

As a piece combining both Regency and American Empire characteristics, this double platform-based sideboard is both early for its form in Ontario, and unusually large. It was, however, a commissioned piece. The straight-corniced broken pediment and capped plinths at the corners are pure Regency; the heavy lion's-paw feet are more typically Empire. The sideboard is of well selected curly maple and curly maple veneer over pine, except for the top and the platform surfaces, which are of cherry. Platform-based furniture, though popular in England from about 1810, in Canada is very uncommon before the 1830s. The sideboard was built, presumably in Toronto, for Chief Justice Sir John Beverly Robinson.

Height: 123.2 cm (48¹/₂ in.);
Length: 222.2 cm (87¹/₂ in.)
The Grange, Art Gallery of Ontario

198.
Tea Chest
Eastern Ontario, c. 1800-10

In a late Chippendale style, this bracket-footed tea chest is of curly maple, constructed with exposed corner dove-tailing and with a pine base. Canadian tea chests, in any form, are most uncommon. The lid is of block-laminated triangles of alternating maple and walnut. The lock plate, though it may be from an earlier piece of furniture, appears original to this chest.

Length: 28 cm (11 in.)
Private Collection

199.
Tea Chest
Eastern Ontario, c. 1825-40

Coffin-lidded Regency or Empire tea chests appear to have been the most typical early style in Upper Canada. This piece is wholly of bird's-eye maple veneering over pine, with cherry ball feet, end handles, and keyhole inlay. The interior contains two lidded and lead-foil-lined tea compartments, and a green felt-lined hole for a small pestle or mixing bowl.

Height: 21 cm ($8^1/4$ in.);
Length: 39.5 cm ($15^1/2$ in.)
Canadiana, Royal Ontario Museum

200.
Tea Chest
New Brunswick, c. 1820-40

This very small chest is of mahogany veneers over a pine box frame, with mahogany ball feet. The string inlays and lozenge keyhole inlay are maple. The interior is divided into two compartments, each with a mahogany-veneered pine lid and a small turned bone handle.

Height: 16.5 cm ($16^1/2$ in.);
Length: 20.9 cm ($8^1/4$ in.)
Private Collection

201.
Small Storage Box
Ontario, possibly Niagara Peninsula, c. 1815-30

Wholly of bird's-eye maple, except for a pine bottom, this box has the simple extended bracket base and applied feet of Chippendale-derivative forms. The corners are constructed with exposed dove-tailing, and the keyhole has a brass liner rather than a surrounding in-lay.

Height: 24.1 cm (9½ in.);
Length: 50.8 cm (20 in.)
Canadiana, Royal Ontario Museum

202.
Cellarette
New Brunswick, Miramichi area, c. 1815-1830

As very specialized pieces of furni-ture, cellarettes or wine boxes were never in common use, and Canadian examples are quite rare. The chest and base of this piece are separate and detachable units (see also fig. 285), wholly of mahogany and with a maple keyhole inlay. The interior lining and the bottle separators are of pine. (Similar example, cf. Dob-son, no. 144.)

Height: 60 cm (23⅝ in.);
Front Width: 44.8 cm (17⅝ in.)
Kings Landing Historical Settlement

203.
Cellarette
New Brunswick, c. 1820-1830

A more elaborate piece than that preceding, this mahogany cellarette stands on reeded legs and pedestal, and has rope-carved moulding separately applied to the edge of the coffin-shaped lid. The chest base and bottle separators are of pine. The English hardware appears original to the piece, including the 18th-century keyhole plate, probably salvaged from an earlier piece.

Height: 65.4 cm (25³/₄ in.);
Width: 51.4 cm (20¹/₄ in.)
Loyalist House, Saint John

204.
Tall-Post Bed
New Brunswick, c. 1785-1810

Four-poster or canopy beds of Canadian origin are most uncommon, as compared to low-post beds, and truly sophisticated beds even more so. This example, wholly of mahogany, has particularly fine Sheraton reeded, vase-turned posts. The lower square-tapered legs, on castors, are outlined on two sides with maple string inlays, as well as a small bell-flower inlay just above each brass end-rail bolt cover. The bell-flower is a particularly New England inlay motif, and probably indicates a Loyalist cabinet-maker.

Height: 214 cm (84¼ in.);
Width: 119.5 cm (47 in.)
Private Collection:

205.
Tall-Post Bed
Quebec City, c. 1825-35

With rope-carved upper sections with alternating right and left twists, this bed has foot-end posts including central leaf-carved sections, while the head-end posts are simply turned. This is a typical treatment. The heavy ball feet suggest probable dating to the 1830s. The bed posts are wholly of mahogany, and the frame rails of oak. The headboard and canopy frame are missing. Heavy neo-Empire rope carving over bulbous turning was the more usual Canadian form (see also figs. 219, 220, 297), while light rope carving over thin turning (see figs. 217, 218) was the exception, and of an earlier date. (Similar example, cf. Ryder, p. 79.)

Height: 214.6 cm (84½ in.)
Canadiana, Royal Ontario Museum

206.
Tall-Post Bed
Ontario, c. 1820-40

While beds with plain-turned posts are certainly more common than examples with reeded or rope-carved posts, the turnings of this piece are particularly extreme. The posts of medium height, combined with the bowed canopy frame, are less often observed than taller posts and flat canopy frames. This bed has its posts and end boards of walnut, with the rope frame bars of oak. The canopy frame is pine. (Similar examples, cf. Shackleton, nos. 208, 211; Pain, nos. 701-05.)

Post Height: 157.5 cm (62 in.);
Width: 131.4 cm (51¾ in.)
Private Collection

207.
Tall-Post Bed
New Brunswick, c. 1820-30

With heavier and perhaps less distinguished posts and turnings than the preceding piece, this bed is wholly of maple, and without a footboard. The canopy frame, of pine, is serpentine arched rather than bowed, and held to the posts, like all such beds, by small iron pins inserted into the post tops. (Similar example, cf. Pain, nos. 701-6.)

Post Height: 175 cm (68¾ in.);
Length: 190.8 cm (75⅛ in.)
Kings Landing Historical Settlement

208.
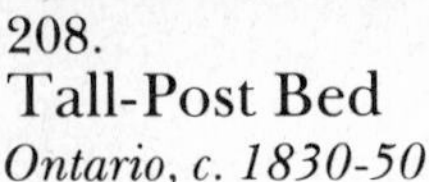

Tall-Post Bed

Ontario, c. 1830-50

The traditional form of canopy bed with plain-turned posts continued to be made in simple form in rural areas well into the mid-19th century, until it was finally rendered obsolete by reasonably efficient domestic heating stoves, and finally by central heating. This bed is entirely of maple, with round rope-frame bars with protruding pins. The flat, pine canopy frame is held in place by short wooden dowels attached to unusual turned upper finials. The original footboard is missing, and the cross-rod appears to be an early replacement. (Similar example, cf. Shackleton, no. 209.)

Height: 195.5 cm (77 in.)
Upper Canada Village

209.

Low-Post Bed

New Brunswick, c. 1810-25

Low-post open beds seem to have appeared as a standard form sometime after 1800, but did not become common until about 1830. Such basic turned-post beds, often with large so-called "cannon ball" finials, were produced all over North America and, except for woods and historical contexts, cannot usually be identified to particular regions. These beds have not been observed with reeded or rope-turned posts, or in other than native woods. This bed, wholly of maple and with original brass frame-bolt covers, is both earlier and finer than most such pieces, but the basic type was made in Canada well into the third quarter of the 19th century. (Similar examples, cf. Pain, nos. 713-27.)

Length: 203 cm (79⅞ in.);
Width: 144.1 cm (56¾ in.)
Kings Landing Historical Settlement

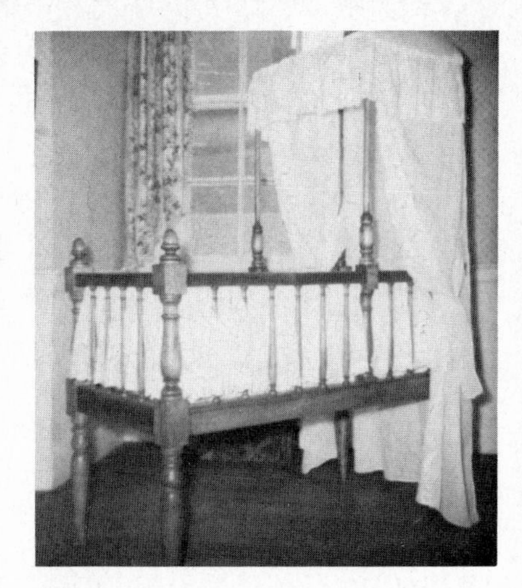

210.
Child's Crib
New Brunswick, c. 1800-20

While those adults who could afford or accomodate them preferred canopy beds in a age of unheatable houses, rarely did children rate such luxury. Canopied at the head end, this small crib has well-turned legs, bars, and canopy frame, and was used with heavy coverings in winter and netting in summer. The crib is wholly of birch, and is permanently framed, not dismountable.

Height: 160.2 cm (63¹/₈ in.);
Length: 122.5 cm (48¹/₄ in.)
Loyalist House, Saint John

211.
Hanging Cradle
Probably New Brunswick, c. 1790-1810

Hanging cradles, other than the later patented and manufactured versions in the late 19th century, only rarely appear. The vast majority of Canadian cradles are home-made box cradles, in infinite variety, typically of painted pine, sometimes hooded, and equipped with floor rockers. With convex legs similar to those on the candle-stands, this cradle has a frame of maple. The suspended box, with exposed corner dovetailing, is of butternut. The frame may be disassembled by removing long end bolts, which screw into rectangular nuts inserted in the ends of the cross-bars. This cradle has been attributed as American, of the Loyalist period, which, as with many such pieces, cannot be positively refuted. The combination of maple and butternut, the legs, and the archaic (in New England) sausage turning of the cross-bar suggest instead a turn-of-century New Brunswick origin, probably by a Loyalist maker. (Similar examples, cf. Shackleton, nos. 235, 236.)

Height: 118 cm (46¹/₂ in.);
Length: 107 cm (42¹/₈ in.)
Kings Landing Historical Settlement

212.
Hanging Cradle
New Brunswick, c. 1820-30; possibily by Alexander Lawrence, Saint John

This elegant cradle, with its thinly turned frame legs, finials, and cradle spindles, is wholly of mahogany. The standing frame is disassembled by removing the end bolts fastened into the cross-bar. The cradle bed is suspended from the frame posts on iron knobbed pins, and loops of iron rod attached to the lower cradle frame ends.

Height: 87.0 cm (34¼ in.);
Length: 116.5 cm (45⅞ in.)
Kings Landing Historical Settlement

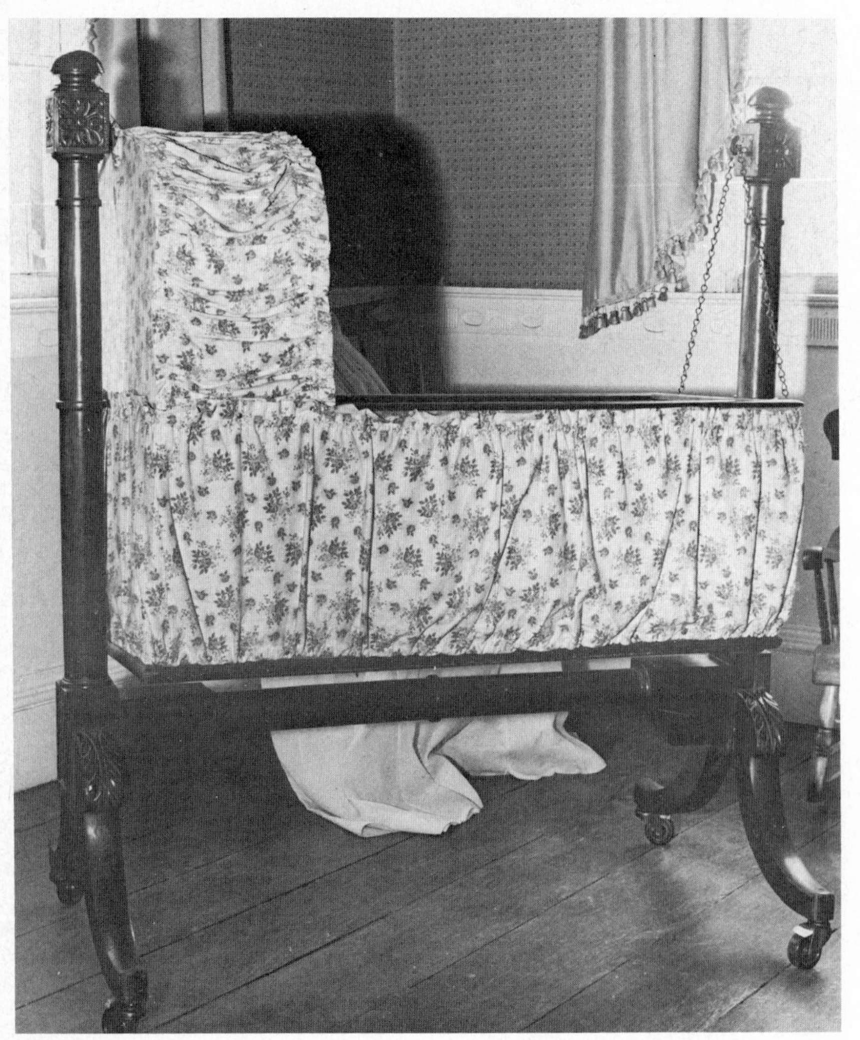

213.
Hanging Cradle
Saint John, New Brunswick, c. 1825-35; attributed to Alexander Lawrence

With straight, spare turnings of the frame posts, and carved knees and upper blocks, this piece has a cradle box of turned spindles, with a head-end bowed canopy hood of steamed hoops. The cradle box is suspended by a light chain over an iron hook at the foot end, and is attached directly through the hood frame. This cradle, like the previous piece, is also entirely of mahogany, and dismounts with end bolts. Another very similar cradle still belongs to descendants of Alexander Lawrence. (Similar example, cf. Pain, no. 746.)

Height: 117.8 cm (46⅜ in.);
Length: 106.8 cm (42 in.)
Loyalist House, Saint John

214.
Chest-on-Chest
New Brunswick, or possibly American, c. 1785-1810

Chests on frames and chests-on-chests are rarely found in the range of Canadian furniture, simply because these earlier 18th-century forms had become obsolete before the beginnings of cabinet-making in English Canada. The original oval drawer pulls and the plain bracket base suggest, however, a later-than-usual dating for such a piece, and the basic austerity suggests, quite possibly, early New Brunswick origin.

The chest is in two sections, with the removable top held in position by the moulding rim attached to the lower section. The piece is wholly of mahogany, with chamfered and fluted corners in the upper section, but without inlays. The secondary wood and drawer structure is pine. The chest was acquired in King's County, New Brunswick. (Similar example cf. Pain, no. 1137.)

Height: 190.2 cm (74⁷/₈ in.);
Width: 106.5 cm (42 in.)
History Division, Museum of Man, National Museum of Canada

215.
Chest of Drawers
Truro, Nova Scotia, c. 1815-20; by James Waddell

With bead-edged birds-eye maple drawer fronts (see also fig. 232), the ends, top, feet, and drawer stretchers of this bracket-footed chest are of birch. The original turned knobs are mahogany, but there are no inlays. The secondary wood is pine. The unusual "secret" long and narrow upper drawer must be opened by finger pressure from underneath.

This chest, a family piece, was given to the Nova Scotia Museum by the great grandniece of its maker.

Height: 114.3 cm (45 in.);
Width: 114.9 cm (45¹/₄ in.)
Nova Scotia Museum

216.
Chest of Drawers
New Brunswick or Nova Scotia, c. 1820

This simple bracket-footed chest is a good example of cosmetic selectivity of wood usage, as the sides and top are of straight-grained maple, while the drawer fronts are of dense bird's-eye maple. The secondary wood is pine. The top drawer lacks a keyhole and lock, while the other keyholes have brass liners. The knobs are replacement, and the square bracket feet of the chest appear to have been cut down at some point.

Height: 115.9 cm (45⁵/₈ in.);
Width: 101 cm (39³/₄ in.)
Kings Landing Historical Settlement

217.
Chest of Drawers
Nova Scotia, c. 1810-20

With square but oddly unbracketed base and feet, this chest also incorporates a stylistically archaic applied moulding, separating the base from the upper section. The feet may have been slightly cut down. The ends and top are of chestnut, all but unknown as a cabinet wood. The drawer fronts are of bird's-eye maple, while the string inlays and the top edge and case veneering are mahogany. The secondary wood is pine. The brass lion's-head pulls are replacements, probably for original wooden knobs.

Height: 97 cm (38¹/₂ in.);
Width: 124.4 cm (49 in.)
Kings Landing Historical Settlement

Sideboard
Montreal, c. 1800-20
See fig. 195

Chest of Drawers
Ontario, Niagara Peninsula
c. 1800-10
See fig. 220

218.
Chest of Drawers
Nova Scotia, c. 1815-30

This chest is a transitional piece, with generic Chippendale square but unbracketed feet, mixed with early Empire half columns. The case is of birch, with curly maple drawer fronts, top edging, and inlaid side-column blocks. The string and band inlays are of maple and mahogany, and the secondary wood is pine. The drawer pulls are replacements, probably for original wooden knobs. The tight ring turning of the half columns (see also figs. 228, 241) is a typical Nova Scotia treatment, but the carved pinwheel in the skirt is incongruous.

Height: 95.9 cm (37¾ in.);
Width: 110.1 cm (43⅜ in.)
Canadiana, Royal Ontario Museum

219.
Chest of Drawers
Nova Scotia, c. 1810

With original but most unusual heavy brass end handles, in the manner of English campaign chests, this simple, early piece is of mixed birch, with well figured curly drawer fronts and skirt, but straight-grained ends and top. The keyhole and drawer edge band inlays are of maple, as is the stringing, while the secondary wood is pine.

Height: 121.9 cm (48 in.);
Width: 120.6 cm (47½ in.)
Canadiana, Royal Ontario Museum

220.
Chest of Drawers
Ontario, Niagara Peninsula, c. 1800-10

As a good example of the early English rather than the Pennsylvania-German influence in the Niagara area, this flared-footed chest has sides and drawer spacers of cherry, with the top, drawer fronts, legs, and skirt of tightly figured curly maple and curly maple veneers. The secondary wood is pine, and the drawer-edge beaded strips and keyhole inlays are walnut. The top drawer, with sectional veneers over pine, is the deepest rather than the most shallow, as is usually the case. (See also fig. 242.) The lion's-head pulls are replacements. The bureau-desk, fig. 89, is a quite similar piece, and perhaps by the same maker. (Similar example, cf. Shackleton, no. 261.)

Height: 111.8 cm (44 in.);
Width: 106.7 cm (42 in.)
Canadiana, Royal Ontario Museum

221.
Chest of Drawers
New Brunswick, c. 1810-20; possibly by Robert Chillas, Saint John

This excellent bow-fronted chest, of mahogany with mahogany veneering over pine on the face and drawer fronts, has a long history with a family known to have ordered furniture from Robert Chillas, though there is no certainty this is one of his pieces. The chest is very similar in its stringing to fig. 90, also with a possible Chillas connection. (cf. Foss, pp. 23-25.) The unusual string inlays are of maple, and a geometric inlaid band separates the case from the base. The remaining brasses are original. Chillas has been established (cf. Ryder, 165) as working from about 1785 to 1824, and was an American Loyalist immigrant.

Height: 110 cm (43³/₈ in.);
Width: 116.5 cm (45⁷/₈ in.)
Kings Landing Historical Settlement

222.
Chest of Drawers
New Brunswick, c. 1805-20.

While curly birch was commonly used as a decorative wood in the Maritimes, matched birch crotch veneer, as in the drawer fronts of this chest, is rare. The veneer, sawed obviously from the same piece of wood, has been used obverse and reverse, leaving a seam in the centre of each drawer. The ends and top are of butternut, and the drawer-front string inlays are maple. The secondary wood, including drawers and birch-veneered base and skirt, is pine. The ring pulls are English, original except for those on the top small drawers, which are replacements.

Height: 113 cm (44½ in.);
Width: 116.5 cm (45⅞ in.)
New Brunswick Museum

223.
Chest of Drawers
Eastern Ontario, c. 1815-20

As a well-proportioned chest with square-footed flared legs, this piece combines plain birch sides, top, drawer stretchers, skirt, and feet with walnut drawer fronts. The drawer fronts are then outlined with quarter-inch curly maple inlaid bands, and the edges of the top and base with a narrower maple band. The brasses may be original. Brass keyhole plates, more an American characteristic, are less common than inlays on Canadian chests. (Similar example, cf. Minhinnick, p. 198; Pain no. 631.)

Height: 86.4 cm (34 in.);
Width: 100.3 cm (39½ in.)
Canadiana, Royal Ontario Museum

224.
Chest of Drawers
Quebec, Eastern Townships, c. 1815-25

A simple, handsome country piece, this chest is of curly maple except for the top, which is butternut and may be an early replacement. In one of infinite adaptations, the apparent drawer cock beading is really integral with the frame, grooved into the structural members. The keyhole inlays (the upper two missing) are bone, and the secondary wood is pine. The drawer pulls are replacements. (Similar example, cf. Shackleton, no. 265.)

Height: 106.7 cm (42 in.);
Width: 107.3 cm (42½ in.)
History Division, Museum of Man, National Museum of Canada

225.
Chest of Drawers
Ontario, c. 1815-25

A similar but finer example, this chest is also of tightly figured curly maple, and also of two boards each combined for the sides and top. The legs are better designed than on the preceding piece, and are integral with the case. The drawer fronts are bordered with inset reeded moulding strips of cherry, and the secondary wood is pine. The knobs are mixed originals and exactly reproduced duplicates.

Height: 92.1 cm (36¼ in.);
Width: 101.3 cm (39⅞ in.)
Private Collection

226.
Chest of Drawers
New Brunswick, c. 1825-35

This somewhat eccentric piece combines a number of techniques not often encountered. The chest is wholly of curly and straight-grained maple, with pine as the interior secondary wood. The elaborate pilaster and frieze inlays are maple and dark horn, to give an appearance of rope-carved appliques. Horn is not a common inlay material. (See also fig. 77.) The keyhole lozenges are not inlays at all, but merely painted diamonds. The French feet are straight, not flared, and the top has an unusually short side overhang. The brasses are incorrect replacements. This piece has been attributed to the Trueman family of Allack, New Brunswick, but on uncertain evidence.

Height: 116.8 cm (46 in.);
Width: 111.5 cm (43⁷/₈ in.)
Kings Landing Historical Settlement

227.
Chest of Drawers
Ontario, Perth County, c. 1820

With two boards each forming the sides and top, this bracket-based, flared-footed chest is wholly of pine. The flared legs are joined by simple serpentine skirting. A lock and brass-lined keyhole was provided only on the top right drawer. The brasses are replacements, but the original pulls also had oval plates. There is no remaining indication of whether the chest was originally painted.

Height: 109 cm (42⁷/₈ in.);
Width: 97.1 cm (38¹/₄ in.)
Private Collection

228.
Chest of Drawers
Nova Scotia, c. 1820-30

With attached flared legs, rather weakly designed, this chest is of bird's-eye maple, with secondary pine, ebonized maple drawer knobs, and tightly ring-turned quarter columns. (See also figs. 218, 241.) The string inlays in the drawer fronts are mahogany, while the keyhole inlays are of bone. The piece was found in coastal southwestern Nova Scotia.

Height: 123.2 cm ($48^1/_2$ in.);
Width: 123.2 cm ($48^1/_2$ in.)
Canadiana, Royal Ontario Museum

229.
Chest of Drawers
Quebec, Eastern Townships, c. 1815-30

This chest is a rather extreme example of the common habit of selecting the finest wood for the most visible areas, and relegating the least fine wood to less visible parts. The façade includes curly birch drawer fronts with mahogany beading strips, combined with curly maple drawer spacers, and bird's-eye maple veneer strips capping the front side edges. The sides and top of the chest, however, are of pine, with exposed dove-tailing at the top corners. The secondary wood is also pine. The brass knobs are early and apparently original.

Height: 99.7 cm ($39^1/_4$ in.);
Width: 106.7 cm (42 in.)
Private Collection

230.
Chest of Drawers
New Brunswick, c. 1820-30

As another example of using several different woods, this wholly-pine chest has its front, legs, skirt, drawer fronts, spacers, and side edges faced with mahogany veneer, with the sides and top left as bare pine. A one-inch-wide mahogany veneer strip is also inlaid into the front edge of the top surface. The drawer knobs are original.

Height: 93 cm ($36^5/_8$ in.);
Width: 91.1 cm ($35^7/_8$ in.)
Kings Landing Historical Settlement

231.
Bow-front Chest of Drawers
Montreal, c. 1805-15

This handsomely proportioned chest is of curly maple, with mahogany drawer-front inlaid edge banding, and maple beading and string inlays. The secondary wood is pine. Canadian bow-fronted chests are far less common than flat-faced examples. The steam or heat bowing of such pieces is always to only a slight curve, never an extreme one. Complex or extreme curves were, instead, block carved. The brass drawer pulls of this chest are original.

Height: 111.1 cm ($43\frac{3}{4}$ in.);
Width: 110.2 cm ($43\frac{3}{8}$ in.)
Private Collection

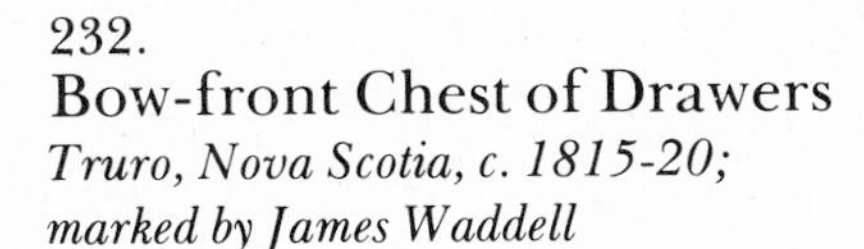

232.
Bow-front Chest of Drawers
Truro, Nova Scotia, c. 1815-20; marked by James Waddell

Another bow-front chest, this piece is a good example of the capabilities of cabinet-makers whose prime occupation was ship-finishing. There were many in the Maritimes. The bowed drawer fronts of the chest are of bird's-eye maple veneer over pine, while the sides, top, and front structure are straight-grained and curly birch. The simple string inlays are of mahogany, and the secondary wood is pine. A full frame baseboard, beneath the lower drawer and of roughly sawed curly maple, is marked *J. Waddell* in pencil on its bottom side.

James Waddell (1764-1851) emigrated from Glasgow to Halifax in 1813, moved to Rawdon, then to Truro about 1815, where he was a cabinet-maker (see figs. 9, 10, 215), and finally to South Maitland, where he was employed as a ship's carpenter. (cf. MacLaren pp. 12-13.) (Similar example, cf. Dobson no. 164.)

Height: 107.3 cm ($42\frac{1}{4}$ in.);
Width: 110.5 cm ($43\frac{1}{2}$ in.)
Private Collection

233.
Bow-front Chest of Drawers
Halifax area, c. 1810-20

A relatively small, simple chest, this piece is of mahogany, with the bead-edged bowed drawer fronts of mahogany veneer over pine. The lozenge keyhole inlays are also of mahogany, rather than, as usual, a contrasting wood. The secondary wood is pine. The brass drawer pulls are replacements.

Height: 104.2 cm (41 in.);
Width: 98.4 cm (38¾ in.)
Canadiana, Royal Ontario Museum

234.
Tall Chest of Drawers
Ontario, Louth Township (Niagara Peninsula), dated 1821; attributed to David Adolphus Simmerman

This is a smaller chest than usual for its type, a woman's size, and is solidly constructed of black walnut, with reeded-corner quarter columns and with full-depth drawer separators rather than the more typical cross-rails backed by drawer runners. A border design in maple, of diamonds and the inscription *M.M. 1821*, is inlaid across the frieze. The inner drawer structure is of pine.

The back of the top centre drawer is marked in pencil *For Samuel T. Moyer* and *by Simm*. The piece is apparently a wedding chest, the initials those of Moyer's wife, and the 1821 date that of their marriage. David Simmerman came to Louth Township from Germany in the late 1780s.

Height: 167.5 cm (66 in.);
Case Width: 97 cm (38½ in.)
Canadiana, Royal Ontario Museum

235.
Tall Chest of Drawers
Ontario, Waterloo County, c. 1820

A larger high chest, also typically Ontario-German, this piece is wholly of pine, and finely grain-painted in a bird's-eye maple pattern. With its reeded dentil-moulded frieze (see also fig. 157), and flared feet, the chest is one of several known similar examples, some of which have unfortunately been reduced to the bare pine. The keyhole plates and half the brass knobs are original; the other knobs are duplicated replacements. Tall single-case chests in Canada are known only from Ontario-German contexts. (Similar examples, cf. Shackleton, nos. 272, 275; Pain 1119, 1139-41.)

Height: 181 cm. (71¼ in.);
Width: 120.6 cm (47½ in.)
Canadiana, Royal Ontario Museum

236.
Chest of Drawers
Aurora, Ontario, c. 1830; by John Doane

With the short ogee bracket feet characteristic of Ontario-German makers, this chest is of tightly figured bird's-eye maple, with secondary pine. The pine top is edged with half-round maple edge moulding which complements the corner quarter columns. The five drawers with overlapping edges have brass-lined keyholes. The brass knobs are replacements, and the chest is known to have had earlier glass knobs, which may also have been replacements. (See also fig. 80.) (Similar example, cf. Shackleton, no. 277; Pain, no. 1124.)

Height: 109.7 cm (43⅛ in.);
Width: 106 cm (39⅝ in.)
Private Collection

237.
Chest of Drawers
Ontario, Niagara Pensula,
c. 1830-40

Wholly of cherry with secondary pine, this bracket-based and ogee-footed chest was found in Jordon, Ontario, and was probably made in that immediate area. The underside of the bottom drawer is dated *1837* in chalk, though this does not necessarily indicate the date of origin. The chest is very similar to the following piece. The glass drawer pulls are replacements. (Similar examples, cf. Pain, nos. 1126, 29.)

Height: 116.8 cm (46 in.);
Width: 113 cm (44½ in.)
Private Collection

238.
Chest of Drawers
Ontario, Niagara Peninsula,
c. 1825-30

This chest, of walnut with secondary pine, in its ogee bracket feet, plain quarter-round columns, and lower cove moulding, is very similar to the previous piece, though it is not by the same maker. The keyholes are brass lined, and the brass knobs, except for replacements on the lower drawer, are original. This piece had a long history with the Sherle family, who moved from the Niagara Peninsula to Waterloo County in the 1830s.

Height: 115.5 cm (45½ in.);
Width: 116.2 cm (45¾ in.)
Private Collection.

239.
Bow-front Chest of Drawers
New Brunswick, c. 1805-20

This handsome chest is wholly of mahogany, with the drawer fronts mahogany veneered over secondary pine. The curve of the steam-bowed drawer fronts is very slight. The fluted, Sheraton-derived flat pilasters are very unusual (see also fig. 214.) and rather incongruous with the light ring-turned, pin-footed legs. The latter, however, as well as the simply panelled ends, are not uncommon even on quite early Maritimes chests. The hardware is original.

Height: 102.2 cm (40¼ in.);
Width: 106.7 cm (42 in.)
New Brunswick Museum

240.
Chest of Drawers
Ontario, Ottawa Valley, c. 1825-35

As on the preceding piece, solid, unbevelled panelled ends appear quite early in the 19th century on Canadian chests, though somewhat later in frontier and agricultural regions than in coastal and urban areas. This chest, wholly of cherry except for pine drawer structures, stands on plain-turned legs. The drawer edges have applied beading strips, and the brasses are replacements. (Similar examples, cf. Pain, nos. 639, 43.)

Height: 97.8 cm (38½ in.);
Width: 106.7 cm (42 in.)
Private Collection

241.
Chest of Drawers
Nova Scotia, c. 1825-40

Chest of drawers with Sheraton-derived extended front corner columns, capped by top extensions, are an uncommon Canadian form, as is other furniture of this style. These pieces are also later in date than American furniture of the extended column type, and usually show Empire characteristics as well. This chest, with a scrolled backboard and lower skirt, is of curly birch, with secondary pine in the drawer structure. The legs and corner columns have small ball feet, and typically Maritimes multiple ring turnings. (See also figs. 218, 228.) The ring drawer pulls appear original to the piece. The drawer edge beading is incised into the drawer fronts, not separate moulding strips. (Similar example, cf. Dobson, no. 165.)

Height: 116.8 cm (46 in.);
Width: 108 cm (42½ in.)
History Division, Museum of Man, National Museums of Canada

242.
Chest of Drawers
Eastern Ontario, c. 1825-40

This chest, with an attached set-back unit of two small drawers and a backboard, is similar to the preceding piece in its ring-turned corner columns and small ball feet. The birch backboard is simply scrolled, and the skirt scalloped. The sides, top, columns, and drawer stretchers are also of birch. The drawer fronts, of bird's-eye maple with maple beading strips, are outlined with inlaid walnut bands, wider on the deep upper drawer (see also fig. 220) than on the lower two. The wooden knobs are original. Set-back drawers, often with mirror mountings, became popular in Canada only after about 1830, though the form itself dates between 1805 to 1810.

Height: 116.8 cm (46 in.);
Width: 99 cm (39 in.)
Canadiana, Royal Ontario Museum

243.
Chest of Drawers
New Brunswick, c. 1830-40

With a definite later Empire influence in the irregular turning of the corner columns, this chest is a good piece for illustrating mixtures of both styles and materials. The chest case is of straight-grained maple. The top backboard, drawer fronts, and the deep skirt are of bird's-eye maple, while the drawer stretchers and drawer edge beading are mahogany. The secondary wood is pine. The drawer pulls replace original wooden knobs. This piece has been attributed to the Trueman family of Allack, New Brunswick, but evidence of this is lacking. (See also fig. 225.) (Similar example, cf. Pain, no. 644; Foss, p. 41.)

Height: 114 cm (44 7/8 in.);
Width: 120 cm (47 1/4 in.)
Kings Landing Historical Settlement

244.
Chest of Drawers
New Brunswick, c. 1815-25

This strange chest was made in two separate units, divided between the second and lowest drawers, as if intended for portability. (See also fig. 102.) It has no carrying handles, however. The ends and top are of pine, while the front spacers and drawer fronts are mahogany, with maple knobs. The huge, maple ball feet are archaic and reminiscent of the 17th century, though they appear original to this piece. (See also fig. 156.)

Height: 95.8 cm (37 7/8 in.);
Width: 97.9 cm (38 1/2 in.)
Kings Landing Historical Settlement

245.
Chest of Drawers
New Brunswick, c. 1825-35

An otherwise ordinary chest, this piece also has heavy maple ball feet, but with a deep groove turned in each. The chest is wholly of mahogany, with the drawer sides of oak, and with other secondary pine. Oak is an extremely uncommon secondary wood in Canadian furniture. The ebonized maple drawer knobs have inset bone centres.

Height: 106 cm (41¾ in.);
Width: 101 cm (39¾ in.)
Kings Landing Historical Settlement

246.
Chest of Drawers
New Brunswick, c. 1825-35

Perhaps by the same maker, this chest has turned feet very similar to those on the preceding piece, but with added lower ball feet. The chest is of mahogany, with the drawer structure and stretchers of pine, and the side edges and drawer stretchers are mahogany veneered. The drawer fronts are outlined with unusual, thin, glued-on reeded strips. The lowest drawer pulls are non-matching replacements; the upper three drawers have their original hardware.

Height: 107.1 cm (42⅛ in.);
Width: 110.6 cm (43½ in.)
Loyalist House, Saint John

247.
Bow-front Chest of Drawers
Nova Scotia, c. 1810-25

An uncommonly small chest, this piece has simply bowed drawer fronts and is of mahogany and mahogany veneering over pine. The top edge is surrounded by a thin, rope-patterned string inlay. The legs, though original, have a typical turning for a Nova Scotia piece. The original wooden knobs are also mahogany, and the veneering of the top drawer front and the drawer stretchers is mismatched, the result of recent restoration.

Height: 85.7 cm (33¾ in.);
Width: 99.1 cm (39 in.)
Private Collection

248.
Chest of Drawers
New Brunswick, Saint John area, c. 1825-35

A chest similar to fig. 245, with a half-round base moulding, this piece is also of mahogany, including the drawer sides. The drawer bottoms and backs are of pine. The pin-tipped, short-turned feet are a common form, and the wooden knobs are original.

Height: 118.1 cm (46 1/2 in.);
Width: 125 cm (49 1/4 in.)
Kings Landing Historical Settlement

249.
Chest of Drawers
New Brunswick, c. 1820

This chest, with mahogany ends and top, has drawer fronts of well-figured mahogany veneer over pine. The knobs are black-stained birch, and the secondary wood is pine. The bracket base and feet are modern replacements, and the piece is known originally to have had short, heavy-turned or bun feet. Disregarding the incongruous original feet, pieces with any early appearance, such as this one and fig. 250, are very often retrofitted with new "Chippendale" bases and feet, and matching hardware.

Height: 101.6 cm (40 in.);
Width: 105.4 cm (41 1/2 in.)
Private Collection

250.
Chest of Drawers
New Brunswick, c. 1820

Rather than the more usual mahogany, this chest is wholly of birch, with drawer-front beading strips instead of moulded overlaps. The secondary wood is pine. The original, square-bracketed feet were cut down at an early date, and then replaced with more fashionable short, pin-footed turnings, which have remained. The hardware is a more recent replacement, but not the first, for original wooden knobs.

Height: 99.8 cm (39 1/4 in.);
Width: 83.3 cm (32 3/4 in.)
Kings Landing Historical Settlement

251.
Chest of Drawers
Eastern Ontario, Brockville area, c. 1840-50

A piece dating considerably later than its design might indicate, this chest is also most unusual in its top wash-stand splash boards, which are original, and attached to three sides of the top. The wood is butternut, with secondary pine, while the keyhole inlays are walnut. The brass knobs are replacements; the originals were probably wooden.

Height to top surface: 108.5 cm ($42^3/_4$ in.); *Width:* 107 cm ($42^1/_8$ in.)
Private Collection

252.
Mirror
Montreal, c. 1810

Before about 1820, or perhaps even later, the generic Chippendale, rectangular, scrolled-bordered mirror seems in Canada to have been the only stylized form. These, and even simply framed, early-looking glasses, are rare. Columned and corniced "Sheraton" mirrors do not seem to appear before the 1820s, and like chests, most have Empire characteristics. This mirror, of known origin, has a mahogany frame with a gilded, carved pine liner. The fret-sawed scroll work, also of mahogany, is thin, and glued to the back of the frame with pine support blocks. Like the card table, fig. 116, the mirror was made in Montreal for Sir James Monk, Chief Justice of the Court at King's Bench from 1794 to 1824.

Height: 115.6 cm ($45^1/_2$ in.); *Width:* 67.3 cm ($26^1/_2$ in.)
Canadiana, Royal Ontario Museum

Bow-front Chest of Drawers
Montreal area, c. 1805-15
See fig. 231

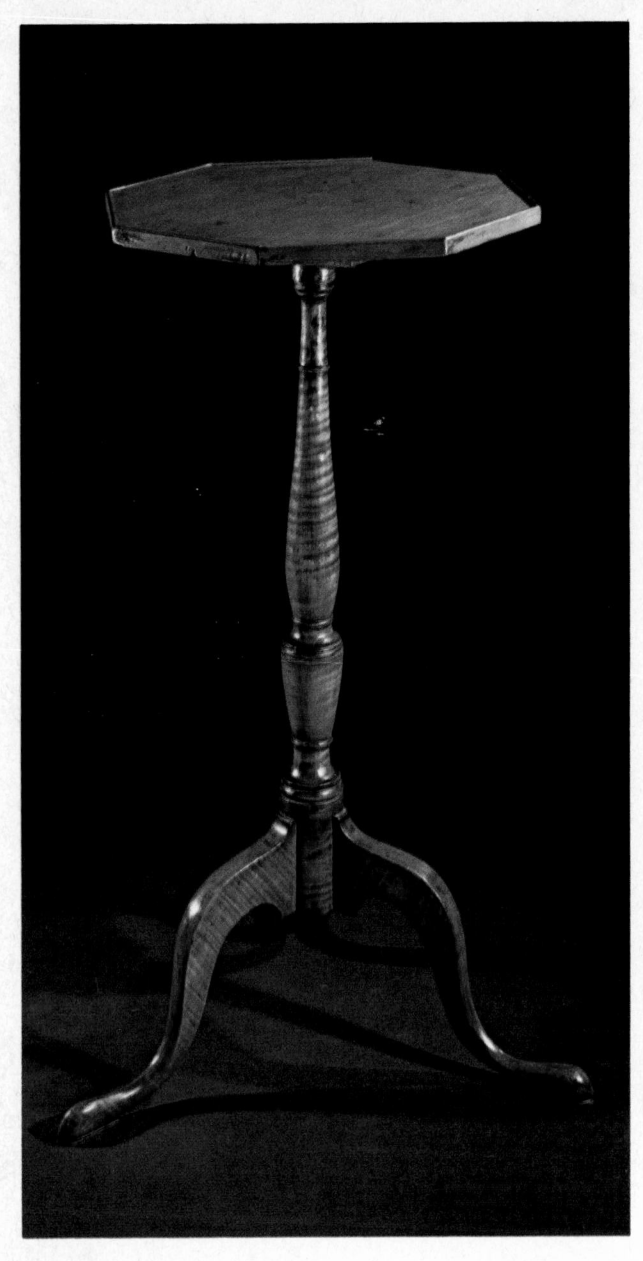

Candle-Stand
Quebec, Eastern Townships
c. 1790-1810
See fig. 267

Work Table
Quebec City area, c. 1810-20
See fig. 291

253.
Box Chest
Nova Scotia, c. 1800-20

As a good example of the Loyalist influence in Maritimes furniture, this chest is a particularly American New England type, with a blanket box and hinged lid on top, and two drawers with moulded front overlaps beneath. The upper two drawer fronts are false. The simple bracket base is typical on box chests of this form. Except for the maple knobs, the piece is wholly of pine, and was probably originally painted. (Similar examples, cf. Pain. nos. 607-19)

Height: 110.5 cm (43½ in.);
Width: 101.6 cm (40 in.)
Nova Scotia Museum

254.
Box Chest
Ontario, Niagara Peninsula, c. 1810-30

Box chests with drawers in a single row above the base and dove-tailed corners are a Pennsylvania form that was carried by tradition to the Germanic-settled areas of Ontario. With three drawers and a bracket base, this chest is of walnut with exposed dove-tailing on all corners. A narrow inlaid banding of cherry surrounds the drawer fronts. The cock beading is attached to the frame, rather than the drawer edges, and the reeding between drawers is incised in the frame, not applied. The secondary wood is pine. Though the originals were probably similar, the brasses and keyhole plates are replacements. (Similar example, cf. Pain, no. 1094.)

Height: 72.4 cm (28½ in.);
Length: 126.4 cm (49¾ in.)
Private Collection

255.
Box Chest
Ontario, Niagara Peninsula, c. 1810-30

With two drawers rather than three, this bracket-footed chest with exposed corner dove-tailing, front and back, is also of walnut. The drawer fronts are outlined with curly maple inlaid banding and the keyhole inlay is also of maple. Similar to the preceding piece, the apparent drawer-edge cock beading is applied to the frame, not the drawer fronts. As with all such chests, the secondary wood of the drawer structure is pine.

This chest was acquired from the Smith family farm in Trafalgar Township, Halton County. The family, however, had originally settled near Grimsby, and moved to Halton County in late 1831, taking this chest with them.

Height: 74 cm ($29^{1}/_{8}$ in.);
Length: 120 cm ($47^{1}/_{4}$ in.)
Private Collection

256.
Box Chest
Ontario, Niagara Peninsula or York County, c. 1825-35.

This three-drawer chest, wholly of pine rather than the usual walnut, and painted, has ogee bracket feet typical of Ontario-German chests of drawers. The corners, though paint-covered, have exposed dove-tailing in the manner of hardwood chests. The small quarter columns opposite the drawers are carved into the dove-tailed corners. The drawer fronts overlap the frame, and the drawer pulls are replacements. This chest was found in the Vaughan-Markham Township area of York County, but may have been brought there by a family migrating from the Niagara Peninsula. (Similar examples, cf. Pain, nos. 1088, 94.)

Height: 84 cm (33 in.);
Length: 116 cm ($45^{5}/_{8}$ in.)
Private Collection

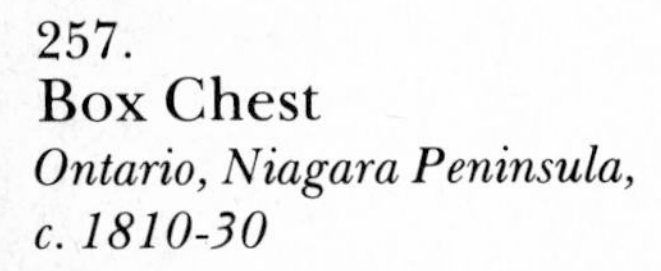

257.
Box Chest
Ontario, Niagara Peninsula, c. 1810-30

Without drawers, this simple bracket-footed, "six-board" chest is probably more typical of pieces built by Ontario-German settlers than are drawered chests. The piece is wholly of walnut, with the usual exposed dove-tailed corners. There is no external hardware, and the keyhole is unlined.

Height: 64.5 cm ($25^{3}/_{8}$ in.);
Length: 125.1 cm ($49^{1}/_{4}$ in.)
Private Collection

258.
Corner Wash-Stand
Nova Scotia, c. 1800-15

Graceful and simple corner wash-stands with light, flared legs were a common English form, and also popular in the New England states. The type seems most uncommon in Canada, this being one of a handful of examples now known (though simple English pieces are abundant). This wash-stand is wholly of pine, with a small drawer in the shelf section. The piece has apparently never been painted. (Similar examples, cf. Pain, nos. 167, 69; Minhinnick, p. 108.)

Height: 101.3 cm (39 7/8 in.);
Width: 57 cm (22 3/8 in.)
Nova Scotia Museum

259.
Wash-Stand
New Brunswick, c. 1820-30

A small, delicate, square stand (see also fig. 293) with lightly ring-turned legs, this piece could have also served as a lamp table. The top, without a bowl opening, has never had splash boards. The top is edge reeded, above a scalloped skirt, and the lower section contains a single wooden-knobbed drawer. The secondary wood is pine. The stand has been attributed to Thomas Nisbet. The mahogany bevelled-frame New Brunswick mirror is an Empire piece of the 1830s. (Similar examples, cf. Pain, no. 168; Minhinnick, p. 106.)

Height: 83.8 cm (33 in.);
Width: 40.6 cm (16 in.)
Kings Landing Historical Settlement

260.
Portable Wash-Stand
New Brunswick, c. 1810-12

As a military field wash-stand with detachable turned and pin-tipped legs, this piece combines New Brunswick cabinet-work with English hardware and interior pewter bowls and utensils. The wash-stand is of mahogany, with secondary pine, and was made in New Brunswick for Lt. Gen. John Coffin, and was used by him during the War of 1812.

Height: 84 cm (34 in.)
New Brunswick Museum

261.
Wash-Stand – Bidet
New Brunswick, c. 1815-30

A most unusual piece, this wash-stand includes an integral bidet, mounted as a drawer at one end, and sliding closed into the frame. The wash-stand proper, with splash board, two flanking drawers, and a small cupboard, is of stained birch and maple, with secondary pine. The cupboard doors, with centre circular veneering, are mahogany veneered over pine. The lowest drawer front is false. The extended bidet, with a tinned iron basin, is of mahogany and birch, also with secondary pine. Though it has square-tapered and folding legs contrasting with the turned legs of the wash-stand, the bidet is original to the piece. The knobs, with bone centres, are original.

Height: 77.6 cm (30 1/2 in.); *Length, bidet closed*: 63.5 cm (25 in.)
Loyalist House, Saint John

262.

Dressing Table

New Brunswick, c. 1815-25

This is a combined dressing table and wash-stand with splash boards on three sides. The frame, top, splash boards, and turned pin-footed legs are of solid mahogany. The wood-knobbed drawer fronts, however, are mahogany veneered over mahogany, while the drawer structures are pine. The separate dressing mirror and base, of mahogany and also of New Brunswick origin, date from the 1830s.

Height: 86.3 cm (34 in.); *Length:* 92 cm (36¼ in.)
Kings Landing Historical Settlement

263.

Dressing Table

New Brunswick, c. 1820-30

Very similar in basic form to figs. 85 and 86, but with straight-turned legs on English offset castors, this piece has a set-back, three-drawer top section with splash boards. The dressing table is of mahogany, with secondary pine, and reeded fan carvings form the corners of the knee opening. All drawers have brass-lined keyholes and locks, and the knobs are original.

Height: 94.5 cm (37¼ in.);
Length: 110.4 cm (43½ in.)
Kings Landing Historical Settlement

264.
Wash-Stand
New Brunswick, c. 1825-35

With two drawers and top splash boards, this mahogany wash-stand has only a lower shelf, attached to square blocks integral with the turned legs. The secondary wood of the drawer structures is spruce rather than the usual pine. The small ball feet indicate a date not earlier than about 1825, and the brass drawer pulls are original. (Similar example, cf. Pain, no. 171.)

Height: 95 cm (37 3/8 in.);
Width: 63 cm (24 3/4 in.)
Kings Landing Historical Settlement

265.
Wash-Stand
Ontario, Waterloo County, c. 1820-40

In a dry sink form, this wash-stand is a bedroom rather than a kitchen piece, and probably by a German immigrant maker. Though of Ontario-German origin, it shows more of a European than North American derivation. Wholly of pine, the cupboard door, front sides, and front rim are all steam bowed. The rimmed sink, probably watertight, has never been metal lined. The brass hinges and latch are original, and the door knob is a replacement.

Height: 78.5 cm (30 7/8 in.);
Width: 68.5 cm (27 in.)
Private Collection

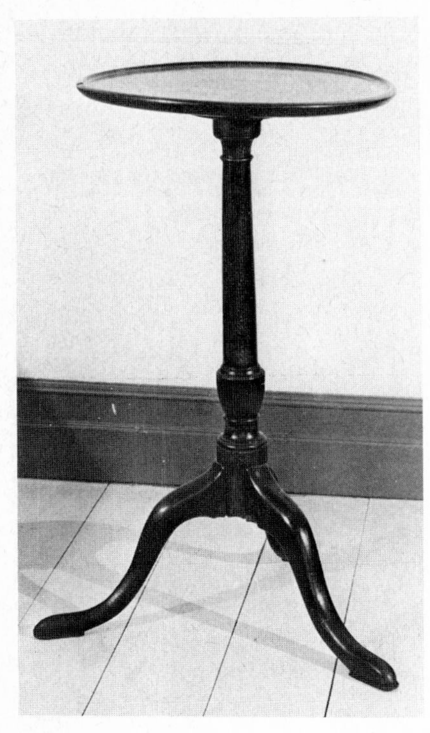

266.
Candle-Stand
New Brunswick, c. 1800-20

The long, straight-tapered shaft above an urn turning in the pedestal of this table is an excellent example of this very common turning form. The dished top (see also fig. 113) and cabriole legs are of mahogany, and the column is birch. (Similar examples, cf. Dobson, no. 32; Shackleton, no. 465; Pain, no. 84.)

Height: 73.4 cm (28⅞ in.);
Diameter: 40.5 cm (16 in.)
Kings Landing Historical Settlement

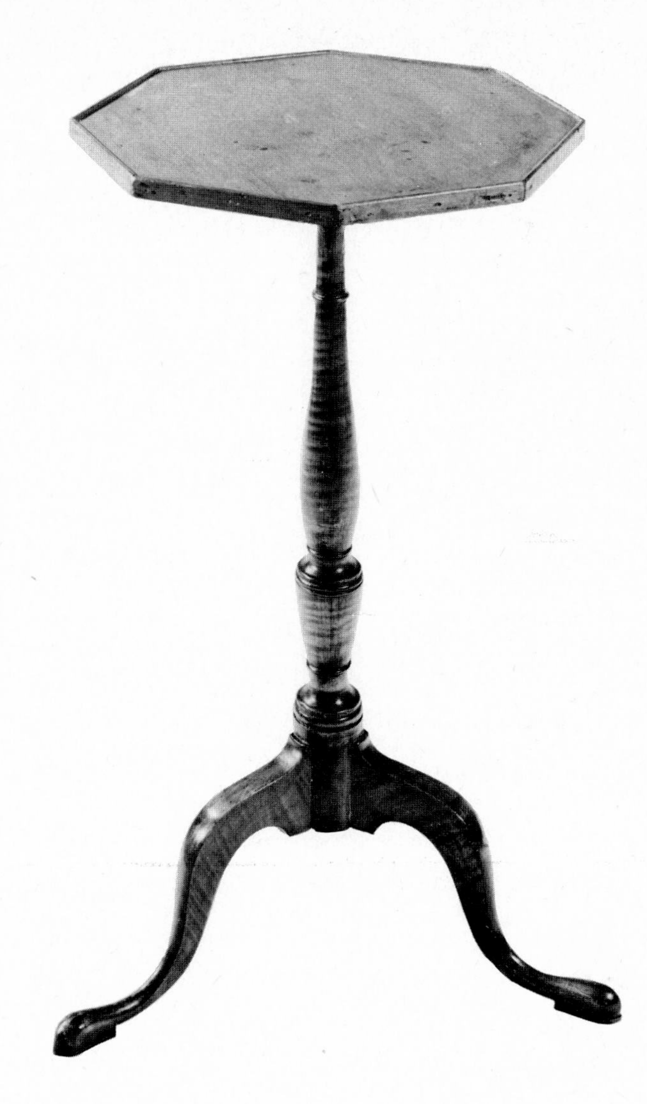

267.
Candle-Stand
Quebec, Eastern Townships, c. 1790-1810

The majority of Canadian candle-stands, if not ungainly, are more heavily structured than they ever needed to be. Very light and delicate pieces are the exception. This very delicately designed stand has an uncommon octagonal top, rimmed with separate bead-moulding strips. The legs and column are of curly maple, while the top and rim strips are of pine. (Similar example, cf. Shackleton, no. 466.)

Height: 77.8 cm (30⅝ in.);
Top Width: 39 cm (15⅜ in.)
Canadiana, Royal Ontario Museum

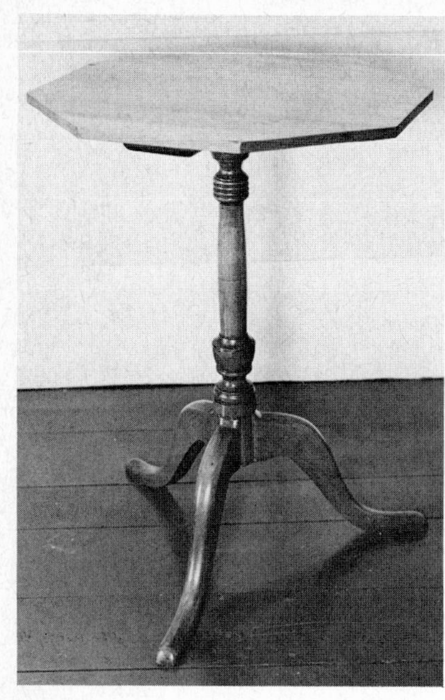

268.
Candle-Stand
Nova Scotia, c. 1810-20

As another lightly but substantially constructed example, this table has an unusual column turning with a rudimentary urn below, multiple rings above, and a bowed centre section. The octagonal top and cabriole legs are of maple, while the pedestal is birch.

Height: 72.4 cm (28½ in.);
Top Width: 51.4 cm (20¼ in.)
Nova Scotia Museum

269.
Candle-Stand
New Brunswick, c. 1810-20

With a heavy-tapered bulbous pedestal, and somewhat out-sweeping cabriole legs, this piece has a top of mahogany, and pedestal and legs of stained birch. The top tilts, in the usual manner, on a wooden pin through a pedestal block and two top underside struts.

Height: 66.3 cm (26⅛ in.);
Diameter: 53.1 cm (20⅞ in.)
Kings Landing Historical Settlement

270.
Candle-Stand
Nova Scotia, c. 1800-20

A particularly well-proportioned piece, this table has an aura of ground-clinging solidity. The angled-corner square top has simply rounded edges, and the piece is wholly of birch. The rounded feet have well-defined applied pads, which seem to be a maker's characteristic. (Similar example, cf. Dobson, no. 32.)

Height: 68.6 cm (27 in.);
Top Width: 36.8 cm (14½ in.)
Canadiana, Royal Ontario Museum

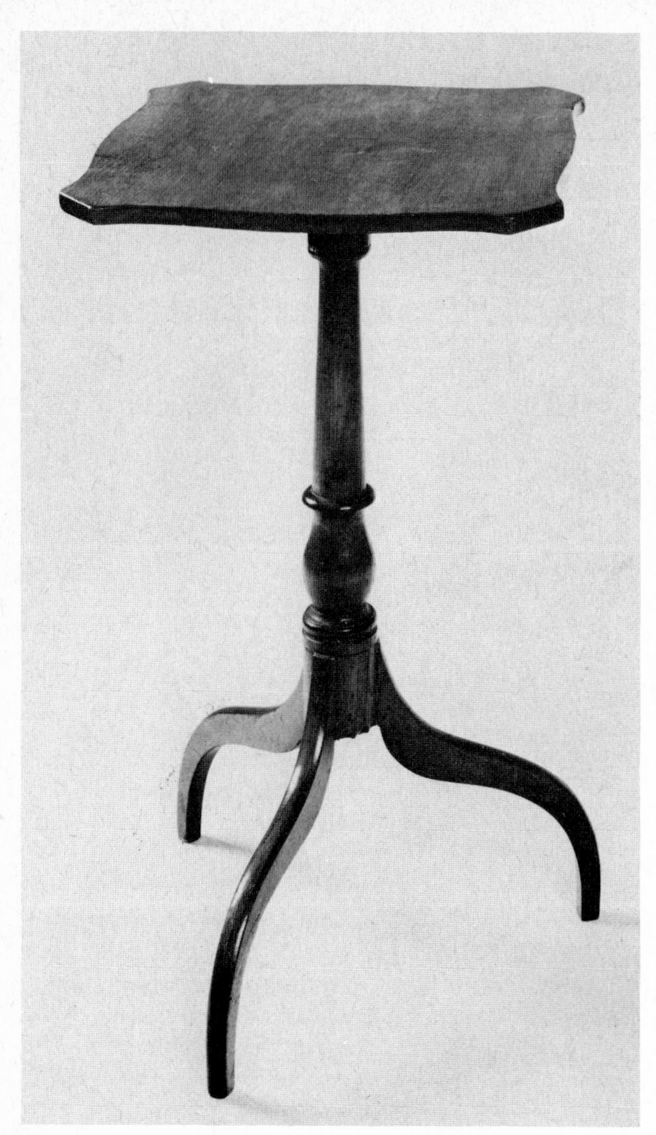

271.
Candle-Stand
Southwestern Nova Scotia, c. 1800-20

While not as common on Canadian tables as the cabriole and snake-footed leg types, various forms of convex or arched legs are occasionally found, primarily in the Maritimes. All are, of course, of English design origin. The table is wholly of birch, and the angled-corner and serpentine-sided tilt-top (see also fig. 274) indicates a New England influence.

Height: 73 cm (28³/₄ in.);
Top Width: 43.2 cm (17 in.)
Canadiana, Royal Ontario Museum

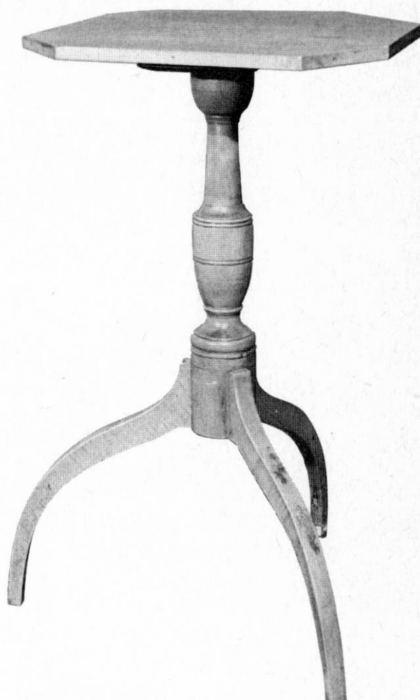

272.
Candle-Stand
Quebec, Eastern Townships, c. 1800-15

With a square angled-corner top, this table has concave legs so strongly arched that the piece seems poised to leap from the floor. The fixed top is of straight-grained maple, the column of birch, and the legs are of curly maple.

Height: 69.6 cm (27³/₈ in.):
Top Width: 43 cm (16⁷/₈ in.)
Private Collection

273.
Candle-Stand
New Brunswick, or possibly New England, c. 1800-15

This piece, and that following, point out the difficulty of differentiating the simpler furniture of the Maritimes from that of northeastern New England. The top and legs are of maple, and the column with a tapered, convex shaft above a turned urn is birch. The ovolo-cornered top is atypical to, but not unknown in, Canada. (See figs. 116, 275.) The table has been attributed as American Loyalist (cf. Foss, p. 16), which is not positively refutable, but the piece seems later than the Loyalist period, and the structural simplicity and combination of woods are typical of the Maritimes.

Height: 71.0 cm (28 in.);
Top Length: 57.5 cm (22⁵/₈ in.)
Kings Landing Historical Settlement

274.
Candle-Stand
Nova Scotia, New Brunswick, or New England, c. 1800-15

Like the preceding piece, the origin of this candle-stand is also an uncertainty. The angled-corner, serpentine-sided top (see also fig. 271) and the overly heavy pedestal are of maple, while the legs are birch, a usual combination. The tight ring turnings on the pedestal are also suggestive, because of widespread occurence, of Maritimes origin rather than New England, though the piece has been attributed, uncertainly, to New England. (cf. Montgomery, no. 81.)

Height: 64.2 cm (25¹/₂ in.);
Width: 41.6 cm (16³/₈ in.)
Henry Francis DuPont Winterthur Museum

275.
Candle-Stand
New Brunswick, c. 1800-15

Spade feet are most unusual on English-Canadian furniture and have been observed only on a few New Brunswick pieces. (See also fig. 194.) The ovolo top (see figs. 116, 273), the column, and the legs are of mahogany, while the top support block is birch. The spade feet, in an unusual two-dimensional adaptation, are formed on the inner and outer edges only. The leg sides are quite flat.

Height: 71.8 cm (28¹/₄ in.);
Top Length: 51.5 cm (20 in.)
Kings Landing Historical Settlement

277.
Candle-Stand
Nova Scotia, probably Halifax area, c. 1825-40

This strange neo-Regency table, with segmented ring turnings in the pedestal, and concave roll-footed legs, is wholly of mahogany. The top, mounted on light crossed struts, is fixed, not tilting.

Height: 73.8 cm (29 in.);
Diameter: 38.1 cm (15 in.)
Canadiana, Royal Ontario Museum

276.
Candle-Stand
Probably New Brunswick, but possibly American, c. 1800-10

Plain concave legs with a pin foot (see also figs. 107, 278) are the least common form on Canadian candle-stands and are rarely encountered. The "birdcage" frame for the tilting top, while not an unusual form in New England, would make this table virtually unique as a Canadian piece. It may well, however, be of New Brunswick-Loyalist origin. The slightly double-elliptic rectangular top is of birch, while the legs, the pedestal with its strong urn turning, and the top support frame are all of mahogany.

Height: 76.1 cm (30 in.);
Top Width: 57.8 cm (22¼ in.)
Loyalist House, Saint John

278.
Candle-Stand
Quebec or Ontario, c. 1825-35

As the fashion and need for small-topped pedestal candle-stands declined in the second quarter of the 19th century, sophisticated versions ceased to be made, and country tables became structurally very simple. This piece, with the uncommon concave legs, is wholly of curly maple except for the pine strut connecting the top to the pedestal.

Height: 73.4 cm (28⁷/₈ in.);
Top Length: 45.5 cm (17⁷/₈ in.)
Private Collection

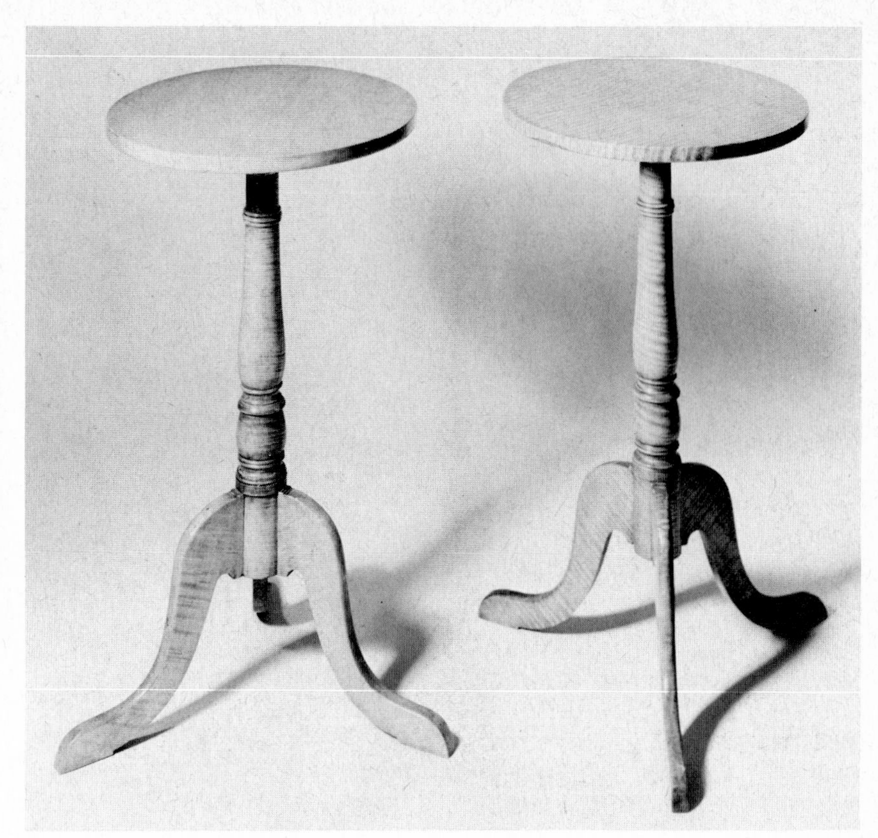

279.
Candle-Stands
Ontario, c. 1840-50

Known pairs of candle-stands, meant for either end of a sofa, are quite rare in a Canadian context, and these examples are also stylistically archaic, as they were made much later than their design would suggest. The tables, with simple plank-cut, flat cabriole legs, are wholly of curly maple. The fixed tops are mounted on single, maple cross-grain struts. (See also fig. 300.)

Height: 73.7 cm (29 in.);
Diameter: 43.2 cm (17 in.)
Canadiana, Royal Ontario Museum

280.
Candle-Stand
Nova Scotia, Lunenburg area, c. 1820-30

Basically English styles translated into the Germanic tradition can result in strange adaptations. Lunenburg County, Nova Scotia, was an area of German and American-Germanic settlement at least as early as the 1750s, with Pennsylvania-German Loyalists immigrating to the colony after the American Revolution. (See also fig. 309.) Wholly of birch under dark paint, this table has cabriole legs mounted so flatly that the base of the pedestal stands only an inch from the floor. The pedestal is turned with the multiple tight rings that seem to have been favoured particularly in Nova Scotia.

Height: 69.2 cm (27¹/₄ in.); *Diameter:* 51.8 cm (20³/₈ in.)
Canadiana, Royal Ontario Museum

281.
Sewing/Writing Table
Saint John, New Brunswick, c. 1820; attributed to Thomas Nisbet

Though all-purpose work tables are a standard form, Canadian sewing tables with suspended work bags are quite rare. Four examples are now known of the Nisbet variety of combination sewing table and writing desk. The upper case of this table is of mahogany veneer over pine, and the interior has mahogany separators over a pine base. The fine-reeded legs, top, and the delicate bowed stretchers are also mahogany. The drawer fronts are edged with thin rope-pattern inlays, with a string-outlined, diamond-patterned band around the lower case edge. The inner drawer structure is pine, and the knobs are of ebony with bone ring inserts.

This table belonged to John Warren Moore of St. Stephen, New Brunswick, who probably acquired it from Nisbet. It remains with a Moore descendant.

Height: 76 cm (30 in.); *Width:* 52.1 cm (20¹/₂ in.)
Private Collection

282.
Sewing/Writing Table
Saint John, New Brunswick, c. 1820; attributed to Thomas Nisbet

Another example, with reeded legs, of the Nisbet form of sewing and writing table, has a unique (in a Canadian context) cover-top inlay of pierced brass sheeting forming a full border. The table is also of mahogany and mahogany veneering over secondary pine. The upper false drawer front, centre drawer, and work bag slide are edged with maple stringing and have their original brass knobs. This table, and the following piece, have the multiple ring turning of the legs that appears as a regional form.

Height: 77.5 cm (30½ in.);
Width: 52 cm. (20½ in.)
Kings Landing Historical Settlement

283.
Sewing/Writing Table
Saint John, New Brunswick, c. 1820-25; labelled by Thomas Nisbet

Of bird's-eye maple rather than mahogany, and with turned rather than reeded legs, this piece has the same leg turnings as the preceding example. The upper drawer front is false; the Nisbet label is in the bottom of the centre drawer. The top cover-edge banding and the keyhole inlays are of mahogany, and the secondary wood is pine. Another nearly identical, but unlabelled, maple example is known in a private collection.

Height: 76 cm (30 in.);
Width: 52 cm (20½ in.)
Canadiana, Royal Ontario Museum

284.
Sewing Table
Montreal, c. 1820-30

With uncommon English ball rather than wheeled castors, rarely seen on Canadian furniture, this sewing table is much more of a standard type, with two drawers and a lower work bag slide (the work bag missing). The table is of mahogany, with mahogany-veneered drawer fronts, and secondary pine. The back of the piece has, in applied bead mouldings, false drawer and bag slide fronts, unusual on a work table. The slender ring-turned legs and the drop leaves were quite popular on small tables after about 1825. On the underside the table is dated *1830* in ink in two places, perhaps, but not necessarily, the date of its making. (Similar examples, cf. Pain, nos. 74-5.)

Height: 71.1 cm (28 in.);
Width, leaves extended: 88.9 cm (35 in.)
Canadiana, Royal Ontario Museum

285.
Sewing Work-Box
New Brunswick, c. 1815-30

A most unusual sewing box with end handles, this piece rests on a separate base frame with turned legs and castors. (See also fig. 202.) The top surface is mahogany veneered as four triangles over pine, while the box and frame are of solid mahogany, with interior pine. The top drawer front is false, and the two lower drawers, like the top covered bin, have internal spacers for sewing material. A very odd three-line inlay in maple outlines neither frame nor drawers, but instead crosses the cover edge and lower box frame, and vertically bisects the drawer ends. The keyhole lozenges are of bone. The upper false-drawer knobs are replacements; the other hardware is original. (Similar example, cf. Pain, no. 76.)

Height: 60.6 cm (23⁵/₈ in.);
Width: 36.3 cm (14¹/₈ in.)
Kings Landing Historical Settlement

286.
Work Table
Ontario, c. 1800-15

The thin square-tapered legs of this table are flared outwards from the corners, through a slight angled cutting of the tenioned frame sides. (See also fig. 176.) An unusually delicate piece, the legs and frame are of curly maple, and the top of cherry. A small drawer, without a pull and opened by finger pressure, is in one side. The secondary wood is pine. The table was found many years ago in Johnstown, Ontario. (Similar examples, cf. Pain, nos. 139-40.)

Height: 71.1 cm (28 in.);
Width: 52 cm (20¹/₂ in.)
Private Collection

287.
Work Table
Ontario, probably Trenton—Belleville area, c. 1800-15

A fine light table, this piece is wholly of cherry except for a drawer structure of pine. Though many examples are known of such relatively plain but well-proportioned tables, the legs of this piece are not typical. The apparent outward flaring was created by tapering only on the inner sides; the legs are not structurally angled. The full-width drawer has its original brass pull. (Similar examples, cf. Pain, nos. 132-39.)

Height: 68 cm (26³/₄ in.);
Width: 50.8 cm (20 in.)
Private Collection

288.
Work Table
Eastern Ontario, or possibly Montreal, c. 1810

More a typical form than the preceded piece, this table has heavier and straight square-tapered legs. The primary wood, however, is mahogany, not cherry — this early usage (for Ontario) of imported mahogany creates doubt about the table's accepted eastern Ontario origin, in favour, perhaps, of Montreal. The drawer front has its original brass knob; the interior drawer structure is pine.

Height: 69.5 cm (27 3/8 in.)
Toronto Historical Board

289.
Work Table
Ontario, Niagara Peninsula, c. 1810-20

Though its woods are mixed, this table is basically of walnut, with the square-tapered legs glued rather than pinned to the frame. The stretchers above and below the walnut drawer front are of cherry, and the string inlays of the top edge and drawer front are maple. The secondary wood is pine. (Similar example, cf. Pain, no. 132.)

Height: 67.5 cm (28 5/8 in.);
Width: 47.5 cm (18 3/4 in.)
Private Collection

290.
Work Table
Montreal area, c. 1800-15

This fine, delicate table with lightly tapered legs is a good example of early straight-line inlaying and stringing. With two shallow drawers, the table is wholly of maple, and secondary pine. The top, drawer fronts, skirts, and upper leg fronts are then inlaid with curly maple banding, this set off by thin maple string inlays across the lower front edge of the frame. The top is edged with separate applied moulding, as are the beaded drawer fronts. Only the lower drawer locks and the brass knobs appear to be replacements.

Height: 68 cm (26$^3/_4$ in.);
Width: 52 cm (20$^1/_4$ in.)
Private Collection

291.
Work Table
Quebec City area, c. 1810-20

In the earliest years of the 19th century, small utility furniture with any real elaboration of inlay work was largely restricted to the Montreal–Quebec area, and is only rarely found from Ontario or the Maritimes. (See also fig. 299.) With two drawers, this table is of mahogany, with mahogany and bird's-eye maple inlays and veneering over pine on the frame and drawer fronts. The top, sides, drawer fronts, and leg fronts are string and motif inlaid in maple and stained maple. The keyhole inlays are blanks; there are no locks. The drawer knobs are replacements. (Similar example, cf. Pain, no. 129.)

Height: 72.4 cm (28½ in.);
Width: 43.8 cm (17¼ in.)
Canadiana, Royal Ontario Museum

292.
Work Table
Nova Scotia, c. 1810-20

A simple but early elongated country table, this cleanly designed yet basic piece is wholly of birch, with a mahogany top that appears to be a later 19th-century replacement. The beaded edges of the drawer are grooved into the drawer front, not applied mouldings. The brass knob seems original.

Width: 43.8 cm (17¼ in.);
Length: 62 cm (24 in.)
Canadiana, Royal Ontario Museum

293.
Work Table, Candle-Stand, or Kettle-Stand
Montreal area, c. 1820-40

This small stand, with its rimmed surface and small, solid pull-out slide with a brass knob, is a special piece; its use is not readily discernible. Portable on its original castors, it may be a reading candlestand or chair-side tea table. The table is wholly of curly maple. The bulbous turning of the legs is reversed from the usual arrangement, with the heavier sections down, giving the piece an appearance of solidity despite its lightness. Though the scalloped frame sections are original, the lower shelf, over the previously open stretchers, is a more recent addition.

Height: 72.5 cm (28½ in.);
Width: 25.9 cm (10¼ in.)
Private Collection

294.
Work Table
Ontario, probably Port Hope – Cobourg area, c. 1820-30

Canadian tables with sophisticated reeded legs are quite rare, certainly more so than examples with rope-carved legs. With small drop leaves as well, supported by pine wooden-hinged arms (see also fig. 298), this table has a frame and legs of cherry, with the drawer fronts and stretchers of well-figured mahogany veneer over pine. The drawer knobs are original to the piece. This table is reasonable evidence that, though solid mahogany as a bulk cargo does not appear in Ontario before completion of the Lachine Canal at Montreal, bundled mahogany veneer in small quantities was occasionally brought in. One other similar table, with nearly identical legs, is known from the same area.

Height: 74.3 cm (29¼ in.);
Width: 46.4 cm (18¼ in.)
Private Collection

295.
Work Table
Southwestern Ontario, c. 1815-25

Also with well-reeded legs, and pin feet, this earlier table, with a top disproportionately heavy for the delicacy of its legs, is of walnut with a single full-width drawer. The lower frame moulding is unusual on such pieces, but consistent with the basic Sheraton design. The secondary wood is pine. The white, opalescent glass knob is early, though not necessarily original to this table. (Related examples; cf. Stewart, p. 138; Shackleton, no. 501.)

Height: 74.9 cm (29½ in.);
Width: 60.3 cm (23¾ in.)
Canadiana, Royal Ontario Museum

296.
Work Table
Probably New Brunswick, c. 1820-30

With its single wide drawer and original wooden knobs, this table is wholly of mahogany, excepting secondary pine in the drawer structure. The pin-footed round legs have the same clustered, tight multiple-ring turnings observed on other Maritimes pieces, a characteristic which seems too widespread and diverse to reflect the work of any single maker or small area.

Height: 71.8 cm (29¼ in.);
Length: 81.3 cm (32 in.)
Kings Landing Historical Settlement

297.
Work Table
New Brunswick, c. 1830

A solid, four-square piece with pin-footed, rope-carved legs, this table has two wooden-knobbed drawers, both with brass keyhole liners. The leg twist changes corner to corner. The table is wholly of mahogany except for the pine drawer structure.

Height: 71.5 cm (28⅛ in.);
Width: 46.5 cm (18⅛ in.)
Kings Landing Historical Settlement

298.
Work Table
Ontario, c. 1830-40

Of especially well-selected, densely figured bird's-eye and curly maple, this table has drop leaves, which slowly began appearing on small work tables after about 1820. The leaf supports are small, hinged pine arms, and the secondary wood of the drawer structures is also pine. The two drawer fronts are outlined with walnut beading strips, and the lion's-head ring pulls are replacements.

Height: 69.5 cm (27⅜ in.); *Width, leaves down:* 46.7 cm (18⅜ in.)
Private Collection

299.
Work Table
Ontario, Belleville area, c. 1825-35

This excellent two-drawer table is one of several known examples with virtually identical turnings and inlays, all clearly by the same maker. The table is of cherry, with bird's-eye maple panel inlays in the upper leg blocks. The drawer fronts, conversely, are of bird's-eye maple with inlaid cherry edge banding and applied beading strips. The drawer structure is pine and the "ebonized" knobs are original. (Similar examples, cf. Pain, nos. 129, 44, 46, 49.)

Height: 72.4 cm (28 1/2 in.);
Width: 49.5 cm (19 1/2 in.)
Private Collection

300.
Work Table or Sofa-end Table
Eastern Ontario, c. 1825-35

Though the transitional leg turnings are rather unusual, this curly maple table is a relatively simple and typical Ontario piece. It is, however, one of an identical and matched pair, unknown in work tables, and rare in candle- or lamp-stands. (See also fig. 279.) The secondary wood is pine and the drawer knob is original. These tables had a long family history in Gananoque.

Height: 71.7 cm (28 1/4 in.);
Width: 52.1 cm (20 1/2 in.)
Private Collection

301.
Work Table
Nova Scotia, Bay of Fundy area, c. 1825-40

Of typically Nova Scotia mixed woods, this table has its legs, drawer stretchers, and back of straight-grained maple, the sides and top of birch, the drawer structures of pine, and bird's-eye maple drawer fronts with rectangular mahogany string inlays. The legs and frame are pinned together, a construction technique that at this period was obsolescent, having been replaced by wholly glued joints. The bulbous-tapered and ball-footed legs have the common Maritimes multiple-ring turnings. The drawer knobs are apparent replacements for earlier knobs of the same sizes. (Similar example, cf. Pain, no. 154.)

Height: 71.5 cm (28 1/8 in.);
Width: 53.3 cm (21 in.)
Private Collection

302.
Work Table
Nova Scotia, c. 1830-40

This well-proportioned table has the strong, double-bulbous leg turnings on small ball feet so typical of the post-1825 to 1830 period. (See also fig. 190.) The table is of birch, the full-width drawer front of curly maple, and the drawer structure is pine. The brass pull is a replacement, probably for an original wooden knob. (Similar examples, cf. Pain, nos. 145, 152.)

Width: 65.5 cm (25 in.);
Depth: 50.8 cm (20 in.)
Canadiana, Royal Ontario Museum

303.
Work Table
Ontario, c. 1830-50

Wholly of bird's-eye maple, except for a straight-grained maple top, this rectangular table has the ball feet common to the 1830s, but is probably somewhat later. The drawer structure is the usual pine, and the brass knob appears original. Though a difficult wood to work, bird's-eye maple was always popular in Ontario, and continued to be used in country furniture as long as individual furniture-making remained a viable craft.

Height: 68.6 cm (27 in.);
Length: 68.6 cm (27 in.)
Canadiana, Royal Ontario Museum

304.
Work Table
Ontario, c. 1820-35

With pin-tipped, light-turned legs, this table incorporated the typical Ontario mixture of frame and legs of cherry combined with a top of curly maple. The single drawer, without bead moulding, has its inner structure of pine. The glass pull is a replacement, probably for a wooden knob.

Height: 72 cm (28 3/8 in.)
Private Collection

305.
Work Table
Nova Scotia, c. 1820-35

This is a table reduced to the basic simplicity that is typical of later country pieces. The frame and legs are of birch, with a curly maple top and drawer front, and secondary pine. The knob is a replacement. Great numbers of tables of this type were made well into the third quarter of the 19th century, in later years often with legs disproportionately heavy for the overall design.

Height: 68 cm (26³/₄ in.);
Width: 53 cm (20⁷/₈ in.)
Canadiana, Royal Ontario Museum

306.
Work Table
Newfoundland, c. 1790-1820

Georgian-period Newfoundland furniture is very uncommon; most known examples date to the mid- or late 19th century. All seem to be of indigenous woods, and no Newfoundland pieces are known in mahogany. This table has a single drawer, with carved edge beading and corner fans. The wooden ball knobs and early keyhole plate are original, though the keyhole plate may be salvaged from an earlier English piece. The legs and front frame of the table are birch, and the sides, back, top, and drawer front are of pine. The under-top moulding is a 17th-century derivation.

Height: 80.1 cm (31¹/₂ in.);
Length: 80.3 cm (31⁵/₈ in.)
Canadiana, Royal Ontario Museum

307.
Work Table
Newfoundland, c. 1800-20

While early Newfoundland furniture in its design is rather removed from the mainstream of English-Canadian cabinet-making, it is still based on English and Scottish country forms, though sometimes archaic. This table, wholly of birch with a pine top, has a very small drawer without a pull, opened by finger pressure from below. The square and slightly tapered legs, pinned to the frame, are beaded on the outer edges in the manner of many Canadian Chippendale chairs. The corner fan, demi-lune, and rosette carving, and the separated scalloping of the front skirts, however, is very remiscent of 17th-century English oak country furniture.

Height: 68 cm (26³/₄ in.);
Length: 74.1 cm (29¹/₈ in.)
Canadiana, Royal Ontario Museum

308.
Work Table
Nova Scotia, Lunenburg area, c. 1820-40

Basically Anglo-American forms translated to the North American-Germanic tradition often resulted in strange stylistic combinations (See also fig. 280.) Of birch with a pine top, this table has unusual, slender leg turnings quite unlike those found on English-derived Maritimes furniture. The entire table is grain painted in red and black, and the top is inscribed, also painted, *to Laticia Thomson.*

Height: 73.3 cm (28⁷/₈ in.);
Length: 76.2 cm (30 in.)
Canadiana, Royal Ontario Museum

309.
Work Table
Ontario, Waterloo County, c. 1820-40

Stylistic throw-backs, even far into the 19th century, were made occasionally in most furniture types, and always in rural areas, more subject to tradition than the pressures of changing fashion. With archaic club-on-ball feet below plain-turned legs, this table is wholly of pine. The frame joints are pinned, a technique largely abandoned by this date in favour of gluing.

Height: 72 cm (28³/₈ in.);
Width: 53.4 cm (21 in.)
Private Collection

Bibliography

English-Canadian Furniture

Burrows, G. Edmond. *Canadian Clocks and Clockmakers.* Oshawa: Kalabi Enterprises, 1973.

Carlisle, Lilian Baker. "Martin Cheney, Elegant Clockmaker." *Canadian Collector,* Feb. 1967, p. 11.

Collard, Elizabeth M. "Montreal Cabinetmakers and Chairmakers; 1800-1850." *The Magazine Antiques,* May 1974, pp. 1132-46.

Dempsey, Hugh A. *Ethnic Furniture*. Calgary: Glenbow-Alberta Institute, 1970.

Dobson, Barbara and Henry. "In Search of a Standard." *Canadian Collector,* Jan./Feb. 1973, pp. 8-17; May/June 1973, pp. 10-25.

———. "What Price Heritage?" *Canadian Collector,* Sept./Oct. 1973, pp. 27-32.

———. *The Early Furniture of Ontario and the Atlantic Provinces*. Toronto: M. F. Feheley Co., 1974.

Duncan, Dorothy. "Some Thoughts on Niagara Furniture." *Canadian Collector,* Mar./Apr. 1977, pp. 33-35.

Dunning, Phil T. "The Evolution of the Windsor." *Canadian Collector,* Mar./Apr. 1974, pp. 12-16.

Elwood, Marie. "Two Halifax Cabinetmakers: Thomas Cook Holder and Henry Arthur Holder." *Canadian Collector*, Sept./Oct. 1976, pp. 16-19.

Elwood, Marie. "18 Chairs from Nova Scotia." *Canadian Collector*, Jan./Feb. 1977, pp. 38-42.

Ferguson, B. W., and Lackey, Thomas. *Decorated Nova Scotia Furnishings.* Halifax: Dalhousie Art Gallery, 1978.

Field, Richard H. "Some Furniture from Prince Edward Island." *Canadian Collector,* Sept./Oct. 1976, pp. 30-32.

———. "Blanket Chests from Prince Edward Island." *Canadian Collector,* Nov./Dec. 1976, pp. 46-47.

Finlay, A. Gregg. *Heritage Furniture: A catalog featuring selected heritage furniture from the collection of the New Brunswick Museum.* Saint John, N.B.: New Brunswick Museum, 1976.

Foss, Charles H. "Two New Brunswick Furniture Craftsmen: Thomas Nisbet and Alexander Lawrence." *Canadian Collector*, May/June 1975, pp. 29-33.

———. "Kings Landing Historical Settlement, New Brunswick." *Antiques*, June 1979, pp. 1212-1227.

Foss, Charles H., and Vroom, Richard. *Cabinetmakers of the Eastern Seaboard.* Toronto: M. F. Feheley, 1977.

Ingolfsrud, Elizabeth, "Antique Beds." *Canadian Collector*, Oct. 1971, pp. 15-17.

———. "Ontario Drop-Leaf Tables." *Canadian Collector*, July/Aug. 1972, pp. 14-16.

———. "Blanket Chests." *Canadian Collector*, Sept./Oct. 1972, pp. 30-31.

———. *All About Ontario Chairs.* Toronto: The House of Grant Ltd., 1974.

———. *All About Ontario Beds.* Toronto: The House of Grant Ltd., 1975.

———. *All About Ontario Chests.* Toronto: The House of Grant Ltd., 1976.

———. *All About Ontario Tables.* Toronto: The House of Grant Ltd., 1976.

———. *All About Ontario Cupboards.* Toronto: The House of Grant Ltd., 1978.

Johannsen, S. K. "The Unknown Furniture Master of Walerloo County." *Canadian Collector,* July/Aug. 1977, pp. 18-23.

MacKinnon, Joan. "Kingston Cabinetmakers before 1867." Unpublished paper for Canadiana Dept., Royal Ontario Museum, Oct. 1974.

———. "A Checklist of Toronto Cabinet and Chair Makers, 1800-1865." History Division, Paper no. 11, Mercury Series, National Museum of Man, Ottawa 1975.

McIntyre, John. "Chairs and Chairmaking in Upper Canada." Unpublished M.A. dissertation, University of Delaware, 1975.

———. "Niagara Furniture Makers." *Canadian Collector*, Part I, May/June, 1977, pp. 50-53; Part II, Sept./Oct. 1977, pp. 50-53; Part III, Mar./Apr. 1978, pp. 24-28; Part IV, July/Aug. 1978, pp. 37-40.

MacLaren, George E. G. *Antique Furniture by Nova Scotian Craftsmen.* Toronto: Ryerson Press, 1961; McGraw-Hill Ryerson, 1975.

———. "The Chairmakers of Nova Scotia." *Canadian Collector,* March 1967, pp. 12-13.

———. "Nova Scotia Furniture" *Canadian Collector*, Oct. 1967, pp. 7-9.

———. *Nova Scotia Furniture.* Halifax: Petheric Press, 1969.

———. "The Windsor Chair in Nova Scotia." *The Magazine Antiques,* July 1971, pp. 124-127.

———. "*Nova Scotia Furniture.*" *Canadian Collector*, Jan./Feb. 1972, pp. 33-35.

———. "Nova Scotia Furniture." In *The Book of Canadian Antiques*, edited by D. B. Webster, pp. 71-90. Toronto: McGraw-Hill Ryerson, 1974.

Minhinnick, Jeanne. "*A Study of Furnishings in Room Use in Upper Canada, 1784-1867*." Report to Historic Sites Branch, Parks Canada, 1964.

———. *Early Furniture in Upper Canada Village.* Toronto: Ryerson Press, 1964.

———. *At Home in Upper Canada.* Toronto: Clarke Irwin, 1970.

———. "Collecting Furniture in Ontario." *Canadian Collector*, May 1971, pp. 53-55.

Minhinnick, Jeanne and Shackleton, Philip. "Early Furniture of Canada: The English and American Influence, 1760-1840." *Canadian Collector,* Jan./Feb. 1974, pp. 25-29.

Nykor, Lynda M., and Musson, Patricia D. *Mennonite Furniture: The Ontario Tradition in York County.* Toronto: James Lorimer & Co., 1977.

O'Dea, Shane. "[Newfoundland] Furniture; Imported and Country Styles to 1850." *Canadian Collector*, Mar./Apr.

1975, pp. 38-41.

Pain, Howard. "Style Influences in the Furniture of Upper Canada." *Canadian Collector,* Sept./Oct. 1978, pp. 32-38.

———. *The Heritage of Upper Canadian Furniture.* Toronto: Van Nostrand Reinhold, 1978.

Rogers, Irene, and MacKenzie, Ruth. "Furniture Making on Prince Edward Island." *Canadian Collector,* Mar./Apr. 1973, pp. 46-49.

Ryder, Huia G. "Elegance of New Brunswick Furniture." *Canadian Collector*, Sept. 1967, pp. 19-20.

———. *Antique Furniture by New Brunswick Craftsmen.* Toronto: Ryerson Press, 1965; McGraw-Hill Ryerson, 1973.

———. "New Brunswick Furniture." In *The Book of Canadian Antiques,* edited by D. B. Webster, pp. 91-109. Toronto: McGraw-Hill Ryerson, 1974.

———. "The Best of Pine and Maple." *Canadian Collector,* May/June 1975, pp. 70-72.

Shackleton, Philip. "Furniture of Upper Canada." *Canadian Collector,* May 1967, pp. 6-8.

———. "Ontario Chairs." *Canadian Collector*, May 1971, pp. 62-64.

———. *The Furniture of Old Ontario.* Toronto: Macmillan, 1973.

———. "Furniture of Old Ontario." *Canadian Collector,* Sept./Oct. 1973, pp. 9-12.

———. "Ontario Furniture." In *The Book of Canadian Antiques*, edited by D. B. Webster, pp. 110-127. Toronto: McGraw-Hill Ryerson, 1974.

Smith, Sheila M. "Jacques and Hay, Cabinetmakers, 1835-1885." Unpublished paper for Canadiana Dept., Royal Ontario Museum, June 1972.

Stevens, Gerald. *Early Ontario Furniture.* Toronto: Royal Ontario Museum, 1966.

———. *The Wiser's Canadiana Collection: Interim Report.* Ont.: Wiser's Distillery Ltd., Belleville, 1967.

Stewart, Don R. *A Guide to Pre-Confederation Furniture of English Canada.* Toronto: Longmans, 1967.

Symons, Scott. *Heritage: A Romantic Look at Early Canadian Furniture.* Toronto; McClelland & Stewart, 1972.

Webster, D. B. "Manitoba Furniture." *Canadian Collector*, April 1969, pp. 18-19.

———. "Quebec furniture with an English accent." *Canadian Homes*, July 1969, p. 7.

———. "Victorian Furniture in Canada." *Canadian Collector,* Nov. 1970, pp. 9-12.

———. "Furniture of English Quebec." In *The Book of Canadian Antiques,* edited by D. B Webster, pp. 53-70. Toronto: McGraw-Hill Ryerson, 1974.

———. "Furniture Sleuthing." *Canadian Collector*, Mar./Apr. 1976, pp. 16-18.

———. "Colonial Elegance: Canadian Furniture of the Georgian Period." *Rotunda* (Royal Ontario Museum), Winter 1977/78, pp. 13-21.

———. "The Identification of English-Canadian Furniture, 1780-1840." *The Magazine Antiques,* Jan. 1979. pp. 164-179.

Yeager, William, ed. *The Cabinet Makers of Norfolk County.* Simcoe, Ont.: Norfolk Historical Society, 1975.

English Furniture

Cescinsky, Herbert. *English Furniture from Gothic to Sheraton.* New York: Dover, 1968.

Cescinsky, Herbert, and Hunter, George L. *English and American Furniture.* Garden City, N.Y.: Garden City Pub. Co., 1929.

Edwards, Ralph. *Sheraton Furniture Designs.* London: Alec Tiranti, 1949.

Fastnedge, Ralph. *English Furniture Styles from 1500 to 1830.* New York: A.S. Barnes, 1964.

Harris, John. *Regency Furniture Designs from Contemporary Source Books: 1808-1826.* London: Alec Tiranti, 1961.

Harris, Eileen. *The Furniture of Robert Adam.* London: Alec Titanti, 1963.

Hinckley, F. Lewis. *A Directory of Antique Furniture*. New York: Bonanza, 1953.

Joy, Edward T. *The Book of English Furniture.* South Brunswick, N.J.: A. S. Barnes, 1965.

MacQuoid, Percy. *A History of English Furniture.* London: Lawrence & Bullen, 1908; New York: Dover, 1972.

Musgrave, Clifford. *Regency Furniture, 1800 to 1830.* London: Faber and Faber, 1961.

Roe, F. Gordon. *Windsor Chairs*. New York: Pitman, 1953.

Wills, Geoffrey. *English Furniture, 1760-1900*. New York: Doubleday, 1971.

American Furniture

Bishop, Robert. *Centuries and Styles of the American Chair,* 1640-1970. New York: Dutton, 1972.

———. *How to Know American Furniture*. New York: E. P. Dutton, 1973.

Bjerkoe, Ethel Hall. *The Cabinetmakers of America*. Garden City, N.Y.: Doubleday, 1957.

Butler, Joseph T. *American Antiques, 1800-1900.* New York: Odyssey Press, 1965.

Comstock, Helen. *American Furniture: Seventeenth, Eighteenth and Nineteenth Century Styles.* New York: Viking, 1962.

Cornelius, Charles O. *Furniture Masterpieces of Duncan Phyfe.* New York: Dover, 1970.

Davidson, Marshall, ed. *The American Heritage History of American Antiques.* 3 volumes. New York: American Heritage, 1968.

Downs, Joseph. *American Furniture: Queen Anne and Chippendale Periods in the Henry Francis du Pont Winterthur Museum.* New York: Macmillan, 1952.

Durant, Mary. *American Heritage Guide to Antiques.* New York: American Heritage, 1970.

Fales, Dean A., Jr. *Essex County* [Mass.] *Furniture: Documented Treasures from Local Collections, 1660-1860.* Salem, Mass.: Essex Institute, 1965.

———. *American Painted Furniture, 1660-1880.* New York: E. P. Dutton, 1972.

———. *The Furniture of Historic Deerfield.* New York: E. P. Dutton, 1976

Greenlaw, Barry A. *New England Furniture at Williamsburg.* Williamsburg, Va.: Colonial Williamsburg Foundation, 1974.

Hummel, Charles F. *With Hammer in Hand: The Dominy Craftsmen of East Hampton, New York.* Charlottesville: Univ. of Virginia Press, 1968.

Kirk, John. *Early American Furniture.* New York: Knopf, 1970.

———. *American Chairs.* New York: Knopf, 1972.

Kovel, Ralph, and Kovel, Terry. *American Country Furniture, 1780-1875.* New York: Crown, 1965.

Lockwood, Luke Vincent. *Colonial Furniture in America.* 3rd ed. New York: Castle-Scribners, 1957.

Maynard, Henry P. *Connecticut Furniture: Seventeenth and Eighteenth Centuries.* Hartford: Wadsworth Atheneum, 1967.

McClelland, Nancy. *Duncan Phyfe and the English Regency, 1795-1830.* New York: William Scott, 1939.

The Metropolitan Museum of Art Guide to the Collections: The American Wing. New York: Metropolitan Museum of Art, 1961.

Miller, Edgar G., Jr. *American Antique Furniture.* Baltimore: Lord Baltimore Press, 1937; New York: Dover, 1966. 2 vols.

Miller, V. Isabelle. *Furniture by New York Cabinetmakers, 1650 to 1860.* New York: Museum of the City of New York, 1956.

Montgomery, Charles F. *American Furniture: The Federal Period, 1788-1825, in the Henry Francis du Pont Winterthur Museum,* New York: Viking, 1966.

Nutting, Wallace. *Furniture Treasury.* New York: Macmillan, 1928. Reprint, 1963.

———. *Furniture Treasury.* Vol. 3. New York: Macmillan, 1933. Reprint, 1966.

Ormsbee, Thomas H. *Field Guide to American Victorian Furniture.* Boston: Little Brown, 1952. Also in paperback.

———. *Field Guide to Early American Furniture.* Boston: Little Brown, 1952. Also in paperback.

Ormsbee, Thomas H. *The Windsor Chair.* n.p.: Deerfield Books, 1962.

Ott, Joseph K. *The John Brown House Loan Exhibition of Rhode Island Furniture.* Providence: Rhode Island Historical Society, 1965.

Otto, Celia Jackson. *American Furniture in the Nineteenth Century.* New York: Viking, 1965.

Parsons, Charles S. *The Dunlaps and Their Furniture.* Manchester, N. H.: Currier Gallery of Art, 1970.

Randall, Richard H., Jr. *The Decorative Arts of New Hampshire, 1725-1825.* Manchester: Currier Gallery of Art, 1964.

———. *American Furniture in the Museum of Fine Arts, Boston.* Boston; Museum of Fine Arts, 1965.

Rice, Norman S. *New York Furniture Before 1840.* Albany: Albany Institute of History and Art, 1962.

Sack, Albert. *The Fine Points of Furniture: Early American.* New York: Crown, 1950.

Sack, Israel, Inc. *American Antiques from the Israel Sack Collection.* 5 vols. n.p.: Highland House, 1970.

White, Margaret E. *Early Furniture Made in New Jersey, 1690-1870.* Newark: Newark Museum, 1958.

Williams, H. Lionel. *Country Furniture of Early America.* New York: Barnes, 1963.

Winchester, Alice, ed. *The Antiques Treasury.* New York: Dutton, 1959.

Trees and Woods

Canadian Forest Products Laboratories. *Canadian Woods: their properties and uses.* Ottawa: Forest Products Laboratories Div., Forestry Branch, 1951.

Core, H. A.; Cote, W. A.; and Day, A. C. *Wood Structure and Identification.* Syracuse, N.Y.: Syracuse Univ. Press, 1976.

Edlin, Herbert L. *What Wood is That? A Manual of Wood Identification.* New York: Viking, 1969.

Fowells, H. A. *Silvics of Forest Trees of the United States.* Agriculture Handbook No. 271. Washington: U.S. Dept. of Agriculture, 1965, 1975.

Hosie, R. C. Native Trees of Canada. Ottawa: Canadian Forestry Service, 1969.

Peattie, Donald Culross. *Natural History of Trees of Eastern and Central North America.* Boston: Houghton Mifflin, 1950.

U.S. Department of Agriculture. *Trees: The Yearbook of Agriculture, 1949.* Washington: U.S. Dept. of Agriculture, 1949.

Index

References to illustrations are in boldface type.